To

_____

From

_____

Date

_____

Published by Christian Art Publishers
PO Box 1599, Vereeniging, 1930, RSA

© 2017
Second edition 2018

Designed by Christian Art Publishers

Images used under license from Shutterstock.com

Scripture quotations are taken from the Holy Bible, New Living Translation®, copyright © 1996, 2004, 2007, 2013, 2015 by Tyndale House Foundation. Used by permission of Tyndale House Publishers, Carol Stream, Illinois 60188. All rights reserved.

Printed in China

ISBN 978-1-64272-001-3 GB151
ISBN 978-1-64272-964-1 GB221

© All rights reserved. No part of this book may be reproduced in any form without permission in writing from the publisher, except in the case of brief quotations in critical articles or reviews.

24 25 26 27 28 29 30 31 32 33 – 21 20 19 18 17 16 15 14 13 12

January 1

Brave Faith

"Have I not commanded you? Be strong and courageous. Do not be afraid; do not be discouraged, for the LORD your God will be with you wherever you go." (Joshua 1:9)

Over the years of your life together as husband and wife, God will take you to unexpected places. You'll face new jobs, addresses, and relationships. You'll tackle challenges and questions that shake you to the core. At the first sight of change, you might be tempted to run back to what's familiar. But when God's leading the way, you're called to face the future with courage.

Where is God taking you today? Which aspects are the most intimidating? How do you feel inadequate to face what's ahead? What kind of disasters fill your imagination? Lay down your fears by trusting that God is in control. Take hold of his promise to be with you every step of the way.

God is keeping you under his wing. Nothing that's ahead will be a surprise to him. He promises to use everything for your good because he loves you. Be strong and courageous!

Lord, you're leading us down unfamiliar roads. Give us confidence in your presence so we're set free from fear. Give us courage to follow you every step of the way.

Amen.

January 2

One Plus One Is One

"For this reason a man will leave his father and mother and be united to his wife, and the two will become one flesh." (Matthew 19:5)

Moving forward means leaving the past behind. If you keep looking over your shoulder, you'll stumble and fall as you travel the road of life. To fully embrace a new identity in marriage, you leave your parents' household and build your own home.

Have you "left" your father and mother? Is your parents' approval more important than your partner's? Do they provide for you financially? Is there pressure to arrange your plans for their benefit rather than yours? You need the privacy to work through decisions and conflict on your own. Have they offered their home as an escape if things don't "work out" in your marriage? Have they given their blessing, respecting you as adults with separate goals, dreams, and life choices?

You're called to honor your father and mother (Exod. 20:12). Their wisdom and help can be a gift. They deserve thanks for supporting you growing up. Ask God for direction in how to move fully into your marriage relationship while still showing kindness and respect to your parents.

Lord, teach us how to leave our past behind and build a new life with each other. Unite our hearts so we can become one. Amen.

January 3

Faith Like a Child

> I led them with cords of human kindness, with ties of love.
> To them I was like one who lifts a little child to the cheek,
> and I bent down to feed them. (Hosea 11:4)

In our fast-paced world, kids grow up in a hurry. Success is defined by self-reliance. Independence. A competitive edge. We're told with an education, the latest technology, and money in the bank, we can handle whatever comes our way.

There's no room in that worldview for childlike faith. You belong to a Father who knows your heart-need for kindness. You don't have to be self-sufficient in tough times. You can cry out for loving comfort when you're hurt or afraid. He binds himself to you with constant love. He reaches out and holds you when you need him most.

Today, remember your God and King is your "Abba, Father" too. Pray about your problems. Bring him your sorrows and disappointments. Ask for him to provide for all your needs. Let him lead you by the hand, trusting he'll take you where you need to go. Have faith, believing he delights in you as his precious children.

Lord, we try so hard to be tough in every situation. Soften our hearts so we remember how much we need you. Thank you for loving us as our kind, faithful Father.

Amen.

January 4

Give What You've Received

> Be kind and compassionate to one another, forgiving each other, just as in Christ God forgave you. (Ephesians 4:32)

Our spouse can become a target when we see them fail. We're tempted to shoot arrows of criticism, judgment, and spite. We can name every flaw, and use their past as a weapon in the present. Gentleness and love are stamped out by angry accusations.

Instead, our spouse can serve as a mirror for our own heart. Their weaknesses reflect our own. We can identify with their lack of self-control, relational struggles, and discouragement. We're reminded of times we've also lost our courage or caved in to temptation. The Lord's grace toward our partner reflects his mercy toward us as well. We're moved to show patience and understanding as we remember our need for Jesus.

Today, put down the arrows that will shatter your partner's hearts. Allow the Lord to develop compassion and kindness between you. Choose to respond with forgiveness instead of anger. Praise God for bearing with you through every struggle.

Lord, teach us to forgive as you've forgiven us. Let us encourage one another to love and obey more fully each day. Fill us with your mercy and kindness.

Amen.

January 5

Better Together

As it is, there are many parts, but one body. The eye cannot say to the hand, "I don't need you!" And the head cannot say to the feet, "I don't need you!" (1 Corinthians 12:20-21)

All believers have unique gifts, passions, and abilities to share with others. Joined together, a fully-functioning spiritual family is formed.

In the same way, a husband and wife unite their different strengths in marriage. The cliché that "opposites attract" proves true – we fall in love with qualities distinct from our own. The shy introvert enjoys his outgoing girlfriend who brings him out of his shell. The free spirit respects the reliable, detail-oriented approach of her fiancé. Discovering how we "fit" is exciting. We feel complete as we join our lives together.

Just as God builds the body with uniquely gifted believers, he builds a family through the strength of each member. Rather than resenting what sets you apart, celebrate each other as God's creation. Ask him to reveal his plan for serving him and each other. Love and depend on each other today.

Lord, thank you for making us unique. Show us how to love and help each other with our gifts.

Amen.

January 6

Love in the Real World

> Love is patient, love is kind. It does not envy,
> it does not boast, it is not proud. (1 Corinthians 13:4)

We find out quickly after the wedding that love is more than feelings – it's hard work! The Lord knows true love calls us to surrender our pride and preferences.

How are you challenged in patience today? Do you partner's quirks and habits get on your nerves? Ask the Lord for a fresh filling of grace to accept your differences.

How can you show kindness today? Give a gift, pitch in with chores, or pay a compliment. Look for opportunities to help and care for one another.

How might you be coveting your spouse? Are you resentful, thinking they have a better job, more fun, and less stress than you? Choose to rejoice today over the blessings you've each received.

How is pride stealing joy from your marriage today? Do you point out your superior parenting, organization, and money management? Do you pressure your partner to be just like you? Ask God to renew your respect for each other's strengths.

Fix your eyes on Jesus – our servant King and his example of perfect love. He'll turn your hearts toward each other and give you joy.

Lord, forgive us when we're impatient, jealous, and proud. Teach us to cherish one another as gifts from you.
Amen.

January 7

Keeping it Real

One person pretends to be rich, yet has nothing; another pretends to be poor, yet has great wealth. (Proverbs 13:7)

It's tempting to control what the world thinks of us. We manipulate our image so we look as attractive, successful, and happy as possible. Struggles and failure are kept behind closed doors. We can make much of our small success, or cover up prosperity with false modesty. We settle for superficial relationships so nobody finds out who we really are.

You're called to authenticity in Jesus. He invites you to bring every sin and weakness into the light of his grace. You lay your need for salvation at his feet and he purifies your hearts. By inviting him into the darkest corners of your life, you allow him to make you new.

Your lives become a story of his transforming work. You can share the miracle of being changed from who you once were. As you become real with others – letting them see who you truly are – the love and power of God are made known.

Lord, give us the courage to be ourselves. Let us lay down the need to impress other people. Let us tell your story of redemption as we openly share our lives.

Amen.

January 8

Love for a Lifetime

"The man who hates and divorces his wife," says the Lord, the God of Israel, "does violence to the one he should protect," says the Lord Almighty. So be on your guard, and do not be unfaithful. (Malachi 2:16)

It cuts a wife to the core when her husband turns his heart away. She notices the subtle glances at other women. She's aware of his visits to pornographic sites online. Her internal alarm goes off when past relationships return in the present. When the walls of faithfulness fall down around your marriage, a wife is crushed in the rubble.

Guard your hearts from unfaithfulness today. Rebuild accountability and boundaries so you're not overcome by temptation. Confess your sin to one another and begin again today.

Take any hatred or bitterness to the Lord in prayer. Let him soften a hardened heart. Choose to put your marriage first, ahead of any other relationship or goal for your life. Turn your fighting with each other into fighting for your marriage.

Close the door of your mind to any thought of divorce. Ask the Lord for strength to keep your promises to one another. Let him rekindle your love, and erase any infatuation or desire to walk away. Let his perfect love teach your hearts to love each other well.

Lord, when our marriage feels difficult, it's tempting to look for a way of escape. Keep us from breaking apart. Guard our love and give us strength to stay together.

Amen.

January 9

The Treasure of Your Marriage

> Every good and perfect gift is from above, coming down from the Father of the heavenly lights, who does not change like shifting shadows. (James 1:17)

When you fell in love, you were excited about all you had in common. You felt complete and happy together. You enjoyed the affection and encouragement you shared. You were certain you were God's "good and perfect gift" made just for each other.

God's love and wisdom for your life hasn't changed. You know that neither of you is perfect, yet your marriage is still part of God's plan to bless your lives. No matter how you've failed each other, God is still good. His Word is always true. He's as strong and able as ever to heal, mend, and make things new. He still offers grace and mercy, no matter how much you've sinned and failed.

Today, thank God for the relationship he created between you. Confess how you've neglected to cherish each other as his good gifts. Praise him for offering all you need for love and life together. Ask him to show his never-changing goodness by restoring your joy in each other. Depend on him for enduring love like his.

Lord, thank you for never changing, so we can trust you all the time. Teach us to be faithful in loving each other and you.

Amen.

January 10

The Privilege of Giving

This service that you perform is not only supplying the needs of the Lord's people but is also overflowing in many expressions of thanks to God. (2 Corinthians 9:12)

Today, you may be the answer to someone's prayer. The meal delivered to a new mother brings relief from her exhaustion.

The visit to an elderly widow comforts her lonely heart. The music prepared for Sunday morning allows the church to worship. Money sent to a struggling family satisfies their landlord for another month. Donated clothing keeps foster children warm in winter. Help with car repairs lets a missionary focus on ministry. The help and encouragement we share is God's way of caring for his people.

Pray and ask God how to serve others today. Consider what you have to give – time, skills, resources – and pray for opportunities to share. Look forward to the thanks God will receive as he directs you to help.

Remember how the Lord met your needs through Christians in your life. Thank him for the blessings you've been given. Praise him for hearing your prayers and moving in people's hearts for you.

Lord, thank you for the family of God. Teach us to serve our brothers and sisters in Christ, loving them in your name. Let all the glory go to you.

Amen.

January 11

Give and You'll Receive

> A generous person will prosper; whoever refreshes others will be refreshed. (Proverbs 11:25)

Is your marriage weak and tired? Is conversation wasted by pointless arguments? Have you lost your partnership by looking out for yourselves alone? Do you feel lonely even when you're side by side? Pour the cool waters of generosity over your dry relationship and watch it come to life.

Pour an extra cup of coffee for your loved one. Give a back rub after a stressful day. Stop at the store for their favorite dessert. Wash the dishes without being asked. Take the kids to the park so your spouse can enjoy a quiet house. Give a listening ear to their worries and dreams. Offer affirming words to build up their confidence. Pray over the burdens your spouse is carrying. Surrender your time and energy so they'll feel heard, valued, and cared for.

Thoughtfulness and kindness are powerful ways to refresh your marriage. Ask God for strength to give and to put each other first today.

Lord, give us your gracious Spirit that gives generously at all times. Show us how to encourage and serve each other freely. Keep us from distraction or selfishness that holds back our love. Amen.

January 12

Help Is On the Way

> Yet the Lord longs to be gracious to you; therefore he will rise up to show you compassion. For the Lord is a God of justice. Blessed are all who wait for him! (Isaiah 30:18)

God doesn't play games with your life. He's not cruel, waiting to see how far you'll bend before you break. He's not indifferent to your stress and pain. He's not manipulative, making you work for his attention. He's not corrupt, saving his blessings for the highest bidder. He's not slow, forgetful, or unsure what to do.

Trust in God's grace today. He's with you in your struggles. He hears every word of your prayers. He hates to see you endure gossip, accusations, and abuse. He has a perfectly orchestrated plan for your life and situation. He loves you as his child – he's compassionate and wants to help.

Pray for patience to wait for God. Ask for faith to believe he's working in ways you can't see yet. Thank him for loving you today, and for all he's going to do tomorrow. Look forward to his coming. In the end you'll see him face to face as the greatest reward of all.

Lord, hard times bring doubt and worry. Teach us to wait for you. Your love and grace are more than enough.
Amen.

January 13

Listen and Learn

> Where there is strife, there is pride, but wisdom is found in those who take advice. (Proverbs 13:10)

Pride is at the root of every argument. We're convinced that we're right. We know our way is best. It would be easier if everyone would just cooperate with our plan. We don't want to slow down and listen to another perspective. We're so busy proving our point, that people's feelings are left in the dust.

What is the conflict between you today? Take time to listen respectfully to each other's ideas and opinions. Ask questions and seek to fully understand your partner. Put the goal of unity ahead of your desire to win. Be open to advice from those with greater experience and wisdom to share. Take your issues to God in prayer, asking him to give insight about what to do.

There's no satisfaction in winning an argument if the relationship is broken in the end. Humble your hearts today to give up the fight. Let your love for each other and for God cover every disagreement.

Lord, forgive us for fighting to have our own way. Give us humble hearts to listen to each other and to you. Teach us to communicate with kindness and respect. Give us your perfect wisdom as we make decisions.

Amen.

January 14

God's Way or No Way

> He replied: "Watch out that you are not deceived.
> For many will come in my name, claiming, 'I am he,' and,
> 'The time is near.' Do not follow them." (Luke 21:8)

We hear the false teachers around us. They promise wealth and prosperity for following Jesus. They ask for money, as if we can buy God's favor. They tell us to follow the rules or suffer God's wrath. They threaten us with the risk of losing our salvation. They require supernatural signs to confirm our position in Christ. They deny the holiness of God, saying wrong is right and good is bad. Deception can lead us away from the One we love.

Be alert, watching who holds influence over your life. Reject those claiming inspiration apart from the Word. Turn away from anyone denying Jesus as the Son of God – "the way and the truth and the life" (John 14:6). Ignore those who promise salvation apart from believing in Christ.

Pray today for wisdom to know who to follow. Study the Scriptures so you know what's true. Worship in a church that holds the Bible as God's inerrant Word. Trust God to give you all you need to follow him without stumbling. Jesus said, "If you hold to my teaching, you are really my disciples. Then you will know the truth, and the truth will set you free" (John 8:31-32).

Lord, guard our hearts and minds from deception. Keep us faithful and true.

Amen.

January 15

The Comfort of Quiet

Then they sat on the ground with him for seven days
and seven nights. No one said a word to him,
because they saw how great his suffering was. (Job 2:13)

It's hard to see your loved one hurting. You can't heal their disease. You can't erase the cruel words of rejection. You can't provide a new job or opportunity. You can't restore the person they lost. You can't replace what's been taken. You can't explain why they're suffering. You feel helpless in the face of their pain – you don't know what to do.

Today, be still. Resist the urge to "fix it" or find someone to blame. Offer the gift of your presence. Clear your calendar so you can stay close. Be willing to listen as they process what's happened. Comfort them through your touch and provide a shoulder to cry on.

Pray for God's healing and help. Ask for insight to understand what your spouse is going through. Let him supply patience and compassion. Thank him for giving you each other so you're not alone. Trust him to do what's needed at the right time. Thank him for his grace that's enough for today.

Lord, show us how to carry this burden together. Bring your comfort and help. Give us hope for all you're going to do. Let us trust in your love.

Amen.

January 16

Watch Your Words

Brothers and sisters, do not slander one another. (James 4:11)

When united in marriage, you begin the process of becoming one. Each of you brings unique traditions, experiences, education, and personalities. As you do the hard work of blending your lives, guard your words and attitudes carefully.

None of us choose our relatives – resist the urge to put down your loved one's family. Find ways to compliment your spouse, even if you don't understand their taste in food, music, or friends. Have patience as you build teamwork in managing your household, money, and schedule. Assume the best in each other before critical words stir up conflict between you.

You'll be tempted to slander if you expect your spouse to be just like you. Remember, you are "fearfully and wonderfully made" (Ps. 139:14). You're chosen and loved by the Lord (2 Thess. 2:13). You're accepted by God (Acts 10:35). Your value is internal, for "The Lord does not look at the things people look at. People look at the outward appearance, but the Lord looks at the heart" (1 Sam. 16:7).

Ask for God's eyes to see each other's worth today. He'll help you to cherish and celebrate one another as you grow in love.

Lord, fill our mouths with words of honor and respect. Teach us to build each other up with praise.

Amen.

January 17

Find Your Lost Temper

> Whoever is patient has great understanding, but one who is quick-tempered displays folly. (Proverbs 14:29)

Our spouse can be disorganized. Forgetful. Distracted. Their quirky habits drive us crazy. When they do that annoying thing again, we're tempted to get angry. We think the louder we yell, the better they'll hear us. We feel justified in our temper – surely if they cared they would change their ways. Yet it's foolish to think an angry outburst will improve the situation. All it can do is tear down our loved one and push him or her away.

Have wisdom today to choose patience over anger. Seek to understand the motives behind your spouse's behavior. Consider if they're tired, overbooked, and overwhelmed. Recognize how they're following the pattern of their upbringing. Appreciate how their skills, gifts, and personality may differ from your own.

Give grace to each other today. Don't assume your partner is deliberately frustrating you. Guard your heart from taking things personally. Seek to listen and understand. Work to find solutions as a team. Forgive, offering the kindness you hope to receive yourself. In this way, build trust and love that lasts.

Lord, quick tempers will tear us apart, but patience knits us together. Let us show the same compassion we receive from you. Amen.

January 18

The Healing Power of Confession

> Therefore confess your sins to each other and pray for each other so that you may be healed. The prayer of a righteous person is powerful and effective. (James 5:16)

Is your marriage "sick" today? Hurtful words, selfish choices, and unresolved conflict create distance between you. You can drift apart, angry and cold toward the one you most want to be close to. As time goes by, you'll struggle to find the way back to each other again.

The Lord provides the medicine for your marriage: confession and prayer. Be willing to admit your part in building the wall between you. Confess the ways you've put yourself first. Apologize for wounding your spouse in the fight to have your way. Ask for forgiveness and a chance to begin again.

Pray for your partner – for healing, help, and wisdom to know what to do. Ask for God's truth and compassion to fill the space between you. Pray for him to renew your love and intimacy as you open up to each other today. Let him tear down the walls and unite you as one again.

Lord, we've sinned against each other and you. We need your grace and help so we're free to love again. Do a powerful work of healing in our marriage today.

Amen.

January 19

Eternally Secure

> Whoever has the Son has life; whoever does not have the Son of God does not have life. I write these things to you who believe in the name of the Son of God so that you may know that you have eternal life. (1 John 5:12-13)

You don't have to be afraid of eternity. Wondering if you're really in the faith. Scared that your sins have turned God's heart away. You can know for certain if you have eternal life: "If you declare with your mouth, 'Jesus is Lord,' and believe in your heart that God raised him from the dead, you will be saved" (Rom. 10:9).

If you truly believe in Jesus today, have peace. If you've called him your Lord, you're his. Leave your doubts behind. Put away your insecurities and trust in his promise. Answer his call to "fight the good fight of the faith. Take hold of the eternal life to which you were called when you made your good confession in the presence of many witnesses" (1 Tim. 6:12).

Pray together for faith to love God, trust in his salvation, and live for him until he comes. Nothing will separate you from his love or snatch you from his hand.

Lord, thank you for giving us life in Jesus. Build our faith so it can't be shaken.

Amen.

January 20

The Humble Road to Greatness

"Whoever wants to become great among you must be your servant, and whoever wants to be first must be slave of all." (Mark 10:43-44)

The headlines are dominated by the dealings of powerful leaders. Magazines highlight celebrities and success stories. Advertising sells the way to grab more attention, status, and prosperity. We're pushed to fight our way to the top.

Jesus calls us to trade in greatness for servanthood. We're to lay down our rights. To put others first. To show mercy and kindness. To love others more than ourselves. No matter how impressive our rank or wealth, we're to surrender ourselves like Christ.

How can you serve today? Who needs a helping hand to move forward? Who is stressed, not having what they need? Who needs comfort and a listening ear? Who needs shelter, rescue, or hope? Who needs what you have to give?

Choose the way of Jesus today. Let pride and selfishness be overcome by humility. Pray and ask for wisdom to pursue his kind of greatness – modesty, love, and willingness to serve. In this way you'll please the One who gave himself for you.

Lord, teach us what it means to be "slaves of all." We want to give and serve with humble hearts like Jesus.

Amen.

January 21

Stick with Jesus

Anyone who runs ahead and does not continue in the teaching of Christ does not have God; whoever continues in the teaching has both the Father and the Son. (2 John 9)

Faith is not a one-time prayer at summer camp. It's not a few good works to ease our conscience. It's not serving God on Sunday and pleasing ourselves through the week. It's not a feel-good message on a t-shirt. It's not a tradition, a lifestyle, or a social activity. Faith is an all-in, life or death, transforming belief in Jesus who died for our sins.

Are you putting your hope for tomorrow in your faith of yesterday? Has that faith endured? Are you still believing? Obeying? Serving? Loving? Praying? Trusting? Are you loving the Lord with all your heart, soul, mind, and strength?

Pray today for faith that lasts for life. Pray for perseverance to keep growing and learning the Word. Pray for trust in God through whatever comes your way. Pray for Jesus to fill you with his love for everyone.

True faith goes on and on, believing until the end. "Here is a trustworthy saying: If we died with him, we will also live with him; if we endure, we will also reign with him" (2 Tim. 2:11-12). Keep believing Jesus. Give your life to follow him. Know you're his forever.

Lord, we want true faith to believe and obey until you come again. Keep us faithful to you and your Word every day.
Amen.

January 22

Heading for Home

> But you must return to your God; maintain love and justice, and wait for your God always. (Hosea 12:6)

Life's distractions and temptations can lead you away from God. Is your family traveling in the wrong direction today?

Is love fading in your house? Do you treat each other with courtesy or rudeness? Are you generous or selfish? Patient or easily angered? Encouraging or critical? Comforting or callous? The further away you wander from God, the less his love fills your lives.

Is your family known for its justice? Are you honest and trustworthy? Do you care for the poor and marginalized? Do you treat each other fairly? Remember God's call to lives of integrity, standing for the truth.

Are you waiting for God every day? Do you continually pray and expect him to answer? Do you search his Word for wisdom? Are you eager to hear him speak through pastors and teachers? Do you depend on him for your daily needs? Have faith, living in eager anticipation of his presence.

If you're distant from the Lord, return to him today. Love one another. Stand for justice. Invite God into every part of your life.

Lord, keep us from wandering away from you. Fill our home with your love and justice. Teach us to wait for you to accomplish all you've got planned.

Amen.

January 23

Grace or a Grudge?

> "When you stand praying, if you hold anything against anyone, forgive them, so that your Father in heaven may forgive you your sins." (Mark 11:25)

Is there anything between you today? Perhaps you're still hurting from words of the past. Frustration over a recent argument. Betrayal from a broken promise. Disappointment from unmet hopes and expectations. Rejection as jobs, families, or friends competes for your spouse's attention. You're wounded by their lust, anger, or selfishness. You're trying to be patient, but resentment is building each day.

Unforgiveness divides both your marriage and your relationship with God. You can't ask for his mercy if you keep it from each other. Take your pain and frustration to God in prayer. Ask for compassion and understanding. Depend on him to make peace in your home. Trust him to help your spouse grow and change. Call on him for humility to see your own need for forgiveness.

Today, lay down what you're holding against each other. Start again, giving the grace you've received through Jesus.

Lord, help us to forgive each other today. Let us show the mercy you've shown to us. Give us a fresh start as we let go of the past.

Amen.

January 24

The Gift of Prayer

Dear friend, I pray that you may enjoy good health and that all may go well with you, even as your soul is getting along well. (3 John 2)

You know your loved one better than anyone else. You're intimately acquainted with their likes and dislikes, hopes and fears, friends and enemies. You know their stress, their aches and pains, their disappointments. You're the keeper of their secrets. The lover of their heart. You know more than anyone else how to pray for their life.

Love each other by praying every day. Ask God to heal your pain and sickness. Ask for strength to keep up with life's demands. Ask him to prosper your work and guard your reputation. Ask him to keep your marriage close and connected. Call on him for wisdom to handle tough decisions. Pray for discernment to understand the Bible and live by its truth. Cry out for courage and rescue when the enemy attacks your faith and family.

Invite God's love and power into each other's lives. Your faith will grow as you see him move in your home. You'll be secure, knowing you're in his hands. The Spirit will make you one as you lift each other up.

Lord, make us faithful to pray for each other about everything. Bring your wisdom, help, and blessings as we pray.
Amen.

January 25

We All Need Jesus

Jesus said to them, "Truly I tell you, the tax collectors and the prostitutes are entering the kingdom of God ahead of you. For John came to you to show you the way of righteousness, and you did not believe him, but the tax collectors and the prostitutes did. And even after you saw this, you did not repent and believe him." (Matthew 21:31-32)

God invites everyone to enter his kingdom. He sees the inner-city mom on welfare. He knows the criminal locked away in jail. He sees the addict. The stripper. The corrupt and cruel among us. The message is the same to all: repent and believe.

Jesus isn't impressed by credentials. Playing by the rules won't get you to heaven. He loves those devastated by guilt and regret. He hears their cry for help and forgiveness. He never turns away "a broken and contrite heart" who believes in him (Ps. 51:17).

We need humility and grace today. Humility to remember our own need for Jesus, and mercy for others who need him too. Thank God today for loving you no matter what you've done. Ask for faith to keep believing and turning away from sin. Lift up the lost around you – believe in Jesus and be set free. Pray for a heart of compassion for everyone.

Lord, keep us free from pride that says we deserve your love. May we keep believing, obeying, and loving the lost in your name.

Amen.

January 26

The Open Arms of God

"So he got up and went to his father. But while he was still a long way off, his father saw him and was filled with compassion for him; he ran to his son, threw his arms around him and kissed him." (Luke 15:20)

Are you "still a long way off" from your Father God today? Perhaps pain and struggle have damaged your trust in his love. The pull of money or success has captured your focus. The Bible and church feel less fulfilling than other activities you enjoy. You're losing the battle against temptation, so you quit trying to obey the Lord. For whatever reason, your heart and mind are far from God.

Don't believe the enemy's lie that God has given up on you. Replace any fear of his anger with confidence in his mercy. Trade in your self-reliance for humility to tell how much you need him. Come as you are – guilty, tired, wounded, full of doubt – and receive his compassionate embrace.

Pray. Confess. Let go of the past. Run toward your Father who forgives and makes all things new.

Lord, we've tried living without you and it's no life at all. Today, we surrender our lives to your control. We trust in Jesus' work on the cross to cover every sin and save us. Keep us close to you forever.

Amen.

January 27

We're in This Together

Let us consider how we may spur one another on toward love and good deeds, not giving up meeting together, as some are in the habit of doing, but encouraging one another – and all the more as you see the Day approaching. (Hebrews 10:24-25)

We weren't meant to follow God alone. We need accountability to do the right thing. We need godly friends to encourage us along the way. We need to remember that this earth isn't our home – we're looking ahead to eternal life with our brothers and sisters in Christ.

Left to yourselves, you'll forget who you are as believers. You'll fall into sin without anybody challenging your choices. You'll become self-absorbed and blind to the needs around you. You'll start living for the "now" instead of keeping your eyes on the horizon of eternity.

Commit to the church as a couple. Participate in worship, service, and friendship with other believers. Invite Christians into your life who set an example of obedience and knowledge of the Word. Look for those who need love and help in difficult circumstances. Invest your time, energy, and spiritual gifts to build up the family of God.

Let God reveal his truth and comfort your pain through others who love him.

Lord, thank you for creating a spiritual family in Christ. Show us how to share our lives with your people.
Amen.

January 28

Kids and the Kingdom

He said to them, "Let the little children come to me, and do not hinder them, for the kingdom of God belongs to such as these." (Mark 10:14)

God loves children. He wants to know them, hold them, and love them. As parents or friends of kids, we have the privilege of introducing them to Jesus. We're to do all we can to help – not hinder – children in coming to him.

Pray for kids' salvation and protection from evil. Pray with them for God's help with their troubles. Invite them to bring their thanks, fears, and questions to him in prayer.

Teach children God's Word. Read Bible stories before bed. Take them to church. Shield them from false teachers who deny the truth. Let them see you study Scripture for yourself.

Worship together. Sing along to worship music. Enjoy God's creation. Take every opportunity to tell God how wonderful he is.

Show love to others. Give kids a chance to give and serve. Lead them in praying for their friends. Encourage them to reach out to those who are hurting or left out. Show them how love is meant to be shared.

A child's faith inspires our own. Their simple trust and open hearts are beautiful to God. Pray today for faith like a little child.

Lord, thank you for your love for children. Show us how to love them in your name.

Amen.

January 29

Pay It Forward

Praise be to the God and Father of our Lord Jesus Christ, the Father of compassion and the God of all comfort, who comforts us in all our troubles, so that we can comfort those in any trouble with the comfort we ourselves receive from God. (2 Corinthians 1:3-4)

On the other side of suffering, we carry a measure of comfort to share. We can identify with the hurt in another's heart.

The childless relate to the pain of infertility. The jobless know the stress of unemployment. The addict knows the ruin of destructive choices. The abused and rejected know the heart's deep longing for safety and acceptance. Those who receive God's grace and healing are especially enabled to share compassion with others.

How has God met you in your pain? Remember how he cared for you. Share your story with those walking the same dark road. Have courage to enter into their grief. Offer words of hope from your experience and God's Word. Give assurance that just as he's been faithful to you, he's faithful to all his children. Remember his power that's strong enough to hold you to the end.

Lord, thank you for meeting us in our darkest hour. Your love is enough to carry any burden and heal any wound. Use us to comfort those who are suffering today.

Amen.

January 30

Learn Before You Teach

"How can you say to your brother, 'Brother, let me take the speck out of your eye,' when you yourself fail to see the plank in your own eye? You hypocrite, first take the plank out of your eye, and then you will see clearly to remove the speck from your brother's eye." (Luke 6:42)

When you marry, your life becomes an open book. It's hard to hide your bad habits and weaknesses from the one who knows you best. It's tempting to point out every error and pressure each other to change. And, it's much easier to focus on someone else's failings than your own.

The Scriptures challenge you to keep your focus inward rather than outward. Keep a sensitive conscience to the Spirit's correction. Take responsibility for your actions, confessing your sins to God and the one you've offended. Study the Word diligently to know his will for your life.

Once you've humbled your hearts to acknowledge your mistakes, you're in a position to encourage one another. You can lovingly help each other do the right thing. You can seek God together to ask him what to do. Then your marriage becomes a place to grow in obedience every day.

Lord, give us eyes to clearly see our sin. Help us to focus on our own obedience instead of trying to change each other.
Amen.

January 31

Give What You've Got

Do not withhold good from those to whom it is due,
when it is in your power to act. (Proverbs 3:27)

To love like Jesus, we can't turn a blind eye to the needs around us. Whether it's taking a sick child to a doctor appointment, holding the door when our partner's arms are full, or giving fair payment to our lawn service, we're responsible to care for those in our lives. Holding back from doing good is the opposite of Jesus' servanthood and sacrifice.

Who needs your help today? What blessings could you share with others? Who needs the gift of friendship to ease their loneliness? Who needs a listening ear or encouraging word? How can you show thoughtfulness to your family as you go about your day? Who deserves a reward or payment for their service to you?

Jesus gave up everything for us – even his life on the cross. He asks us to give out of the good we've received from his hand. Experience the joy of loving others in Jesus' name.

Lord, prompt our hearts to serve and give generously to those around us. Let us share our time, energy, resources, and love. Teach us to be thoughtful and kind to one another.

Amen.

February

February 1

Don't Be Scared

Are not two sparrows sold for a penny? Yet not one of them will fall to the ground outside your Father's care. And even the very hairs of your head are all numbered. So don't be afraid; you are worth more than many sparrows. (Matthew 10:29-31)

Few of us stand out in a crowd. Our influence is small. Our talent is far from extraordinary. We don't have power to keep ourselves secure. We don't have money to buy our way out of trouble. When trials and enemies come, we're helpless and afraid.

Jesus said you'd have trouble in this world. He understands your struggle to do the right thing. He sees the enemy scheming, lying, and tempting you to sin. He knows the world hates you for loving him. Even so, he says, "Don't be afraid."

God is not surprised by your struggle. He knows everything about you. You're his treasures – chosen, loved, and bought with the price of his life. This testing will build your faith and endurance. In all of it, he's working for your good. He'll strengthen you, comfort you, and love you until the end.

Pray to take hold of his promise today: "Peace I leave with you; my peace I give you. I do not give to you as the world gives. Do not let your hearts be troubled and do not be afraid" (John 14:27).

Lord, give us courage when it's hard to live for you in this world.

Amen.

February 2

Stand in the Gap

We do not want you to be uninformed, brothers and sisters, about the troubles we experienced in the province of Asia. We were under great pressure, far beyond our ability to endure, so that we despaired of life itself. (2 Corinthians 1:8)

God has called his people to dangerous places. They share the Word where it's forbidden. They rescue children from slavery. They stand for justice for the oppressed. They bring spiritual peace to those in the middle of war. They supply food for the hungry, shelter for the homeless, and work for the poor. They take back ground from the enemy for God's kingdom.

The cost of obedience is high for many. They suffer violence, disease, and even death for the sake of Christ. As their brothers and sisters, we can be blinded by our safety and comfort. How do we stand with God's servants today?

Learn, give, and pray. Discover how missionaries are serving around the world. Read their stories and support them as God leads you. Send gifts and encouraging letters. Share the needs you discover with others, inviting them to care. Most of all, pray. Cry out to God for their safety, strength and courage. Ask for his favor and victory in their battles. Remember them when they feel alone in the fight.

Lord, in the security we enjoy, we can forget the pressure on our brothers and sisters. Meet their needs, give them hope, and guard their lives.

Amen.

February 3

Twisting the Truth

Now the serpent was more crafty than any of the wild animals the LORD God had made. He said to the woman, "Did God really say, 'You must not eat from any tree in the garden'?" (Genesis 3:1)

The gateway to sin is through doubting God's Word. "Did God really say" sex was just for a married man and wife? "Did God really say" to submit to those in authority? "Did God really say" to be generous with our hard-earned money? "Did God really say" to keep slander, coarse jokes, and gossip out of our conversations? "Did God really say" to be an active part of his church family? When we don't take God at his Word, sin is sure to follow.

Today, pray and ask God to show if you're making excuses for your actions. If you're compromising the truth. If you're living to please yourself instead of him. If you're resisting the Word, afraid of the cost to obey. If you're doubting his wisdom and goodness in your life.

God loves you. He knows the peace and blessings that come through obedience. Surrender to him as the Lord of your life today.

Lord, protect us from the enemy's lies. Give us faith to trust and obey your Word.

Amen.

February 4

Touch, See, and Believe

> He said to them, "Why are you troubled, and why do doubts rise in your minds? Look at my hands and my feet. It is I myself! Touch me and see; a ghost does not have flesh and bones, as you see I have." (Luke 24:38-39)

Our emotions are deceptive, making us feel like God is far away. Trials and pain create doubt in his love. Enemies and persecution stir up fear, and we wonder if we're safe in his hands. Delayed answers to prayer shake our trust that he's listening. We lose faith in what we can't see, despite his promise to be with us always, to the very end of the age (Matt. 28:20).

Pray for eyes of faith to see Jesus. He doesn't always show up in the way you expect. Your difficulty may be his loving hand of discipline. Your friend's encouraging word is his voice of love. The food on your table and roof over your head is his faithful provision. Your loving marriage is his gift of comfort. His Word is always at hand to give truth and wisdom. He's not absent or hiding from you today. Let go of your doubt and believe he's with you.

"Be strong and courageous. Do not be afraid; do not be discouraged, for the LORD your God will be with you wherever you go" (Josh. 1:9).

Lord, you're alive, you're here, and your love never fails. Make us sure of you today.

Amen.

February 5

The Temper Trap

> Do not make friends with a hot-tempered person,
> do not associate with one easily angered, or you may
> learn their ways and get yourself ensnared. (Proverbs 22:24-25)

Is anger taking hold in your home today? It's inevitable that bitterness and rage will impact each member of the family. A parent who lashes out and punishes harshly will make their child bitter and discouraged (Col. 3:21). A spouse who's easily offended will divide the marriage and stifle love (Prov. 17:9).

Sarcasm is contagious. Angry insults crush respect and kindness. A hot temper breaks trust. Walls are built around the heart to defend against the next explosion. How is your household suffering the effects of anger today? Freedom is found in Christ. By forgiving as you've been forgiven, resentment and bitterness fade away. By the power of the Spirit, you learn kindness, gentleness, and self-control. He makes you his new creation, frees you from the power of darkness, and gives you everything you need to overcome.

Pray today for rescue if anger is doing damage in your family. Trust him to fill you with love and peace as you depend on him. Praise him for the healing he'll bring as you submit to him in everything.

Lord, forgive us for the angry words and actions that hurt each other's heart. Heal our wounds and teach us your way of peace.

Amen.

February 6

A Teachable Heart

Avoid foolish controversies and genealogies
and arguments and quarrels about the law,
because these are unprofitable and useless. (Titus 3:9)

Are we concerned with being right or righteous? In our sin, we can turn the Scriptures God gave into an object of debate and division. Instead of responding to the Word with a humble heart, we use it to condemn those around us.

Perhaps your Bible reading gives you a sense of moral superiority to your neighbor. Maybe the appeal of your studies is to come out on top in a discussion. Secret fears can drive you to learn God's "rules" to earn his love. The Bible can become a tool to boost your pride rather than renewing your heart and mind.

Consider how the Bible is shaping your life together. Does it challenge you to love and obey the Lord? Is it leading you to worship? Is it helping you respond in mercy to those who are lost in their sin?

Ask God for a fresh perspective on his Word today. Pray for a pure desire for knowledge and understanding. Find freedom from legalism and conflict with others. Let the Lord's love and wisdom fill your life as you seek him.

Lord, thank you for your Word that teaches the way of salvation. Help us to know your truth and live in your will. Keep us humble as we seek to understand the Bible more and more. Amen.

February 7

Give Grace, Get Grace

> "Do not judge, or you too will be judged. For in the same way you judge others, you will be judged, and with the measure you use, it will be measured to you." (Matthew 7:1-2)

It's a lot easier to judge others than to examine ourselves. We hold a gavel in our hand, declaring people guilty for not living up to our standards.

We decide how our brother should handle his emotions. How our teenage neighbor should be modest. How our sister should save her money. How our pastor should preach. How our friends should raise their children. How our boss should lead the department. We create our own definition of right and wrong, apart from the Word of God.

Let God be God today. Trust him to deal with others' sin in his way, in his timing. Believe the Spirit is able to provide the wisdom that's needed. Remember how you need forgiveness every day. "Indeed, there is no one on earth who is righteous, no one who does what is right and never sins" (Eccles. 7:20). We all would be lost without Jesus.

Pray for humility today. Ask the Lord to make you sincere. Kind. Free from hypocrisy. Obedient to his Word. Let his love and mercy fill your heart.

Lord, keep us from trying to take your place and judge other people. Fill us with your grace toward everyone.
Amen.

February 8

The Wealth of the Word

> By wisdom a house is built, and through understanding it is established; through knowledge its rooms are filled with rare and beautiful treasures. (Proverbs 24:3-4)

We can build a mansion with boards and bricks. We can paint, decorate, and landscape the yard. We can fill its rooms with expensive furniture, clothes, and toys. Yet a house without God's wisdom is missing the greatest treasures of all.

Pray for God to establish your home today. Depend on his Word for knowledge and understanding. Learn how to raise your kids and honor your marriage. Let it teach you how to work and rest, show hospitality, and care for your neighbors. Submit to his will with your money and possessions. Find strength to cope with enemies and trials that come your way. The truth of God will make your house secure:

"Therefore everyone who hears these words of mine and puts them into practice is like a wise man who built his house on the rock. The rain came down, the streams rose, and the winds blew and beat against that house; yet it did not fall, because it had its foundation on the rock" (Matt. 7:24-25).

Praise God for the gift of his Word as he leads your family today.

Lord, make our house a home that's filled with grace, truth, and love. May we treasure your Word and live for you.
Amen.

February 9

Never Alone

"When you pass through the waters, I will be with you; and when you pass through the rivers, they will not sweep over you. When you walk through the fire, you will not be burned; the flames will not set you ablaze." (Isaiah 43:2)

Are you drowning in grief today? Are you buried beneath waves of pressure and stress? Are people's needs and expectations crushing you under their weight? Are you feeling the heat of threats to your good name? Is anger burning in a difficult relationship? In your most desperate hour, the Lord is with you.

Today, tell God your deepest fears. What feels overwhelming? Which situation seems hopeless? What have you lost that can never be replaced? Who are your enemies? What is too hard to possibly handle on your own?

Trust God's promise to never let you go. "We are hard pressed on every side, but not crushed; perplexed, but not in despair; persecuted, but not abandoned; struck down, but not destroyed" (2 Cor. 4:8-9). Don't let the storms and fires today shake your faith in his love. He's going to bring you safely home.

Lord, when we're hurting and afraid, give us faith to believe you're here. Give us hope and peace as we trust you through it all.

Amen.

February 10

A Firm Foundation

As for everyone who comes to me and hears my words and puts them into practice, I will show you what they are like. They are like a man building a house, who dug down deep and laid the foundation on rock. When a flood came, the torrent struck that house but could not shake it, because it was well built. (Luke 6:47-48)

Is a tsunami bearing down on your life today? Are financial pressures, broken relationships, or life's demands sweeping away your stability and hope? Sickness can strike, children rebel, and possessions are lost. You wonder how to build anything that lasts.

True security is found in the Word of God. Its wisdom gives answers to the challenging questions of life. It guards you from sinful, destructive choices. It points the way to knowing the Lord and experiencing his joy in every situation. When you live by the Bible and hold to faith in Jesus, you cannot be shaken.

If the foundations of your life are crumbling, take hold of the Word. Discover the peace and confidence that come through knowing his promises. Understand his will so you can follow where he leads. Find peace in his unshakeable truth.

Lord, teach us your Word so we can do what it says. Be the foundation of our lives.

Amen.

February 11

Righting our Wrongs

"Therefore, if you are offering your gift at the altar and there remember that your brother or sister has something against you, leave your gift there in front of the altar. First go and be reconciled to them; then come and offer your gift." (Matthew 5:23-24)

No matter our good intentions, we let each other down. We forget our debts, break our promises, and wound with our words. Our busy lives distract us from meeting others' needs. We carry on, too stubborn or careless to try to work it out.

The Lord challenges you to make things right when you've done wrong. Before you enter into worship, pursue peace in your relationships. Have the humility to confess the sin. Pay the debt. Apologize for the hurt. Undo the damage as much as you're able. Freely approach the Lord with a clean conscience, knowing you've done all you can to reconcile.

Pray for peace with everyone today. Ask for courage to obey, and for mercy and forgiveness to heal the past. Rejoice in the unity that can be found in him.

Lord, you know the ways we've failed to love. Show us the way to peace and reconciliation. Give us your grace and help to restore what's been broken.

Amen.

February 12

The School of Prayer

> One day Jesus was praying in a certain place. When he finished, one of his disciples said to him, "Lord, teach us to pray, just as John taught his disciples." (Luke 11:1)

God has compassion for inexperience and insecurity about prayer. He's glad to teach the way to approach the Father.

We're invited to come to him to worship. We can bring our needs and ask for help. We can seek forgiveness and ask for a heart of mercy for others. We can lean on his strength to resist sin and the devil.

Join together in prayer today. Praise God for his majesty, holiness, and salvation through Jesus. Give him your needs and concerns. Confess your sins. Ask for his grace to love everyone. Seek his deliverance from the enemy's schemes and your temptation to fall.

Commit to pray together as a couple, for "where two or three gather in my name, there am I with them" (Matt. 18:20). When you're apart, continue to lift each other up. Let the Lord bind you closer to himself and each other as you grow in prayer.

Lord, we need you to teach us to pray. Thank you for receiving our worship, forgiving our sins, and providing for our needs. May we know you more fully as we call on you in prayer.
Amen.

February 13

Who Am I?

*When I consider your heavens, the work of your fingers,
the moon and the stars, which you have set in place,
what is mankind that you are mindful of them,
human beings that you care for them?* (Psalm 8:3-4)

The God who moves the winds across the globe knows every breath you take. The Creator who named every star in the universe knows every hair on your head. The eternal One who's outside of space and time knew exactly where he'd place you in human history. The God whose thoughts "outnumber the grains of sand" is thinking about you all the time" (Ps. 139:18). He knows where you go, what you do, and what you think and say. No detail of your life is a secret.

He pays such close attention because he loves you. He made you. He prepared you for each other. He has plans for your lives right now and for eternity.

Today, do you feel small and unimportant? Do you feel invisible, like you don't matter? Be encouraged – you're loved with an everlasting love (Jer. 31:3). You were bought at a price. You're seen and known. You bear the image of God. You're temples of the Holy Spirit. You're friends of Jesus and children of God. You're his treasure and he'll never let you go.

Lord, we don't understand why you care for us so much. Thank you for loving us every moment.

Amen.

February 14

Remember the Romance

> Daughters of Jerusalem, I charge you: Do not arouse
> or awaken love until it so desires. (Song of Songs 8:4)

When you fell in love you dreamed about your future. Your favorite moments were spent together. Your desire for each other grew every day. You were eager to know the affection and intimacy of marriage. You dreamed of sharing everything for the rest of your lives.

Fast-forward to life as husband and wife. Desire gives way to distraction. Communication is hard work. Time alone is difficult to come by. Romance takes effort. Intimacy drops low on the list of what's important. You want to "arouse or awaken love" but don't know where to begin.

Today, put aside your work, parenting, and responsibilities to focus on your loved one. Remember why you love and like each other. Share how you find one another attractive. Offer thanks for ways your spouse has helped and cared for you. Plan a special date just for fun. Hold hands in the car. Buy a personal gift to say "I love you." Listen, laugh, and anticipate tender moments ahead.

We value what costs us the most. Do whatever it takes to put each other first and rekindle the joy of your marriage.

Lord, help us connect and cherish one another. Let our love grow deeper and stronger every day.

Amen.

February 15

Dying to Live

> Whoever finds their life will lose it, and whoever loses their life for my sake will find it. (Matthew 10:39)

Everyone is looking for joy and happiness in life. We think it's found in love and romance. Kids and family. Careers and money. Houses, cars, and the latest technology. Beauty and strength. Popularity and attention. Travel and excitement. The harder and longer we search, the more impossible it is to find.

Jesus is "the way, the truth, and the life" you're searching for (John 14:6). The life he gives is abundant, free, and never ends. When you believe in him, you die to yourselves. You give up your sins, selfish desires, and pride to live for him alone. You're crucified with Christ and you no longer live, but Christ lives in you. The life you're living in the body is by faith in Jesus, who loved you and gave himself up for you (Gal. 2:20).

You have a choice: to live to please yourself, or to give up everything for Jesus. You can be self-reliant or depend on him for everything. You can go your own way or trust in his Word. You can chase after wealth and comfort, or give and serve in his name. Let go of it all and believe – find true life in Jesus today.

Lord, let us find our life in you forever.

Amen.

February 16

Hope in the Desert

> For three days they traveled in the desert without finding water. When they came to Marah, they could not drink its water because it was bitter. (That is why the place is called Marah.) So the people grumbled against Moses, saying, "What are we to drink?" (Exodus 15:22-24)

Have you searched and waited for what you need, only to be disappointed when it comes? The job you accepted is a dead-end street. Rude neighbors take the joy out of your new home. Your hard-earned savings are wiped out by unexpected bills. You think you're getting to your destination, but troubles get in the way.

How has the "water" you've found let you down? Pray and ask the Lord to take care of you. Hold on to hope and confidence that he'll provide what you need. Don't let the obstacle in front of you shake your faith. Resist the temptation to worry and complain while you wait.

Trust that this trial is for your good, "because we know that suffering produces perseverance; perseverance, character; and character, hope. And hope does not put us to shame, because God's love has been poured out into our hearts through the Holy Spirit, who has been given to us" (Rom. 5:3-5).

Lord, forgive us for doubting your goodness in this situation. Give us faith to believe you'll meet our needs. Thank you for the hope we have in you.

Amen.

February 17

Relief and Rest

> "Take my yoke upon you and learn from me, for I am gentle and humble in heart, and you will find rest for your souls. For my yoke is easy and my burden is light." (Matthew 11:29-30)

We all wear a "yoke" – we're tied to someone or something. Who's in authority over you today? What is influencing your worldview? Who is your source of knowledge and wisdom? How are you dealing with failures and disappointments? What gives you hope for tomorrow?

Jesus wants to set you free from the world's lies and the burden of sin. He offers forgiveness you don't have to earn. He promises wisdom for the asking, without looking down on your questions. He rescues you from empty religion – traditions and obligations that falsely promise to win God's favor. He provides spiritual gifts and the strength to use them. He accepts you completely, releasing you from pressure to please other people. He gives you hope and a future that no one can take away.

Find rest in Jesus today. Learn from his humility and gentleness. Stop working and striving to be "enough." Lay down your heavy burdens as you receive his love.

Lord, teach us to rest in you. Thank you for taking the burden of our sin and giving us life. Let us learn to love like you.

Amen.

February 18

Leave Room to Share

"When you reap the harvest of your land, do not reap to the very edges of your field or gather the gleanings of your harvest. Do not go over your vineyard a second time or pick up the grapes that have fallen. Leave them for the poor and the foreigner. I am the Lord your God." (Leviticus 19:9-10)

In the name of financial stewardship, we cling to every last penny. In our push to maximize our days, we plan and schedule every minute. Yet according to God's priorities, our time and money are meant to be shared.

Leave room in your budget for giving. Leave generous tips. Add extra groceries to your cart for the food pantry. Share your resources with the poor and hurting. Modify your spending and financial goals to include the needs of others. Allow God to show his love in tangible ways as you give.

Share the gift of your time. Enjoy family nights to connect with your loved ones. Free up weekends to share your table with friends and neighbors. Keep your schedule flexible enough to serve and share life with others. God loves people and will move through the hours you share.

Look for someone who's in need or lonely today. Give to them out of all the Lord has given to you.

Lord, keep us from holding your blessings for ourselves. Teach us to create margins in our life to share with others. Let us love in your name.

Amen.

February 19

Showing Off Jesus

Not to us, Lord, not to us but to your name be the glory,
because of your love and faithfulness. (Psalm 115:1)

Every day we have a choice – to bring glory to God or to ourselves. We can work hard to serve others in Jesus' name or pursue our own success. We can train our kids to obey the Word, or use their success to boost our reputation. We can make healthy choices to care for the body God created or to look attractive to others. We can prepare our home to show loving hospitality or to impress the neighbors. Everything we do is an opportunity to praise the Lord or seek attention for ourselves.

How can you glorify the Lord in your lives today? Generosity, compassion, humility, and selflessness reveal him to everyone you know. Gratitude for his gifts tells others of his faithfulness. Your joy and peace in hard times testifies to his constant love. Forgiving your enemies paints a picture of God's great mercy. Your plans and priorities show what's important to the heart of God.

Every talent, possession, and achievement is an opportunity to make God's name great. Seek his glory in all things.

Lord, deep down, we crave attention and success. Show us how to magnify your name in all we do. There's no limit to your love and faithfulness – be glorified in us each day.

Amen.

February 20

Friend or Foe

> Jesus knew their thoughts and said to them, "Every kingdom divided against itself will be ruined, and every city or household divided against itself will not stand." (Matthew 12:25)

On the battlefield, soldiers fight a common enemy. If they turned their weapons against each other, the enemy could win without firing a shot. Will you face the battles of life together or become divided in the struggle?

Your marriage will face opposition of every kind – financial setbacks, rebellious children, interfering in-laws, sexual temptation, health crises, or busyness and stress. Strength to overcome is found in unity. Each challenge is a new opportunity to encourage, help, and grow closer to each other and to God.

Today, meet your "enemy" as a united front. Pray together for God's wisdom and help. Set aside any blame, criticism, or resentment you're aiming at your partner. Value the insight and abilities you each bring to the situation. Make Jesus your ally through prayer and reading the Word. Take courage in knowing that together, you can stand strong and achieve victory in the end.

Lord, show us how to be one with each other – and with you – in the battles we face today.

Amen.

February 21

Help or Hate?

> If you come across your enemy's ox or
> donkey wandering off, be sure to return it.
> If you see the donkey of someone who hates you
> fallen down under its load, do not leave it there;
> be sure you help them with it. (Exodus 23:4-5)

The mark of God's people is grace. We help the undeserving. We show kindness to our enemies. We do good to those who hate us. We let go of our right to retaliate. We show God's compassion in a bitter, angry world.

Pray for opportunities to help your unfriendly neighbor. Have patience with your backbiting coworker. Let the rude driver get ahead of you on the highway. Support your difficult relatives in hard times. Show empathy when others suffer. "Love your enemies, do good to those who hate you, bless those who curse you, pray for those who mistreat you" (Luke 6:27-28). Take every chance to do right by everyone.

When you love the ones who don't deserve it, you're living like Jesus. When you're generous and helpful you're children of light. You give your enemies an up-close look at the love of God that can save their souls.

Lord, we want to shine your light in the world. Fill us with your love so we can bless our enemies. Make us faithful in doing good to everyone.

Amen.

February 22

Walking in Wisdom

Your word is a lamp for my feet, a light on my path. (Psalm 119:105)

When surrounded by a confusing array of choices, it's hard to know which way to go. When blocked on every side with no way to move forward, you feel angry and trapped. Whether you're at a crossroad or a dead-end street, God is ready to guide your steps.

Look to God's Word for wisdom in what to do. He'll tell you his priorities. He'll warn you about the dangers of sin and the enemy. He'll share how to make peace with others, and he'll teach you how to pray. The Spirit will speak through the Bible's living pages and counsel your heart and mind. "All Scripture is God-breathed and is useful for teaching, rebuking, correcting and training in righteousness," – let it shine God's light on your path (2 Tim. 3:16).

Follow the map of God's Word today. Commit to read and study, and ask the Lord to help you understand. In his great love he'll be faithful to speak into your situation today.

Lord, thank you that we don't have to make our way through life alone. Teach us to depend on your Word. Show us which way to go, and give us hearts that want to follow wherever you lead.

Amen.

February 23

Brick by Brick

> Therefore encourage one another and build each other up, just as in fact you are doing. (1 Thessalonians 5:11)

You don't have to work in construction to be a builder. You can focus your days on building a career or education. A family or social life. A bank account or physical fitness. A reputation or sense of style. A hobby or vacation plans. In the busyness, it's easy to forget God's call to build each other up in your marriage.

Each encouraging word lays a brick in the foundation of your life together. Comforting words are a lifeline in grief. Affirming each other's abilities gives courage to chase your dreams. Tenderness and "I love you's" give relief from a harsh, critical world. Speaking God's truth resists every attack of the evil one. Your words have the power to bring hope and help when your partner needs it the most.

Commit to building each other up through encouragement. Put away the wrecking ball of a critical, negative spirit. Let God's love flow through your words to bring joy and strength to your home.

Lord, teach us to be faithful in encouraging one another. Open our eyes to see how we can build each other up. Thank you for the gift of marriage, letting us face life's challenges together. Amen.

February 24

The Field of Faith

> Sow righteousness for yourselves, reap the fruit of unfailing love, and break up your unplowed ground; for it is time to seek the LORD, until he comes and showers his righteousness on you. (Hosea 10:12)

Is your heart hardened today, unable to receive the "seeds" of truth? Has the Bible become dry and boring? Is it a chore to serve other people? Does God's moral law seem hard and unreasonable? Is prayer just a formality? Would you rather please yourself than the Lord?

Pray and ask God to break up the soil of your heart. Be honest and confess any sin you're holding on to. Read the Scriptures every day to remember what's true. Pray for a thankful heart for all he's poured into your life. Ask for deeper love – a willingness to lay yourselves down for God and the ones you're called to serve.

God wants to transform your lives. He'll make you holy and pure. You'll be his shining lights in a dark world. You'll receive the grace and love he's promised to give. "Blessed are those who hunger and thirst for righteousness, for they will be filled" (Matt. 5:6).

Lord, keep our hearts open and ready to receive your love. Make us righteous as we seek your face every day.
Amen.

February 25

Only Jesus

"You do not want to leave too, do you?" Jesus asked the Twelve. Simon Peter answered him, "Lord, to whom shall we go? You have the words of eternal life." (John 6:67-68)

Following Jesus doesn't guarantee an easy life or a quick fix to every problem. When burdens feel too heavy or the cost of obedience is high, it's tempting to give up on God. We can lose hope and decide to go our own way.

The world will say to trust in money instead of our Provider. To rely on doctors and self-help instead of our Healer. To make our own rules instead of submitting to our Lord's Word. To trust in our own strength, our own plans, and our own goodness to get us through.

Is Jesus your source for life today? Abide in him, have faith in him, and obey him in everything. Keep your eyes fixed on him when the world is calling your name. He'll keep every promise to save you, protect you, and keep you as his own forever.

Lord, give us faith that's never shaken. Be our Truth, our Shelter in the storm, and the King of our life. Thank you for your love and salvation.

Amen.

February 26

A Faithful Father

> Awake, LORD! Why do you sleep? Rouse yourself!
> Do not reject us forever. Why do you hide your face
> and forget our misery and oppression? (Psalm 44:23-24)

When our problems go on and on with no relief in sight, we can feel forgotten. We're backed into a corner with no one on our side. The stress and hurt are compounded by our loneliness. We feel angry – how could God leave us when we need him the most?

Today, remember God's promise:

"He will not let your foot slip – he who watches over you will not slumber; indeed, he who watches over Israel will neither slumber nor sleep" (Ps. 121:3-4).

You're never alone or forgotten. Nothing you face is too small or difficult for God to handle. He's with you all the time. Despite your fears and emotions, he's always faithful.

Pray together today for strength to believe. Give him your problems to carry. Tell him you're discouraged. Call on him to protect you and meet your needs. Find peace as you trust him to watch over you.

Lord, it's hard for us to see you're here. Help us to believe you care. Let us rest in you since you never sleep.

Amen.

February 27

Giving our Best

> Abel also brought an offering – fat portions from some of the firstborn of his flock. The LORD looked with favor on Abel and his offering. (Genesis 4:4)

What we give tells a lot about our hearts. The more time and preparation the gift requires, the more it says, "You're important to me." The greater the attention to detail, the more it says, "You deserve the best." The greater the personal cost and sacrifice, the more it says, "I love you."

Consider what you're offering the Lord today. Do you make time to seek his face, or fit him around the edges of your schedule? Do you give generously or keep your blessings for yourself? Do you give help to the family of God, or only what's most easy and convenient? Do you give him your future or make plans to please yourself? Do you give him obedience or carry secret sins? He knows by your gifts if he has your heart.

Today, bring him a pleasing offering. Pray and thank him for his love. Ask him what he wants you to do, and obey him together. Reach out to care for others in his name. Repent of any sins you're holding on to. Offer him all you have to use as he pleases.

Lord, all we have is yours. Show us how to give you the best of our time, energy, and resources. Let us love without holding back.

Amen.

February 28

Life in the Spirit

"Whoever believes in me, as Scripture has said, rivers of living water will flow from within them." By this he meant the Spirit, whom those who believed in him were later to receive. (John 7:38-39)

We can't begin to measure "how wide and high and long and deep is the love of Christ" (Eph. 3:18). We're given his great salvation. His perfect Word. His prayers for us this very moment at the Father's right hand. His promise of a future with him forever. The gift of the Spirit to help us until he comes again.

The Holy Spirit is your teacher, guiding you into the truth of the Word. He prays for you when you don't have the words. He gives you power to overcome sin and darkness. He gives wisdom and understanding to know what's right. He binds your hearts together. He makes your lives bear spiritual fruit: love, joy, peace, patience, kindness, goodness, faithfulness, gentleness, and self-control. He's God's seal of ownership, claiming you as his own forever.

Pray and praise God for the Spirit today. Ask for him to fill you with his love, strength, and holiness. Be at peace, knowing he's with you until the end.

Lord, keep us in step with the Spirit so we can know and love you more every day.

Amen.

February 29

Faith or Foolishness?

> Then they called on the name of Baal from morning till noon. "Baal, answer us!" they shouted. But there was no response; no one answered. And they danced around the altar they had made. (1 Kings 18:26)

The nation of Israel turned away from the living God to worship idols. Bowing down to a statue can seem ridiculous in modern times, but it's just as easy today to misplace our trust and devotion.

We can count on a job or lottery ticket to pay the bills instead of our Provider himself. We can pursue health through fad diets or science alone instead of crying out to our true Healer. We can invest in a relationship that fills our time but empties our spirit – ignoring our best friend, Jesus. We can bolster our self-worth through perfectionism and performance, forgetting we're fully accepted by a loving Father. We forget our God and put faith in what can be seen and touched.

Today, ask for faith to trust in God alone. Take your struggles and pain to him in prayer. Praise him for his faithful love and power. Believe his promises to care for you in his way, in his perfect timing. He is real, he's here, and he loves you forever.

Lord, forgive us for trying to find our own answers to life's problems. We want to trust in you alone. Build our faith and show us your power.

Amen.

March

March 1

Freedom to Follow

> Turn to me and have mercy on me, as you always do to those who love your name. Direct my footsteps according to your word; let no sin rule over me. (Psalm 119:132-133)

As much as we love the Lord our God, we wrestle against sin and evil in this life. Addictions crush our willpower. Lies become easier than telling the truth. Cravings overpower our conscience. By continually giving in to sin, it takes root in our lives and rules over us.

God has mercy on you in your weakness. When you cry out to him for help, he promises freedom. He gives you strength to repent and live in obedience again. He works in your heart so you love him more than anything. He delivers you from the power of your habits and addictions – you become slaves to righteousness and servants of love.

What sin are you battling today? Pray for help and deliverance. Let God restore your heart and mind through Scripture. Trust in him for strength to escape whatever is holding you back from living for him. Submit yourselves fully to Jesus, "who loves us and has freed us from our sins by his blood" (Rev. 1:5).

Lord, set us free from the sins holding power over us today. Make us holy as you are holy. Teach us to obey you faithfully. Let us rest in your love that never fails.

Amen.

March 2

Fight for Your Friends

Be merciful to those who doubt; save others by snatching them from the fire; to others show mercy, mixed with fear – hating even the clothing stained by corrupted flesh. (Jude 1:22-23)

You're in a battle every day. You struggle against "the powers of this dark world" and "spiritual forces of evil" (Eph. 6:12). You put on the full armor of God – his truth, righteousness, peace, faith, salvation, and the Spirit – and you stand your ground. You're able to obey, living in victory over sin and the enemy.

Yet while you're strong in Jesus, many around you are falling today. They're doubting God's love. They're tempted by sins and addictions. They're corrupting themselves with lust, greed, and pride. They're trading the truth of the Word for the enemy's lies. They're headed for pain and destruction as they turn away from Jesus.

Be God's rescuers today. Love your friends enough to tell the truth of the Bible. Pray with them for faith to believe the gospel. Show compassion as you warn your loved ones of spiritual danger. Guard your hearts and minds so their sin doesn't make you stumble.

Praise God for your salvation – you're secure and alive in him. Let his love move you to "rescue those being led away to death" today (Prov. 24:11).

Lord, you've saved us and given us confidence in your love. Show how to take your truth and deliverance to a world lost without you.

Amen.

March 3

Live to Serve

Now that I, your Lord and Teacher, have washed your feet,
you also should wash one another's feet. I have set you an
example that you should do as I have done for you. (John 13:14-15)

*J*esus showed his love through his humility. As he bent down to wash away the filth of the streets from his friends' feet, he set a perfect example for us to follow. His Word tests our hearts to see if we're willing to serve like him.

Consider how you can "wash each other's feet" today. Prepare your spouse a meal, charge their phone, run an errand, mow the lawn – relieve the burden of their to-do list with simple helps.

Be willing to clean up their mess. Pay the bill they forgot to mail. Throw in a load of their laundry. Fill up their gas tank and check the tires too. Pick up their prescription and a fresh box of tissues. Reschedule their cancelled meeting. Let them know you're ready to catch them if they're falling.

Choose three kind, humble acts of service you can give each other today. Follow the example of our Lord Jesus as you show your love. Let your marriage be filled with acts of caring and help.

Lord, teach us to serve each other with humility like Jesus. Let our love grow as we fill our home with kindness.

Amen.

March 4

Watch Your Words

> In your anger do not sin; when you are on your beds,
> search your hearts and be silent. (Psalm 4:4)

Personalities clash. Goals collide. Fatigue and stress erase your patience. You frustrate each other despite your best intentions. Tempers flare and conflict pushes you apart. Walls go up as you close your ears and hearts to one another. Out of God's wisdom, he tells you how to find peace again.

First, be careful with each other when you're angry. Show self-control with your words and actions. Be slow to accuse or blame. Take time to calm down before working through your issue. Give respect and kindness, even when you disagree. Have a humble heart to forgive.

Second, focus on your own heart and behavior. Consider the part you played in the matter. Be willing to listen; do all you can to understand each other's feelings. Confess any wrong you've done and ask for forgiveness. Let go of any desire to win or have the last word. Do all you can to make peace.

The Lord can use your struggle to uncover selfishness and pride. Trust him to use your difficult days to make you more like Jesus.

Lord, we want to be at peace with each other. Overcome our anger with your love.

Amen.

March 5

The Light of Love

Dear friends, since God so loved us, we also ought to love one another. No one has ever seen God; but if we love one another, God lives in us and his love is made complete in us. (1 John 4:11-12)

To an unbeliever, it seems crazy to believe in a God you can't see. Yet the Lord has chosen to reveal himself to the world through the love of his children. When you give to each other, you display your generous Father. When you show compassion and gentleness, you reveal your tender Shepherd. When you stand together on his Word, you offer truth to a world lost in deception. When you rescue the suffering, the trafficked, and the marginalized, you portray the Deliverer to everyone.

How is God revealed in your life today? Which acts of kindness and generosity echo the heart of God? How do your gracious words convey his mercy? Every time you love, God's love is shining in the darkness.

Remember today how the Lord has shown his love to you. As you share that love, rejoice in knowing he's living in you and making his love complete in your life.

Lord, thank you for your limitless love. Show yourself to the world by loving others through our lives.

Amen.

March 6

A New Day

> [Love] does not dishonor others, it is not self-seeking, it is not easily angered, it keeps no record of wrongs. (1 Corinthians 13:5)

When we're hurt or offended, we try to forgive but it's hard to forget. We bring up past failures in the heat of an argument. We joke and complain to family and friends about our partner's mistakes. We pull away from our loved one, waiting for them to let us down again.

Commit to honor one another today. Tear down the pile of rocks – memories of the past – that you throw when you're angry. Lay down your desire to defend yourself. Seek each other's good. Guard your spouse's reputation by respectful words that build them up.

Today can be a new beginning. The past can remain in the past. You can forgive as the Lord forgave you: "I, even I, am he who blots out your transgressions, for my own sake, and remembers your sins no more" (Isa. 43:25).

Lord, give us a fresh start today. Help us to fully forgive as you forgave us. Guard our hearts from holding grudges about the past. Fill our marriage with mercy and grace.

Amen.

March 7

Sorrow for Sin

> "Even now," declares the Lord, "return to me with all your heart, with fasting and weeping and mourning." Rend your heart and not your garments. (Joel 2:12-13)

You vowed to be faithful and cherish one another. Yet inevitably, you hurt the one you love. Your pride can keep you from admitting what you've done. You offer a quick "I'm sorry," without remorse for the pain you've caused. Your spouse – and the Lord – can see through your excuses. They know if you're truly sincere.

Put your heart behind your words today. Do what's needed to prove your love. Get serious about winning your battle with temptation. Bring your sins into the light so you can be forgiven and clean. Pray and ask God for renewed devotion to him and your marriage. Be willing to give up anything that's putting distance between you.

God doesn't want outwardly religious people – he wants children who love him with all their soul, mind, and strength. You don't want a showy romance with your partner – you want a deep, committed love that grows for a lifetime. It's time to love completely, without compromise.

Lord, forgive us for taking our sins so lightly. Help us to love you and each other without holding back.

Amen.

March 8

Take Out the Trash

> Get rid of all bitterness, rage and anger, brawling and slander, along with every form of malice. (Ephesians 4:31)

*I*f you sit down to watch TV, you'll find plenty of hatred and violence to view. Whether it's a screaming match on a reality show, a violent criminal drama, or a harsh political debate, hateful conflict is everywhere.

God's people shine as lights in the world as we live in his peace. We turn from fury to friendship. From grudges to grace. From hostility to helpfulness. From malice to mercy. The compassion and forgiveness of God cannot share a place with any kind of hatred.

Ask the Lord for a peacemaker's heart to obey his Word: "Do not envy the violent or choose any of their ways" (Prov. 3:31). Ask for the Spirit's fruit of self-control to guard every word and action when you're angry. Build a reputation of integrity and restraint in every situation. Show gentleness and kindness, even to your enemies. In this way, you display the love and goodness of God to everyone.

Lord, keep anger and violence away from our door. Teach us self-control, and make us your peacemakers in this world.
Amen.

March 9

Religious or Reborn

My sacrifice, O God, is a broken spirit; a broken and contrite heart you, God, will not despise. (Psalm 51:17)

It's easy to fill our schedules with all kinds of religious activity – Sunday worship, Bible study, charitable giving, service projects – in an effort to do good and please God. Yet in the busyness of serving him, we can miss the power of his presence. We can drown out the Spirit's voice convicting us of sin.

Take some time to be quiet with the Lord, both alone and as a couple. Ask him to reveal any sins damaging your relationship with him and each other. Examine the "sacrifices" you're making of giving, helping, and working: are they motivated by true love and compassion for others, or are you building up your self-image and reputation? Are you feeling resentful of the time and resources you're spending in God's name? Allow the Lord to rekindle the love for him that moved you in the beginning.

Freedom is found in confession. Guilt and shame shut out the joy and success of your marriage and our ministry. God is eager to forgive and make things new. Offer him the sacrifice of your hearts today.

Lord, forgive us for substituting religion for relationship with you. Make us clean and new.

Amen.

March 10

Sick and Tired

> He came to a broom bush, sat down under it and prayed that he might die. "I have had enough, Lord," he said. (1 Kings 19:4)

We suffer persecution. Depression. Exhaustion. Rejection. We try as hard as we can but it's just not enough. We give our love and attention but relationships fail. We work and plan but can't ward off disaster. Our strength runs out and we're ready to quit.

Where do we go when we've "had enough"? The Lord meets our weakness with mercy:

"As a father has compassion on his children, so the Lord has compassion on those who fear him; for he knows how we are formed, he remembers that we are dust" (Ps. 103:13-14).

God doesn't expect you to handle everything yourself. He offers his strength, his wisdom, and his hope in every struggle. He promises to lift you up when you're brought down. Take your burned-out emotions to him in prayer. Ask him to point the way to go. Rest in him, knowing he cares for you and he's in control.

Lord, we've had enough. We don't have the strength to go on. Give us rest as we trust you to care for us. Thank you for your love that never lets us go.

Amen.

March 11

Loyalty Lost

> If an enemy were insulting me, I could endure it; if a foe were rising against me, I could hide. But it is you, a man like myself, my companion, my close friend. (Psalm 55:12-13)

Our marriage vows promise faithful love through any hardship the future might bring. We commit to weather the storms of life side by side. Yet when the source of pain is our spouse – not our circumstances – our commitment is tested the most.

The intimacy of marriage leaves us more vulnerable than any other relationship. Our partner knows our deepest fears and greatest dreams for the future. They have the power to inflict great harm through angry words and selfish actions. These wounds are difficult to heal and forgive. Our trust and security can be shaken to the core.

Have courage today to bring your hurt into the light. Give your spouse freedom to share their pain. Confess any sin and seek forgiveness. Do whatever is necessary to restore truth, hope, and peace to your relationship.

In Christ, all things can be made new. As you receive his help and forgiveness, let him fill you with strength and love.

Lord, you know how we've hurt each other's hearts. Set our marriage free from pain and sin. Give us your grace today.
Amen.

March 12

Overflowing Love

"Give, and it will be given to you. A good measure, pressed down, shaken together and running over, will be poured into your lap. For with the measure you use, it will be measured to you." (Luke 6:38)

We worship a generous God. "Those who seek the LORD lack no good thing" (Ps. 34:10). He "has blessed us in the heavenly realms with every spiritual blessing in Christ" (Eph. 1:3). "His goodness and love will follow me all the days of my life, and I will dwell in the house of the LORD forever" (Ps. 23:6). He loves to pour his mercy and kindness into the lives of his people.

We're called to give like him. We meet betrayal with forgiveness. We respond to poverty with help and mercy. We build up discouragement with hope. Whether it's our time, energy, or compassion, we give out of what we've received from our Father.

It's been said that we can't out-give God. He's eager to repay your meager gifts of grace with lavish love from heaven. Who needs your friendship today? A second chance? A meal or a blanket? A listening ear? Give, and receive so much more.

Lord, it's easier to judge and point fingers than to show mercy. Let us give your grace without holding back. Show us who needs a gift of love today.

Amen.

March 13

Serving God's Servants

She said to her husband, "I know that this man who often comes our way is a holy man of God. Let's make a small room on the roof and put in it a bed and a table, a chair and a lamp for him. Then he can stay there whenever he comes to us." (2 Kings 4:9-10)

Our faith and lives are blessed when we open our home to the people of God. It takes intentional effort to invite godly, mature believers into our life. The benefits of sharing our resources are priceless – we receive friendship, wisdom, and prayer as we learn to follow the Lord more fully.

How can you make space at your table for other Christ-followers today? Do you make room in your budget to support the work of ministry? Is there margin in your schedule for quality time with other believers? Are you inviting others to speak into your marriage and Christian life?

Seek the Lord together for help in showing generous hospitality. Discover the amazing truth that the more you reach out and give, the more you'll receive from God's hand.

Lord, give us courage to reach out for friendship and encouragement. Show us how to align our time and resources with your priorities. Thank you for the blessings you have in store as we share our lives with others.

Amen.

March 14

Good News to Tell

All this is from God, who reconciled us to himself
through Christ and gave us the ministry of reconciliation:
that God was reconciling the world to himself in Christ, not
counting people's sins against them. And he has committed
to us the message of reconciliation. (2 Corinthians 5:18-19)

We trust in the Word of John 3:16, that God loved the world so much that he sent his Son. Through faith in him we're given eternal life. We, who were God's enemies, are named as friends of Jesus. We're delivered from slavery to sin and made sons and daughters of God. In Christ, we're fully reconciled to God and belong to him forever.

You take the power of this reconciliation into every relationship. When you're attacked with anger and hatred, you can respond with patience and love. When you encounter loneliness and pain, you can offer friendship and comfort. When you meet guilt and shame, you can share the life-giving message of God's salvation.

The story of reconciliation is written into your lives – be ready to share it with those who are separated from God today.

Lord, thank you for giving us Jesus. Thank you that nothing can ever separate us from your love. Let us carry your message of reconciliation to those who need you today.

Amen.

March 15

Gentle Strength

Let your gentleness be evident to all. The Lord is near. (Philippians 4:5)

Gentleness is a fruit of the Spirit. When you stay close to God through prayer and the Word, it overcomes your temper. It keeps you from demanding your way. It softens your tone. It offers a quiet, listening ear. It creates a safe place for affection and intimacy. It builds trust.

The world is watching your marriage. They see the courtesy and respect between you. They recognize your self-control, keeping you from lashing out when you're angry. They hear the tenderness in your words. They know your compassion when your loved one is sick or stressed. Your gentleness stands out in the crowd – it's evidence of the love of God.

Today, remember the Lord is near to you. Ask him for an even greater measure of tenderness toward each other. Pray for calm in the storm. Give each other the mercy he's shown to you. Take care of each other's hearts. Let the gentleness of Jesus fill your home.

Lord, keep us from harsh words and actions. Teach us to be careful with each other's feelings. Just as you're our refuge, make our marriage a safe haven in a harsh, angry world.

Amen.

March 16

Letting Go

> Then he fell to the ground in worship and said: "Naked I came from my mother's womb, and naked I will depart. The Lord gave and the Lord has taken away; may the name of the Lord be praised." In all this, Job did not sin by charging God with wrongdoing. (Job 1:20-22)

At birth and in death, we hold nothing in our hands. The years between are filled with God's gifts. Yet we never know if today's gains will be tomorrow's losses. If we'll have to give up our dearest treasures. If the ones we love most will be taken from our lives.

When we lose what's important, we have a choice: to be angry at God or trust that he's good. To feel betrayed or believe his love is perfect. To become bitter or praise God for wisdom that's higher than our own.

What is God removing from your life today? Release your grip and give it to him freely. Know he's in control. Have faith he's able to supply all you need. Love him as the One who can satisfy your heart. Receive his comfort. "And the God of all grace, who called you to his eternal glory in Christ, after you have suffered a little while, will himself restore you and make you strong, firm and steadfast" (1 Pet. 5:10).

Lord, whether you give or take, you are worthy of praise. Teach us to trust in your love all the time.

Amen.

March 17

The Power of Prayer

He has delivered us from such a deadly peril, and he will deliver us again. On him we have set our hope that he will continue to deliver us, as you help us by your prayers. Then many will give thanks on our behalf for the gracious favor granted us in answer to the prayers of many. (2 Corinthians 1:10-11)

Someone in your life is desperate for God's deliverance. Perhaps they face the breakdown of their health or marriage. Their child is about to self-destruct. Financial security has collapsed. Spiritual doubts have their faith hanging by a thread. Without God's miraculous intervention, hope is lost.

Who is counting on your prayers today? Exercise your faith in God's power and love on their behalf. Cry out to him for rescue, believing all things are possible. Offer your prayers to God as a sacrifice of love for those who need him.

Your prayers will do more than help. They'll allow you to participate in the good work God will do. They'll expand the faith of many as they see him move in mighty ways. They'll increase the glory the Lord receives. They'll join with others' prayers, knitting the family of God more closely together.

Pray faithfully today, and prepare to celebrate all that God will do!

Lord, bring your powerful deliverance today. You know the fear and suffering, the doubt and grief. Show your love and bring your comfort.

Amen.

March 18

Faith and Family

> Then they can urge the younger women to love their husbands and children, to be self-controlled and pure, to be busy at home, to be kind, and to be subject to their husbands, so that no one will malign the word of God. (Titus 2:4-5)

Whether you're running errands, responding to e-mails, or caring for your family, the world is watching. God displays himself to everyone through your daily lives, without you having to say a word.

A gentle response to a child's tantrum gets noticed. Faithfulness and respect for your husband stand out. Diligent service to your family and community displays Jesus' love. Integrity and kindness are a breath of fresh air in a me-first culture.

Ministry begins at home, where you're needed the most. It's where faith is proven as you cope with life together. You see each other at your worst, yet you're called to love through it all. That kind of remarkable love is a shining light to the lost. It presents a beautiful testimony of God's perfect love for everyone. As you submit to his Word in your home, his Word speaks to everyone who "reads" your life.

Lord, let our life at home be a witness of your love to the world. Teach us your ways and give us your heart of kindness. Amen.

March 19

One Mind, One Purpose

Also in Judah the hand of God was on the people to give them unity of mind to carry out what the king and his officials had ordered, following the word of the LORD. (2 Chronicles 30:12)

God has a calling on your lives, to obey him together in everything. Today, what is God telling you to do? How much are you to give? Who is he asking you to help? How are you called to teach, comfort, and serve? What sins need confessing? Where are you sent to share his gospel? How is he leading you into grace, kindness, and love? To follow God's Word to the fullest, you need the same heart and mind to obey.

Pray and ask God to help you know his will. Surrender your lives to his control. Ask for his Spirit to help you think as one. Set aside your pride, fear, and doubt. Seek wisdom from the Word. Depend on God for strength to do whatever he asks.

Jesus knew how much we would need each other. He prayed before returning to the Father, "Holy Father, protect them by the power of your name, the name you gave me, so that they may be one as we are one" (John 17:11). Live in unity and joy as you follow him.

Lord, we want to do your will together. Make us like-minded and ready to do all you ask.

Amen.

March 20

The Battle Is the Lord's

> Moses answered the people, "Do not be afraid. Stand firm and
> you will see the deliverance the Lord will bring you today.
> The Egyptians you see today you will never see again. The Lord
> will fight for you; you need only to be still." (Exodus 14:13-14)

Is your enemy coming after you today? Do you want to turn around and run? You can't buy your way out of trouble. You can't argue or persuade your accuser to back down. There's no defense against the disaster bearing down on you. Panic sets in as there's nowhere to turn.

The Lord wants to meet you in your fear. "Stand firm," he says. Today's enemy will be gone tomorrow. Be still!

Take hands together and face your fear. Pray and trust in God, your deliverer. Call on him to show his power for you. Focus on his strength, not your weakness. No matter what happens, he's not going to let you go. He didn't bring you this far to abandon you now. Quiet your pounding hearts and wait for him to show up and fight.

Jesus tells us, "In this world you will have trouble. But take heart! I have overcome the world" (John 16:33). Nothing you face can separate you from his love. Rest in that promise today.

Lord, without you we're beaten. Bring your deliverance today. Help us to be still and believe you're with us.

Amen.

March 21

You Plus Who?

> Do not be yoked together with unbelievers. For what do righteousness and wickedness have in common? Or what fellowship can light have with darkness? (2 Corinthians 6:14)

Unless you live on a deserted island, you've partnered with others in your life. Who is aligned with you in business? In recreation and social activities? In service to your community? You will pattern yourselves after those you share your daily lives with.

God knows the risk to your faith and obedience if you're tied closely to the world. A ladder-climbing, materialistic friend won't support your call to generosity or self-sacrifice. A non-believing business partner may reject your desire for financial integrity. The co-leader of your child's team may resist your efforts to coach in a godly way. Trying to live for Christ in an atmosphere opposed to his truth will wear you down.

Ask God for discernment in your partnerships today. Ask him to reveal which relationships threaten your faith. Renew your commitment to live in obedience and share the gospel without apology. Seek out strong Christians to encourage and build you up. Remember your identity as children of God.

Lord, we need the support of believers to live for you in this world. Join our lives together with your people.
Amen.

March 22

When More Is Less

> Then he said to them, "Watch out! Be on your guard against all kinds of greed; life does not consist in an abundance of possessions." (Luke 12:15)

Building a household requires dishes, furniture, linens, appliances – an endless list of stuff. As our belongings accumulate, it's difficult to discern between needs and wants. We begin to crave a larger home, nicer car, and a more comfortable standard of living. We can lose our gratitude and contentment with what we have.

The Lord challenges us to examine our heart attitude. Are we trusting him to meet our needs or going into debt for nonessentials? Do we give cheerfully to others or complain that we don't have enough? What is our true source of happiness?

In God's kindness he shares the secret of the abundant life – Jesus Christ. We're set free from chasing after the things of this world. We're spared the disappointment of placing our hope in money. We're offered eternal treasures in heaven that can never be lost. The greed in our hearts is overcome by peace, hope, and joy as we live for the Lord.

Lord, thank you for giving us life in you that's better than anything this world can offer. Teach us to be content with all you've given, and trust you for everything we need.
Amen.

March 23

He's Always Enough

> I know what it is to be in need, and I know what it is to have plenty. I have learned the secret of being content in any and every situation, whether well fed or hungry, whether living in plenty or in want. (Philippians 4:12)

Your journey of life will lead through paths of peace and blessing, and valleys of struggle and pain. You'll move through seasons of weakness and health. Financial burdens and prosperity. Loneliness and belonging. Conflict and peace. Through all the ups and downs, the Lord is faithful and never changes.

You don't have to be afraid or angry when hard times come. He is just as good in your hardship as in your abundance. In every situation, you can praise him for his love and power in your lives. You can be content and peaceful knowing he has a good purpose for everything you face. Your well-being is found in knowing him instead of in your circumstances.

Are you in a place of plenty right now? Do you suffer with needs that shake your faith? Find rest in your loving Father who sees all, remains by your side, and bears all your burdens.

Lord, we don't need anything but you to be all right. Help us to trust you to care for us in every way. Teach us to be content with all you've given.

Amen.

March 24

Love for a Lifetime

> Many waters cannot quench love; rivers cannot sweep it away. (Song of Songs 8:7)

Your marriage is under attack every day. Schedules and stress crowd out quality time. Exhaustion takes over intimacy. Friends, kids, and relatives compete for your attention. Conflict breaks trust and steals your peace. The world's culture battles your commitment to purity and faithfulness. So many weddings are followed by divorce – you wonder if your love will survive.

God gives hope that authentic love can survive any storm. Praise him today for the strength to keep your marriage vows. Thank him for his rescue from struggles that could have torn you apart. Remember those who gave a word of encouragement when you needed it most. The source of your love has the power to keep you together.

Identify any threats to your marriage today. Take steps to be close and connected. Make a plan of defense to protect you from harm: prayer, godly counsel, and putting each other first. Remember why you fell in love in the first place. Dream about your future side by side.

Lord, keep our marriage strong and full of love. Show us how to grow as one. Let us abide in you so your goodness can fill our relationship.

Amen.

March 25

Stick with Jesus

"Remain in me, as I also remain in you. No branch can bear fruit by itself; it must remain in the vine. Neither can you bear fruit unless you remain in me." (John 15:4)

Your heart's desire is a fruitful marriage. You want to encourage instead of tear each other down. You hope for humility to serve instead of demanding your way in pride. You desire intimacy and oneness, rather than conflict and separation. You long for unconditional love that gives grace at all times. The ideals for your relationship are high, but in weakness you fall short every time.

The key to a godly marriage is Jesus. Confess your sins and failure when you let each other down. Study his Word to learn how to build each other up. Submit to wise counsel as you learn kindness and respect. Grow in understanding of God's grace, so you can extend the same compassion to each other. Trust that Jesus will make you the husband and wife he desires you to be.

The Word promises that in Christ you're made new. He can transform the most broken marriage through his love. Cling to him, and trust him to bring life and joy to your home.

Lord, draw us close to you as we pray and study your Word. Bear the fruit of your love in our lives. Make our marriage grow in godliness from this day forward.

Amen.

March 26

Your Work Is Worth It

> Therefore, my dear brothers and sisters, stand firm. Let nothing move you. Always give yourselves fully to the work of the Lord, because you know that your labor in the Lord is not in vain. (1 Corinthians 15:58)

The "work of the Lord" isn't easy. It's challenging to provide for others' needs. It takes effort to show hospitality. It requires diligent prayer and Bible study to teach the truth. We need faith to keep believing. Our courage is tested as we share the gospel. Our wisdom and strength are stretched as we raise children in the Lord. Humility is needed to forgive and show compassion. Loving the Lord demands our heart, soul, and strength.

Take heart today as you follow Christ. Don't be afraid of his enemies. Don't worry about wearing out or giving up. Don't believe the lie that your labor is for nothing. It's worth it. You might not see results today, but God is always at work. He promises to supply all you need. He promises to stand for you. "No, in all these things we are more than conquerors through him who loved us" (Rom. 8:37).

Pray for God to renew your passion for his work. Depend on him for all you need. Praise him for the wonderful things he'll do through your obedience.

Lord, we want to serve without holding back. Use our lives to show your love.

Amen.

March 27

Love Is Brave

> There is no fear in love. But perfect love drives out fear, because fear has to do with punishment. The one who fears is not made perfect in love. (1 John 4:18)

We carry some terrible secret worries. Will God accept me after what I've done? Will I ever win this battle with sin? Is God going to give up on me?

We carry insecurity into our marriage as well. If I gain more weight, will he want someone else? If I lose my job, will I lose her respect? Are we ever going to figure out how to be happy?

God has the answer to every question: love. When you trust in his perfect love, you're no longer scared of the future. You don't worry that your mistakes will erase your salvation in Jesus. Threats of abandonment and rejection melt away.

In marriage, unconditional love breaks the cycle of fear as well. You can give yourselves to each other without the fear of divorce. You're motivated to work through issues since you're in it for life. You can be honest and real – you know you're on each other's side no matter what.

Release your fears through prayer, praising God for his perfect love. Celebrate your marriage and the vows you're keeping for life. Discover the peace that only love can bring.

Lord, increase our faith so we're "perfect in love" and free from fear. Bind our marriage together in Jesus' love.
Amen.

March 28

Peace or Panic?

> You will not fear the terror of night, nor the arrow that flies by day, nor the pestilence that stalks in the darkness, nor the plague that destroys at midday. (Psalm 91:5-6)

In the car accident, the heart attack, the corporate downsizing, or the miscarriage, it's always the same: we didn't see it coming. We can lay awake every night wondering if tragedy might strike tomorrow. We hope our perfect performance, healthy habits, and a frugal budget will protect us from disaster. Yet despite our best efforts, security is out of reach.

Peace is found in the love of our Father God. He gives quiet rest as you put your trust in him. His power and strength defend you from your enemies. His healing touch restores your health and strength. When you suffer through trouble, he brings comfort and help. You never walk through anything alone.

Be reassured by his promise to never waste your pain. In the end, he restores what's lost. He repairs what's broken. He allows you to comfort others as you've received comfort. He makes you more like Jesus.

Whether he shields you from life's storms or holds your hand through the hurricane, God is good. He will never leave or forsake you. Find rest in him today.

Lord, nothing can keep us from trouble in this broken world. Teach us to trust you in everything. Give us rest as we put our lives in your hands.

Amen.

March 29

Goodbye, Guilt!

Godly sorrow brings repentance that leads to salvation and leaves no regret, but worldly sorrow brings death. (2 Corinthians 7:10)

It's painful to admit we've hurt the one we love. We've chosen to please ourselves, ignoring the cost to our spouse. We've been overcome by anger and torn each other down. Insults and criticism have tainted our conversation. We've bent the truth, misplaced our priorities, and neglected to help when it's needed. We've fallen short of the love we're called to give each day.

In light of all the failure, you could become stuck in regret. You could give up on yourselves and lose hope for the future. Insecurity and shame could make you hide from God and pull away from your spouse.

The Lord is eager to turn your sorrow into joy. Confess your sin and receive his forgiveness and salvation. Accept his gift of a clean heart and a new beginning. Let him take your eyes off the past, so you can focus on the future he has in store.

Let go of regret and shame today. Holding on will crush your faith in Jesus and bring destruction to your marriage. Trust in God's faithfulness to forgive and make you new.

Lord, forgive us for our sins against you and each other. Set us free from the shame and guilt of the past. Thank you for your promise to forgive and give new life in Jesus.

Amen.

March 30

Forgiven and Free

> Who will bring any charge against those whom God has chosen? It is God who justifies. Who then is the one who condemns? No one. (Romans 8:33-34)

Guilt and shame steal the joy from your relationship with God and each other. Sexual sins of the past create doubt if you'll know pure intimacy in marriage. Regrets over financial choices crush your faith in God to provide. Angry words and broken promises create insecurity as you feel unworthy of love. Memories of sins and mistakes build up like a wall, separating you from those who love you most.

Who is your accuser today? How have you attempted to pay for sins of the past? In your heart, do you think you're unforgiven and beyond repair? Are you God's precious child or his broken mistake?

Consider how God sees you in Christ: Forgiven. Justified. Redeemed. Innocent. Called. Chosen. Loved. No one can require you to pay for sin that's already covered by the cross. Reject the shame that recites your list of failures – in God's mercy he "remembers your sins no more" (Isa. 43:25).

Give him your sins and regrets. Receive his kindness and love. Share the gifts of grace and compassion with each other today.

Lord, help us to remember we're yours. Deepen our knowledge of Christ to trust more fully in your love. Set us free from fear, guilt, and shame.

Amen.

March 31

Never Alone

*A father to the fatherless, a defender of widows,
is God in his holy dwelling. God sets the lonely in families,
he leads out the prisoners with singing.* (Psalm 68:5-6)

Not everyone holds memories of a happy childhood. A husband bears scars from abuse. A wife knows the sting of rejection and the shame of her parents' sin. It's hard to trust again after you're failed by those who should love you the most.

The Lord knows every wound and stands for you today. He offers himself as the perfect, loving Father you never had. He promises justice for every sin against your innocence. He sets you free from the fears and lies of the past. He provides the gift of your marriage – a safe, lifelong haven where constant love can be found.

Thank God for each other in prayer today. Praise him for making you a family, safely kept under his wing. Remember your beautiful vows to love, cherish, and remain faithful for life. Leave the past behind and look forward to the future you're building together.

No matter the regret of what should have been, today is a day to celebrate. You have the eternal love of God himself and a partner by your side.

Lord, thank you for rescuing us from loneliness and pain. You've set us free and given us love. We praise you for making us a family.

Amen.

April

April 1

Who's the Boss?

"No one can serve two masters. Either you will hate the one and love the other, or you will be devoted to the one and despise the other. You cannot serve both God and money." (Matthew 6:24)

No matter how independent we feel, we're under the power of something or someone. God knows how quickly our hearts succumb to the pull of money – we'll sacrifice our time, relationships, and values to acquire more and more. The craving for success can take authority over our lives.

God challenges you to make a choice: let him take control, or give yourselves over to money. Devote yourself today to following Christ. Let him determine your goals instead of looking at the bottom line. Obey him when he directs you to give what you've earned to bless someone else. Pursue treasure in heaven instead of status and comfort on earth.

If you're exhausted from chasing after more, find rest in God today. He promises to meet your needs. He offers a future in glory with him, outshining anything this world can offer. He rules over you with love, holding back no good thing. Serve God – not money – and find peace.

Lord, thank you for offering us more than money could ever buy. Make us faithful in serving you and you alone.
Amen.

April 2

Think Before You Speak

Even fools are thought wise if they keep silent,
and discerning if they hold their tongues. (Proverbs 17:28)

Your silence can bless your partner as much as your words. Holding back a sarcastic remark or critical comment protects your loved one from pain. Silencing excuses and lies builds trust. Refusing to nag or complain communicates respect. Restraining harsh accusations gives a chance to hear their side of the story. Energy spent on listening – rather than constant talking – allows true understanding to grow.

Think through your recent conversations. Which words created tension and conflict? What made your spouse feel rejected or unimportant? How did you attempt to manipulate each other to get what you wanted? When were you driven to have the last word at any cost?

Today, choose to be still. Give your undivided attention to hear what your spouse has to say. Breathe deeply and pray when you're tempted to lash out. Quietly honor each other's opinions and ideas. Smile, make eye contact, and show affection so your love is conveyed without a word.

Lord, teach us to listen to you and each other. Give us wisdom to use our words with love and care. Heal our relationship from the wounds of damaging speech.

Amen.

April 3

Pray for Today

Praise be to the Lord, to God our Savior,
who daily bears our burdens. (Psalm 68:19)

God never gets tired of hearing your troubles. He doesn't want prayer to be your last resort. He wants to hear every detail of your joys, sorrows, and worries. He cares about you every moment, not just in times of crisis. He invites you to talk to him every day, about every issue you face.

Jesus taught you to pray for your daily bread. He says to "Rejoice always, pray continually, give thanks in all circumstances; for this is God's will for you in Christ Jesus" (1 Thess. 5:16-18). Neglecting to pray every day denies God's love, power, and strength to provide all you need.

What are your burdens in this moment? Pray together, sharing how you're weak and tired. Stressed and frustrated. Confused and lost. Bare and spent. You'll never give him anything too heavy to carry. You'll never use up the mercy and love he's holding for you. You'll never have questions his wisdom can't answer. He'll care for you, fight for you, and keep you until the end. Commit to pray every day he gives you until he comes.

Lord, forgive us for trying to bear our own burdens. Teach us to pray all the time, trusting you to care for us.

Amen.

April 4

The Joy of Truth

Love does not delight in evil but
rejoices with the truth. (1 Corinthians 13:6)

In marriage, we hold a powerful position of influence in each other's lives. We can "spur one another on toward love and good deeds" or "cause people to stumble" (Heb. 10:24, Matt. 18:6). We can encourage faith in the Word or fall into doubt as we believe the enemy's lies. We can pursue obedience to God together, or we can tolerate sin and rebellion in our home.

Is there any evil taking root in your household? Are you passive about violence or perversion in your entertainment? Is your marriage bed pure? Has bitterness or anger been stealing peace from your family? Is anyone tearing down your confidence in the Word of God or your marriage vows?

Which truths are delighting your heart today? Is God the anchor for your soul? Does his peace sustain you through hard times? Are you placing your identity, your future, and your possessions in his hands? Are you fully open with one another, confident in the faithful love between you?

Pray that your household would be filled with God's light and holiness. Put away any relationship or activity that tempts you to reject his truth.

Lord, let us love one another by living by your Word. Give us the strength to turn away from evil. Make us holy as you are holy.

Amen.

April 5

The Gift or the Giver

> When I fed them, they were satisfied; when they were satisfied, they became proud; then they forgot me. (Hosea 13:6)

You've known God's generosity. He's met all your needs "according to the riches of his glory in Christ Jesus" (Phil. 4:19). He has kept his promise to take care of you since he "knows what you need before you ask him" (Matt. 6:8). He's proved he is "able to bless you abundantly, so that in all things at all times, having all that you need, you will abound in every good work" (2 Cor. 9:8). He's given protection. Friendship. Food and clothes. Friends and family. Homes and jobs. There are too many blessings to count.

When we're comfortable and satisfied, we can forget the One who provided it all. We give credit to our abilities and hard work. We praise our own good sense and planning. We think we're self-sufficient and deserving of even more.

Instead, choose to be grateful. Pray and thank God for all you have. Recognize him as your source of strength. Be content, knowing he's given exactly what you need for today. Rely on him for your daily bread. Never forget the Father who loves and cares for you.

Lord, we want to remember you as our provider each day. Thank you for every single blessing you've given.

Amen.

April 6

Lasting Love

> It [love] always protects, always trusts, always hopes, always perseveres. Love never fails. (1 Corinthians 13:7-8)

Nothing damages our heart like the betrayal of a friend or loved one. Marriage is designed to be a safe haven in this world – free from gossip, slander, and abuse. Our vows promise a lifetime of love, without giving up or walking out.

Are you living in the hope of your love today? Protect each other's feelings with gentleness and respect. Guard each other's security with mindful use of your time and money. Stand up for each other with critical in-laws or disrespectful children.

Create an atmosphere of trust. Be ready to account for where you go, who you see, and what you're watching. Keep your promises and live in integrity all the time.

Have high hopes for each other – expect the best and show grace for the worst. Trust in God to work out your weaknesses and make you like Christ. Support each other's goals and dreams as their strongest cheerleader.

Never give up. Banish the word "divorce" from your vocabulary. Do whatever it takes to overcome your differences and live as one.

God's love never changes. When we commit to our marriage through thick and thin, his love shines in our home.

Lord, turn our hearts to each other. Give us strength to keep our vows no matter what. Let us love as you love us.
Amen.

April 7

Love Speaks

Wounds from a friend can be trusted,
but an enemy multiplies kisses. (Proverbs 27:6)

Sometimes the truth hurts! It's hard to hear we've made a mistake. Our tempers can rise when our opinions or decisions are challenged. We don't like to be told our attitude needs adjustment. We can feel attacked and hurt when a friend or loved one draws attention to our sin.

Constructive criticism is a gift, however, when it opens your eyes to your weakness. The pain of correction is better than the destruction of sin. You're given a chance to change and grow. You're set free to make amends and begin again.

An enemy is glad to leave you in the mess you're making. Their flattery betrays your need for the truth. There's no kindness in remaining silent as you become entangled in wrong choices. Show true friendship in your marriage today by speaking the truth in love. Lean on one another for valuable insight. Encourage each other to submit to God in everything, knowing true joy and peace are found in him.

Lord, give us courage to hold each other accountable for our actions. Help us receive the truth with humility and love. Bless our marriage as we seek to obey you in everything.

Amen.

April 8

Risky Relationships

Do not be misled: "Bad company
corrupts good character." (1 Corinthians 15:33)

With the best of intentions, we can fall in with those who reject Christ and the Word. We hope to share our faith and the truth of the Gospel. To demonstrate love through friendship and help. To encourage godly choices. To spare them painful consequences of their sin. However, by trying to lift others up we can become dragged down ourselves.

Who are your closest friends and partners today? Are they fellow believers, encouraging you to follow Christ wholeheartedly? Do they dismiss, criticize, or show hostility to your faith? Examine your relationships to see if they benefit or hinder your walk with God.

Ask for wisdom by the Spirit to recognize others' influence on your character. Let him guide you in caring for others without risking your faith. Pursue godly relationships that build you up to obey without compromise. Ask the Lord to guard your heart as you love others in his name.

Lord, we need believers in Christ to encourage us in following you. Give us wisdom to guard our hearts in every relationship. Let us abide in you as we shine your light in the world.
Amen.

April 9

The Model of Marriage

> Join together in following my example, brothers and sisters, and just as you have us as a model, keep your eyes on those who live as we do. (Philippians 3:17)

No matter how long you've been married, your love can teach a lesson to everyone. The truth of the Word is shown in your wise conversations.

Your hospitality and giving show God's generosity. Your unity reflects the oneness of Christ and the church. Your affection and self-sacrifice display the heart of Jesus. Your trust in God to provide challenges others to believe his promises. Faithfulness and sexual purity reveal God's holiness to all who know you.

Be encouraged, knowing your marriage is a ministry to others today. Pray for your relationship to shine the light of Christ. Ask him to make you an example of obedience for others to follow. Seek him for wisdom to know which way to go. Depend on him for greater love and grace toward each other every day. Trust him to use you to lead others to saving faith in Jesus.

Lord, let our marriage please you in every way. Use our love to reveal your truth and goodness to everyone.

Amen.

April 10

Leaning and Learning

*Those who trust in themselves are fools,
but those who walk in wisdom are kept safe.* (Proverbs 28:26)

We take pride in standing on our own two feet. We want to pay our own way and solve our own problems. Asking for help or advice feels embarrassing. We think we're weak or failing if we can't handle every situation by ourselves.

You can't fool God by your attempts at independence. He knows your limitations. He's aware of how hard your lives can be. He allows you to struggle under the weight of trouble so you learn to lean on him.

Take a look at your challenges today. Are you trying to get through them alone? Are you stuck – unable to move forward – as you keep your issues to yourself?

Seek God in prayer and study his Word for insight. Call out to him for help. Reach out to mature, experienced believers for wisdom. Invite the Lord into your situation and trust him to provide all you need.

Lord, we can't solve our problems on our own. Only you can fully supply our needs. Give us your wisdom and help as our loving Father. Teach us to trust you in every situation.
Amen.

April 11

Hope for Tomorrow

"I will repay you for the years the locusts have eaten – the great locust and the young locust, the other locusts and the locust swarm – my great army that I sent among you. (Joel 2:25)

In our broken world we suffer loss. We experience the painful consequences of our actions. Disease and disasters take our loved ones too soon. Treasured possessions are damaged, lost, and stolen. We're insulted for trusting God's Word. Fear and frustration threaten our peace every day.

God knows what you endure in this life. He knows all you're forced to give up or leave behind. Be comforted, knowing he'll restore what you've lost. In his perfect timing, whether now or in eternity to come, he'll bless you with more than you ever had before.

Do you feel like everyone's against you? Look forward to an outpouring of God's mercy. Do you feel discouraged and depressed? Have hope, since joy will come in the morning. (Ps. 30:5). Have you given grace to your enemy, even in the pain? God will overwhelm you with even more grace – "a good measure, pressed down, shaken together and running over, will be poured into your lap" (Luke 6:38).

Trust him to give back more than was ever lost in the end.

Lord, you see our grieving. Give us faith to trust in your love that holds so much in store.

Amen.

April 12

Celebrate Salvation

When God saw what they did and how they turned from their evil ways, he relented and did not bring on them the destruction he had threatened. But to Jonah this seemed very wrong, and he became angry. (Jonah 3:10-4:1)

As children of God we receive forgiveness and salvation. We're blessed with acceptance, protection, and help from our Father. Our lives are filled up and overflow with his grace.

Yet as we celebrate his great mercy toward us, we're not always happy when he gives it to others. We struggle when he forgives our enemies. When he rewards those who haven't worked as hard as we have. When he brings honor to those who've done shameful things. We want God's mercy to flow into our lives while his justice pours out on others.

It takes humility to remember we depend on his compassion too. Nothing we've done has earned God's favor. He didn't choose us because we're special – we're his because we're loved.

Pray for a merciful heart today. Cry out to him to save the lost. Share his message of love with those who are trapped in their sins. Let anger be washed away by the kindness of Jesus.

Lord, none of us deserve your gift of love and life. Fill us with compassion for those who need salvation. Give us your heart of mercy.

Amen.

April 13

The Gift of Grace

A person's wisdom yields patience;
it is to one's glory to overlook an offense. (Proverbs 19:11)

It takes wisdom from God to pick your battles with your spouse. In the daily routine of sharing life together, they will surely let you down. You have a choice each time you're offended – to confront them or let it go.

Ask the Spirit to reveal your motives before you respond to each other's behavior. Are you seeking to have your own way? To feel superior? To receive payback? To vent your emotions? To control or change who they are?

When you feel frustrated, seek peace and unity as much as possible. Keep accusations and critical words from filling your conversation. Listen and try to understand your loved one's point of view. Offer patience and forgiveness. Give them another chance to love you better tomorrow. Remember how you've received grace in the past.

It's worth confronting sin if it's harming your family or your partner's walk with God. With the Spirit's help you can discern whether to speak or be still. You can trust him to work in your spouse's heart and give you peace all the time.

Lord, keep us from pride and selfishness that stirs up anger between us. Let us choose to show mercy and patience. Thank you for love and peace in Jesus.

Amen.

April 14

Your Father's Joy

The LORD your God is with you, the Mighty Warrior who saves. He will take great delight in you; in his love he will no longer rebuke you, but will rejoice over you with singing." (Zephaniah 3:17)

Do you secretly wonder if God is angry with you? Is he offended by your sins, refusing to listen to your prayers? Is he running low on patience, ready to punish if you fail again? When you give up on yourselves, you can believe the lie that God is done with you too.

You serve a God who keeps his promises. He will forgive when you confess your sins. He'll never use the past to shame you in the future. He's continually making you new. When he looks at you, he sees the righteousness of Jesus.

God loves you completely. He's thrilled to know everything about you. He celebrates every victory in your life. He's making perfect plans for your tomorrow and eternity. He's gifted you with amazing talents to use for his kingdom. He cherishes you. He's by your side every moment. Pray and ask for faith to believe in God's great love today.

Lord, thank you for loving us just the way we are. Your grace and love have changed our lives forever.

Amen.

April 15

Do Your Duty

This is also why you pay taxes, for the authorities are God's servants, who give their full time to governing. Give to everyone what you owe them: If you owe taxes, pay taxes; if revenue, then revenue; if respect, then respect; if honor, then honor. (Romans 13:6-7)

It's hard to pay taxes to a government you don't trust. You work hard for your money – it feels unfair to hand it over. Will your leaders waste your tax or use it wisely? Help the poor or line their own pockets? Serve their citizens or promote their own agenda? You wonder how to submit without stress or frustration.

As you pay what you owe today, remember who's in charge. You obey the Lord when you obey his servants. You honor his name when you respect the authorities he puts in place. You rely on him as your source when you have to let things go.

Today, choose God's way of peace. Trust him to protect you through your leaders. Keep a clean conscience by doing what's right. Set an example of honor and faith to everyone.

Lord, teach us to willingly submit to authority in your name. Be pleased as we give what we owe.

Amen.

April 16

A Teachable Heart

*See if there is any offensive way in me,
and lead me in the way everlasting.* (Psalm 139:24)

*I*t's a great deal easier to find fault with your spouse than yourself. In the middle of a disagreement, you're offended by your partner's tone, attitude, and choice of words. You want God to show them the error of their ways. You pray they'll change their ways. This flies in the face of the psalmist's prayer for God to identify the offensive way in me.

It takes a heavy dose of courage and humility to submit to self-examination. Ask for the Spirit to reveal any "offensive way" in you – rudeness, self-centered choices, demeaning language, or any sinful habit that's camping in the backyard of your life. Ask him to teach you his "way everlasting" – repentance and obedience produced by authentic faith in Jesus. Chances are, cleaning up the mess in your own heart won't leave much room to critique your spouse.

God is faithful in keeping his promise to finish the work he's begun in your lives. You can patiently trust him to shape you both and draw you closer every day.

*Lord, thank you for correcting us and showing how to live in your ways. Fill us with patience and mercy as you lead us.
Amen.*

April 17

Keep Believing

> They replied, "Believe in the Lord Jesus, and you will be saved – you and your household." (Acts 16:31)

The very first step of obedience we take is believing in Jesus. We worship him as the Son of God. We receive forgiveness for our sins, knowing his death on the cross paid the penalty for them all. We praise him as creator of everything. We love him as our friend. He's the Word. Our way to the Father. The promised King. He's the reason we have life forever.

What next? We keep believing until Jesus comes again. Trust in the Word and do what it says. Worship as part of God's family. Give, help, and serve others in his name. Pray continually, expecting him to answer. Be filled with "all joy and peace as you trust in him, so that you may overflow with hope by the power of the Holy Spirit" (Rom. 15:13).

Today, remember when you first believed. Thank God for your salvation. Make him the Lord over your house. Praise him for the life you have now and forever.

Lord, thank you for Jesus, for salvation, and for hope. Give us strength to believe until you take us home.

Amen.

April 18

Moving On

"Forget the former things; do not dwell on the past. See, I am doing a new thing! Now it springs up; do you not perceive it?" (Isaiah 43:18-19)

A sure way to start a fight is accusing your partner with, "You're just like your mother!" or, "You're exactly the same as your dad!" Your identity is stripped away and replaced by the past mistakes and failures of your parents.

God promised to make you new when you believed in Jesus and received his Spirit. Your father may have abandoned the family, but you're given a deep commitment to stay. Your mother may have raged in anger, but you're filled with God's peace and gentleness. Addiction, sexual sin, abuse, pride, bitterness – these sins are dead in the past as you find freedom in Christ.

Your true Father is God himself. Trust him to continue his work in your heart and life. Pray for his power to break free from the bondage of yesterday. Let him silence the enemy's lies that you'll never be able to change.

Honor one another with words of hope that God is doing a new thing in each of you. Keep looking forward in joyful anticipation of all that's to come.

Lord, give us eyes to clearly see your work in each of us. Continue to set us free from the pain and sin of the past. Fill us with hope as we trust you to make us new.

Amen.

April 19

Free to Obey

God is faithful; he will not let you be tempted beyond
what you can bear. But when you are tempted, he will also
provide a way out so that you can endure it. (1 Corinthians 10:13)

God knows the temptations we face each day, despite our resolve to do what's right. Gossip draws us in at the office. Children provoke our temper. Online shopping leads to overspending. Insecurity makes us exaggerate our success. Conflict in our marriage creates resentment. At every turn we feel the pull of selfishness and pride.

What temptations are you resisting today? Are you giving ground to sin, believing there's no way out? Take heart in knowing God is with you. He's in control and knows the battle you face. He promises to provide strength and a way of escape. Pray for wisdom to recognize his path to freedom.

Encourage one another in following God. Read Scripture together to keep your hearts and minds conformed to the truth. Let go of excuses or fears keeping you in the grip of sin. Remember past victories and how you've grown in your faith. In joy you can say, "You are my hiding place; you will protect me from trouble and surround me with songs of deliverance" (Ps. 32:7).

Lord, thank you, Father, for giving us all we need to overcome temptation. Keep us close to you so we can walk in obedience all the time.

Amen.

April 20

Our God, Our Source

"The God who made the world and everything in it is the Lord of heaven and earth and does not live in temples built by human hands. And he is not served by human hands, as if he needed anything. Rather, he himself gives everyone life and breath and everything else." (Acts 17:24-25)

God doesn't need help to keep the earth spinning. We can't do him any favors. We can't add to what he's made. We can't make him more wonderful and perfect than he already is.

We love because he first loved us. We serve because he moves us and gives the strength to do it. We show grace to others because we've received his mercy. We live because he gave us breath. He's the true source of everything we are.

Today, put God on the throne of your heart. Let go of any pride or self-centeredness that denies who he is. Thank him for the life he created for you. Praise him for your marriage and home. Give him glory for the good you've been able to share with others. Offer all you have – your possessions, abilities, and your very selves – as an act of worship.

Recapture your awe of the Lord of heaven and earth. Be still and know that he is God.

Lord, you are worthy of praise and glory forever. Our lives are yours to use as you will. We love you.

Amen.

April 21

The Gift of Wisdom

If any of you lacks wisdom, you should ask God, who gives generously to all without finding fault, and it will be given to you. (James 1:5)

As you walk the path of life, you'll encounter dead ends that stop you in your tracks. Crossroads will bring confusion about which way to go. You'll grow tired and frustrated when progress feels slow. You won't know if you should keep going, turn around, or stop walking altogether.

To the Lord, there is no such thing as a foolish question. You can ask him for wisdom about any step to take. When your thoughts are clouded by doubt or discouragement, he gives clarity and renews your purpose. He's ready and willing to provide discernment in every situation.

Which decisions are before you today? What problem or conflict seems impossible to solve? How are you struggling to keep your priorities in order? Should you play it safe or take a leap into the unknown? Seek the Lord in everything and allow him to guide your way.

Lord, we need your help to know what to do. Thank you for your generous promise to give us your wisdom. Help us to trust you as we follow your leading.

Amen.

April 22

Known and Loved

> But who can discern their own errors?
> Forgive my hidden faults. (Psalm 19:12)

We can be blind to our weaknesses. We don't notice how we're inconsiderate. How we interrupt or "tune out" when a loved one is trying to talk. How we put ourselves first in line. How our quick temper hurts feelings. How we fail to keep our word. How we look for praise instead of affirming others. How our sarcasm or criticism puts people down. We don't realize the wake of hurt and frustration we leave behind.

Pray today and ask God to reveal your hidden faults. Ask him how to love and serve others more fully. Consider how pride or selfishness has kept you from kindness. Let him show how you've had your own way instead of surrendering to him. Ask for patience to bear with others too.

God knows you inside and out. He loves you completely with all your imperfections. He's compassionate and ready to forgive. He's faithful to help when you want to obey. He keeps his promise to finish the work of making you like Jesus. Rest in his grace today.

Lord, forgive us for the ways we fail without even knowing it. Thank you for your patience and mercy. Let us trust you to make us new.

Amen.

April 23

Work it Out

Is it possible that there is nobody among you wise enough to judge a dispute between believers? But instead, one brother takes another to court – and this in front of unbelievers! The very fact that you have lawsuits among you means you have been completely defeated already. (1 Corinthians 6:5-7)

Believers are called to tear down walls. To be humble, putting others first. To give up our rights for the good of our brothers and sisters. To love like Jesus – giving, serving, and helping. To be patient and slow to anger. To show mercy and pray all the time. "Blessed are the peacemakers, for they will be called children of God" (Matt. 5:9).

But despite their calling, Christians choose to battle in court. They ruin their testimony to the world by attacking each other. The wisdom of the church is thrown away for legal counsel. No matter how much money is won, the believer loses much, much more.

Strive for unity today. Choose to love instead of fighting for your rights. Love others more than the money or property they owe. Depend on your godly leaders to mediate your trouble. Remember the world is watching – let them see honesty, kindness, and love.

Lord, you're our true source of wisdom and justice. Let us live in peace with everyone, showing Jesus' love to the world.
Amen.

April 24

The Hope of Heaven

"Men of Galilee," they said, "why do you stand here looking into the sky? This same Jesus, who has been taken from you into heaven, will come back in the same way you have seen him go into heaven." (Acts 1:11)

Jesus will come back. This truth changes everything as you wait. You don't have to fear tomorrow. No disaster can keep you from his love. No power or authority can hold back his kingdom. The future is in his hands.

You have purpose for today. As gospel-bearers, you share the hope of salvation. You can invite others to receive Jesus and wait together for his coming.

You're able to let go of this world. Knowing your treasure in heaven, you don't depend on material things to make you happy. You live to please Jesus instead of people. Your true home is in heaven with him.

You seek a reward. Today's choices affect tomorrow. You pursue love and obedience, waiting to hear "Well done, good and faithful servant!" at the end (Matt. 25:21).

Take heart in knowing you'll be home soon. The struggles of today will fade in the beauty and joy of eternity with Jesus. Find joy as you look forward to his coming.

Lord, give us joyful expectation of you coming to take us home. Let us share your good news, walk in obedience, and have hope as we wait.

Amen.

April 25

Think, Speak, Love

May these words of my mouth and this meditation of my heart be pleasing in your sight, Lord, my Rock and my Redeemer. (Psalm 19:14)

When we fall in love, our attention is consumed by our partner. The moments together are the best part of the day. Their character and interests are exciting to discover. We do all we can to express our love and make each other happy.

It's the same when you love the Lord. Your words are an act of worship. You please him by admiring his creation – how his glory is shown in the skies. He's glad when you study his Word, treasuring it as the perfect source of truth. You depend on it for wisdom, letting it influence every part of your lives. You surrender to him by submitting to its teaching.

You also worship the Lord with your thoughts. When you ponder what the Word has to say. When you're introspective, looking for anything in your life that's out of step with him. When you're overwhelmed with gratitude for what he's made.

Today, honor God with your words and thoughts. Make him the center of your attention. Keep his Word in your conversation. Think about how wonderful he is all the time.

Lord, we want our words and thoughts to make you happy. Keep us focused on your Word and the beauty of all you've made. Amen.

April 26

Together Forever

"So they are no longer two, but one flesh. Therefore what God has joined together, let no one separate." (Matthew 19:6)

Marriage is a miracle of God taking two people and making them one. As husband and wife, you create a single household. You pursue mutual goals. You share in exclusive intimacy. You join paths for a lifetime, devoted to one another's well-being. Nothing but death is meant to separate you.

Is anything or anyone coming between you today? Perhaps busy schedules are crowding out time to connect. Friends may criticize your spouse or make light of your commitment. Family members might compete for your loyalty. Job demands may steal energy and attention away from home. Your marriage might feel buried at the bottom of the pile, and you find yourselves drifting apart.

Find your way back to each other today. Take courageous steps to put your relationship first. Confess what you've allowed to divide you. Recommit to loving one another wholeheartedly. Talk and touch, and give your undivided attention. Remember why you love one another so very much.

Lord, thank you for making us, "us." Protect our marriage — don't let anything tear us apart. Show us what it means to be one.

Amen.

April 27

Love or Liberty

"I have the right to do anything," you say – but not everything is beneficial. "I have the right to do anything" – but not everything is constructive. No one should seek their own good, but the good of others. (1 Corinthians 10:23-24)

In our culture, we fight for our rights. Battles rage as people demand the freedom to live as they please. We're told as long as our choices don't hurt anyone, we can do what we like. Yet as believers, we're called instead to choose the way of love.

You've received God's grace and your life is guided by the Spirit. You're set free from the law of sin and death. "Be careful, however, that the exercise of your rights does not become a stumbling block to the weak" (1 Cor. 8:9). You might be free to drink what you like, but it can tempt a recovering alcoholic. You're free to choose what movies to watch, but it can hinder your friend in his struggle with lust. You can express your political views, but can stir up anxiety in those afraid of the future. Your actions impact others more than you know.

Lay down your rights today. Do all you can to help others obey the Lord with a clean conscience. Let love guide all you do.

Lord, make us humble and willing to give up our freedoms for the good of others. Let us love like you.

Amen.

April 28

Our Holy Home

> Nothing impure will ever enter it, nor will anyone who does what is shameful or deceitful, but only those whose names are written in the Lamb's book of life. (Revelation 21:27)

Impure. Shameful. Deceitful. The words describe our world so well. Pornography and sex-trafficking are rampant. Abortion, poverty, abuse, and violence create pain and fear. Corrupt leaders use their power for selfish gain. Our peace and joy are buried under a world of suffering and sin.

Praise God for the hope of eternity with him! He promises a future of beautiful perfection. Purity. Holiness. Rest. Truth. Belonging. Healing. Life. The ugliness and death filling the headlines will disappear as he makes all things new. Our longing for Jesus will be fully satisfied.

Allow God's promises for tomorrow to refresh your heart today. Trust him to hold on to you and bring you safely home. Believe that the darkest days will fade away in the light of God's glory. He is coming – soon!

Lord, keep our eyes fixed on you when the evil of this world is overwhelming. Give us endurance and hope as we wait for you. Make us holy and fill us with your truth so we can shine your light in the darkness.

Amen.

April 29

Remember the Romance

> My beloved spoke and said to me, "Arise, my darling,
> my beautiful one, come with me." (Song of Songs 2:10)

Your days are busy and distracting. The demands on your time and energy leave you depleted. You "divide and conquer" the to-do list, running in opposite directions. After a while, you find yourselves distant and irritable. You wonder how the romance disappeared.

Today, take a moment to say, "I love you." Offer the gift of your undivided attention. Hold your loved one close. Say why you're proud to know them. Tell how they make your heart beat faster. Remember why you fell in love in the beginning.

Pray and ask God to refresh your marriage. Ask him to break down any barriers between you. Put each other first above whatever competes for your attention. Make a plan to get away and rekindle your love. Look forward to growing closer than you've ever been before. Have hope for tomorrow, for "Many waters cannot quench love; rivers cannot sweep it away" (Song of Songs 8:7).

Lord, we don't want anything to come between us and steal our love. Provide time and space for us to enjoy one another. Bind us together in you.

Amen.

April 30

Never Give Up

Jesus replied, "Moses permitted you to divorce
your wives because your hearts were hard.
But it was not this way from the beginning." (Matthew 19:8)

Marriage is hard work! It takes effort to communicate and understand each other. It's difficult to merge two unique personalities, passions, and plans for the future. The pressures of work, parenting, and bills steal the fun and romance you wish for. You can grow apart over time and wonder what's keeping you together.

Is it worth it to stay any longer? You've fought the same battles over and over. You're hurt, lonely, and frustrated. Walls have built up that seem too thick to tear down. Hope is lost for tomorrow.

The answer lies in softened hearts. Humility to admit where you're wrong. Sincere regret for the ways you've wounded each other. Forgiveness, kindness, and devotion each day. Looking for the good in one another. Putting "us" ahead of "me". Loving each other as Christ loves you.

Pray for God to turn you toward each other today. Give up the bitterness and negative expectations you carry. Let go of the past and what you think you deserve. Choose love, and see the miracle that Jesus will do in your marriage.

Lord, our love got lost along the way. Do a powerful work in our marriage, to renew our commitment and heal what's broken. Let us love as you've loved us.

Amen.

May

May 1

Safe in His Arms

He brought me out into a spacious place;
he rescued me because he delighted in me. (Psalm 18:19)

We can feel trapped by the pressures of life. Financial burdens squeeze our budget. Health issues torment our days with relentless pain. Rebellious children keep anxiety high and confidence low. Demands at work and home dominate every waking moment, giving no room to breathe. Juggling the needs of elderly parents and young children takes every bit of strength. We're crushed under the weight, with no relief in sight.

The Lord takes no pleasure in your pain. He's caring – not critical – when you're exhausted. He knows full well when circumstances are too hard and painful. He knows when it's all just too much.

God delights in you today. He offers comfort, peace, and hope for tomorrow. He's strong enough to rescue you, his precious child. Take your eyes off your situation and fix them on Christ. Cry out to him in prayer as your deliverer. Run to him as your strong tower. He will bring you through to the other side.

Lord, we're trapped and tired. Bring us out to your "spacious place" to find safety and rest. Thank you for your love that never ends.

Amen.

May 2

Keep Up the Fight

For our struggle is not against flesh and blood, but against the rulers, against the authorities, against the powers of this dark world and against the spiritual forces of evil in the heavenly realms. (Ephesians 6:12)

The devil is determined to ruin your marriage. He knows a godly husband and wife portray Christ's love for the church. He's aware that when "two or more are gathered" in prayer, God is with them. He can see the encouragement and strength found in your family. He'll do whatever he can to destroy what God has joined together.

Resist him by putting on the armor of God. Fill your minds with the Word so you can recognize his lies. He'll whisper that divorce is the answer. That your spouse doesn't really love you. That a sexual experience outside of marriage won't hurt anyone. That God cares more about your happiness than your wedding vows.

Hold tightly to your salvation and faith in God's forgiveness. When the enemy works to divide or harden your hearts, show grace instead. When he tempts you to sin, live in obedience by the power of the Spirit. Show kindness and integrity to your partner at all times.

You have all you need to stand firm in God today. Resist the devil, and he will flee from you (James 4:7).

Lord, give us strength to stand firm when the enemy attacks our marriage. Protect us from his schemes that would tear us apart.

Amen.

May 3
Bridal Shower
The Eyes of Love

> You are altogether beautiful, my darling;
> there is no flaw in you. (Song of Songs 4:7)

They say that love is blind. But true love isn't blind, it's full of grace. It focuses on your loved one's strengths. It assumes the best and holds hope for the future. It offers forgiveness after failure. It trusts that God is working. It cherishes and admires. It commits for life. It loves like Jesus loves you.

Name the ways you appreciate each other today. Describe the unique qualities you admire. Talk about how God has especially designed you for each other. Share what you find appealing and attractive. Dream about how you'll enjoy each other for life.

Give the gift of mercy today. Let go of past regrets, failures, and negative expectations. Silence any criticism or complaining. Show the same patience and kindness you've received yourselves.

Remember the "wide and long and high and deep" love of Christ, and let it overflow into the love between you. Pray and thank God for bringing you together.

Lord, thank you for creating our marriage. Let us love each other as you love us — with grace and joy every day.

Amen.

May 4

Count to Ten

> My dear brothers and sisters, take note of this:
> Everyone should be quick to listen, slow to speak and
> slow to become angry, because human anger does not
> produce the righteousness that God desires. (James 1:19-20)

In the middle of conflict it's easy for emotions to take over. Being right becomes more important than being kind. Angry words do damage not easily forgotten or erased.

Ask God to help you slow down the pace of your conversations. Put energy into listening instead of making your point. Let go of the desire to win or have your way – the price of hurt, broken trust, and regret will cost too much.

God desires peace and righteousness for you and your marriage. You can place your concerns, questions, and conflict in his hands. You can seek his truth instead of declaring your own. You can trust him to work in your partner's heart instead of having to "fix" them yourself. In God, you're set free to love in perfect unity.

Lord, teach us to listen to each other and to you. Keep us from harsh words and selfish hearts. Give us patience and self-control by your Spirit.

Amen.

May 5

The Ones Who Made a Difference

I thank my God every time I remember you. (Philippians 1:3)

Our hearts and lives are profoundly impacted by others. We remember the teacher who believed we could do great things. The coach who pushed us to be all we could be. The pastor who brought the message of God's grace into our broken life. The mentor who encouraged us to rise above the past. The parents and grandparents who helped us on the road to maturity. The friends who've celebrated life with us each step of the way. Our spouse who committed to love us for life. We wouldn't be who we are without the people in our life.

Praise God today for loving you through others. Name them one by one, and remember the encouragement they've given. Take the time to express your gratitude for how they've blessed you along the way.

Consider how you might also be the answer to someone's prayer. Offer your time and support to those who need a friend. Bring God's love into every relationship as you help and serve in his name.

Lord, thank you for caring for us through the love of other people. Through them, you've shown your grace, kindness, and truth. In the same way, use us to bless others in your name.

Amen.

May 6

Truth and Trust

Do not lie to each other, since you have taken off your old self with its practices and have put on the new self, which is being renewed in knowledge in the image of its Creator. (Colossians 3:9-10)

A strong marriage is built on honesty and openness. Trust is broken by secrets and broken promises. Respect is earned through truth-telling and keeping your word. If you can fully trust and believe in your spouse, intimacy and happiness will flourish.

How would you measure the trust in your marriage today? Have little white lies and excuses crept into your conversation? Does your spouse have confidence in your spending habits and sexual purity? Do you protect each other's confidence and reputation? Do you second-guess one another's account of where you've been and what you're up to? Identify any areas where integrity is breaking down.

Ask God for courage to give up your secrets. Ask him for grace to forgive each other's mistakes. Follow through with keeping your promises – it's never too late to do the right thing. Renew your commitment to fully share your lives with one another. Stand firm against temptation to lie or avoid the truth. Praise God for your new life in Christ!

Lord, set us free from the trap of lies, secrets, and broken promises. Make us like Jesus as we live in your truth.
Amen.

May 7

Hearing and Doing

> Do not merely listen to the word, and so deceive yourselves. Do what it says. (James 1:22)

We recognize the road signs, but don't mind edging a few miles over the speed limit. We glance at a recipe but use an extra pinch of spice. We set the GPS but ignore its direction as we choose a shortcut. We review instructions to assemble new furniture, but skip steps to finish more quickly. We can listen to all kinds of advice or directives, but do our own thing in the end.

The consequences of ignoring the Bible's direction are more serious for your lives. If you hear but ignore God's call to honesty, your lies can cost you your job or relationships. Tuning out his call to purity can open the door to sexual sin and adultery. Dismissing his will for your finances finds you discontent and buried in debt. Every command in Scripture is given in love, so God's goodness can fill your lives.

Is there any part of God's Word that is challenging you today? Put your faith into action as you do what it says. Let the truth of God prove true in your life as you obey him fully.

Lord, teach us your Word, and give us the courage to obey what you say. Create authentic faith in us as we surrender to you.

Amen.

May 8

God Knows Best

> Stop trusting in mere humans, who have but a breath in their nostrils. Why hold them in esteem? (Isaiah 2:22)

A financial planner can't guarantee you'll have enough money. A doctor can't keep sickness from your door. Your best friend's advice won't make you an ideal parent. Your boss can't promise a satisfying career. Your in-laws don't know the best plan for your life. Your marriage can't provide constant security, affection, and self-worth. When you put your lives in others' hands, you're always disappointed.

Only God is your perfect Source of wisdom. Only he can give you love that never fails. He's never selfish, never confused, and never afraid of tomorrow. You can count on him to be strong for you all the time. He'll always tell the truth. He'll never leave or be taken away. Everything he says and does is for your good.

Consider who you're depending on today. Let your needs be met by the Lord. Give him your fears and troubles, confident in his help. Pray for power "to grasp how wide and long and high and deep is the love of Christ" (Eph. 3:18).

Lord, forgive us for putting our trust in others instead of you. Teach us to depend on your Word, your strength, and your love. We praise your name above any other.

Amen.

May 9

Pray in Every Way, Every Day

Pray in the Spirit on all occasions with all kinds of prayers and requests. With this in mind, be alert and always keep on praying for all the Lord's people. (Ephesians 6:18)

The greatest gift you can give your loved one is faithful prayer. As the one who knows your spouse's deepest struggles, fears, and temptations, you're able to pray for every facet of their life.

Pray diligently for your partner's walk with God. Ask for the Word to renew their mind and give them wisdom. Call out to God for victory over sin and doubt. Let him direct you in serving him together.

Ask for God's blessing on their work each day. Look to him for strength and endurance. Trust him to provide opportunity and prosper one another's talents.

Seek God to know how to encourage and comfort your spouse. Ask for eyes to see and understand their troubles. Pray for patience and compassion when they fail. Look to him to fill you with his grace in every situation.

Prayer invites the power of God into the life of your spouse and your marriage. Trust him to do more than you could ask or imagine!

Lord, help us to pray continually for one another. Let us love each other well by bringing our needs and praises to you. Amen.

May 10

The Wisdom of Worship

Let the message of Christ dwell among you richly as you teach and admonish one another with all wisdom through psalms, hymns, and songs from the Spirit, singing to God with gratitude in your hearts. (Colossians 3:16)

Music has forever been woven into the life of God's people. It's not just a gift to enjoy – it has a powerful impact on our faith.

Music teaches us: The Psalms – an entire book of songs in the Bible – give knowledge of the God we serve. We learn about his power to save. His mercy on our weakness. His comfort when we're hurting. His loving faithfulness that's worthy of our trust.

Music corrects us: Biblical songs, hymns, and psalms remind us of God's holiness. They touch our hearts and convict us of sin. Singing words of truth awakens us to see our false beliefs and faulty actions. We're moved to draw near to the One who makes us clean and new.

Music gives thanks: It provides a way to express love and gratitude to our Father. It gives a voice to the wonder we feel for our awesome God. It allows us to join as one with other believers, praising him together.

Today, sing to God! Receive his truth and tell him "thank you" through music.

Lord, thank you for giving the gift of music through your Spirit. Let us know you more fully and praise your name as we sing.

Amen.

May 11

Ready to Go

> Don't let anyone look down on you because you are young, but set an example for the believers in speech, in conduct, in love, in faith and in purity. (1 Timothy 4:12)

Perhaps you're young in years today. Your marriage relationship is fresh and new. You're growing in knowledge and life experience. You're still figuring out God's direction for your family and career. People are eager to give advice and influence your decisions.

Or maybe you're young in your faith. You're a newly-adopted child of God, getting to know your Father better every day. You're learning the power of prayer. You're discovering the treasures of the Word. You're eager to know God's will and do whatever he says.

Be encouraged – you're ready and able to serve the Lord today. He'll use the love and purity of your marriage as an example to others. He'll show his character through your integrity. He'll love and care for people by your generosity. He'll reach the lost through your witness. You have the same Spirit as the most mature believer or godly couple. You've received an equal share of his power, giving you everything needed for life and godliness (2 Pet. 1:3).

Don't worry about living up to people's expectations today. Keep your eyes fixed on Jesus. Love him and set an example of obedience for everyone.

Lord, give us your wisdom and make us pure. Let our faith encourage everyone to believe in you.

Amen.

May 12

Steady and Sure

> You will keep in perfect peace those whose minds
> are steadfast, because they trust in you. (Isaiah 26:3)

Every day brings people and problems determined to steal your peace. You can't make everyone happy, and they let you know if you fail. You can't control your circumstances. You can't make other people change or see your point of view. You can't erase your problems. But you can trust in God in the middle of it all.

Through faith, God gives a new way of thinking about your struggles. He shows his power and faithfulness in the Word. He promises to use every hard thing for your good. He invites you to pray. He gives wisdom to know what to do. When you depend on him, you're not thrown into panic in hard times. His peace is constant as you believe in him.

Do you have peace today? Share your stress with God in prayer. Invite him to search your heart, testing you to know your anxious thoughts (Ps. 139:23). Encourage each other to trust him by remembering his help in the past. Keep worry and complaining out of your conversation. Stay steady together as you believe in him.

Lord, we don't want our faith to be shaken by anything. Help us to focus on you and your love so we can know perfect peace. Amen.

May 13

Full of Joy

> All the days of the oppressed are wretched, but the cheerful heart has a continual feast. (Proverbs 15:15)

Life isn't always easy. Difficult people and circumstances cause frustration and stress. It's tempting to focus on what's hard and lacking in your situation. Pessimism says the bad outweighs the good. The future seems dark. When troubles come, they prove your negative expectations to be true. Gratitude slips away and prayers grow silent.

A cheerful person, however, keeps their focus on the Lord. You count your blessings. You pray, anticipating God's faithful response. You live in a constant state of "feasting" – delighting in today's joys and the hope of eternity to come. You trust that God is in control, believing he'll use every trial for your good in the end.

Is your heart hungry for happiness, or are you feasting on God's goodness today? Take a moment to list the ways he's helped and provided for your needs. Remember answered prayers. Look at all he's given, beyond what you deserve. Bring the Lord an offering of praise for what he's done. Let him bring gladness to your hearts.

Lord, let us choose joy today. Keep our hearts from worry or complaining. Thank you for your wonderful love in our lives. Amen.

May 14

The Way of Peace

"I tell you, love your enemies and pray for those who persecute you, that you may be children of your Father in heaven." (Matthew 5:44-45)

Even at his death, Jesus showed compassion for the soldiers who nailed him to the cross. He lifted them up in prayer, asking for God's mercy: "Father, forgive them, for they do not know what they are doing" (Luke 23:34). As we experience abuse, persecution, and attack in our own lives, we're called to do the same.

Who is your enemy today? Who is threatening your reputation, safety, or peace? Who is demeaning your faith in God? Take them to the Lord in prayer. Trust in his power to defend you and your family. Allow him to work justice on your behalf. Ask him to soften your enemy's heart, and for their eternal salvation in Christ.

Pray for strength to respond to hatred with love. Take every opportunity to show kindness, suppress gossip, and seek peace. Resist conflict; speak the truth with gentleness and respect. Let the Spirit guide you in all you say and do. Allow the Lord to show his perfect love through your life.

Lord, defend us from our enemy today. Help them to know the love of God and live in your peace. Give us strength to love through it all.

Amen.

May 15

The Marriage Manual

All Scripture is God-breathed and is useful for teaching, rebuking, correcting and training in righteousness, so that the servant of God may be thoroughly equipped for every good work. (2 Timothy 3:16-17)

The world is confused about how to achieve a healthy, happy marriage. No book can offer a ten-step program to create perfect intimacy. No doctor has an instant solution for a wounded heart. No online "expert" has a foolproof method to communicate openly, resolve conflict, and hold on to love for life. It's impossible for two imperfect people to create a perfect relationship, no matter how hard they try.

God knows your struggle. He gave the Bible to help as you move through life together. He promises to equip you for the "good work" of loving each other in marriage. Scripture speaks when selfishness and anger begin to tear at the fabric of your relationship. It teaches the true meaning of humility and self-sacrifice. It reminds you of God's instructions to stay pure and faithful. It warns of the danger of loving money and status in this world. God's Word provides wisdom for every situation you'll face.

Saturate your marriage with the Bible. Let it bring perfect help and peace into your life together.

Lord, teach us how to love each other like Jesus as we study your Word.

Amen.

May 16

Listen and Love

Sin is not ended by multiplying words,
but the prudent hold their tongues. (Proverbs 10:19)

It's difficult to be quiet when we're eager to prove a point. It's hard to slow down and listen in the middle of a disagreement. Tensions rise and we lose self-control. Our relationship is broken under the weight of too many words.

It's better to listen than to insist on being heard. Ask the Lord to give you hearts that seek to understand. Allow one another to freely share ideas and feelings. Give undivided attention without interruption or criticism. Take time to consider each other's point of view before presenting your own. Pursue unity above all.

When you have an idea or concern to share, think before you speak. Choose your timing and words carefully to avoid offense. Speak the truth in love, with gentleness and respect. Only say "what is helpful for building others up according to their needs, that it may benefit those who listen" (Eph. 4:29).

Ask the Lord for humility to listen and learn from each other. Let his wisdom and love guide your conversation. Enjoy the closeness that will fill your marriage as you honor one another.

Lord, make us quick to listen and slow to speak. Give us your wisdom to communicate with love and respect. Keep us from harming our marriage through our words.

Amen.

May 17

The Lie of Legalism

> To the pure, all things are pure, but to those who are
> corrupted and do not believe, nothing is pure. In fact,
> both their minds and consciences are corrupted. They claim
> to know God, but by their actions they deny him. (Titus 1:15-16)

We're saved by God's mercy and love. No amount of money, good works, or rule-following could rescue us from hell. Our hope is in Jesus – his death paid for our sins. His resurrection gives eternal life. His Spirit gives us wisdom and the strength to obey. We can't earn salvation by working, and we can't lose it by failing. Life is found in Christ alone.

Be careful when others tell you how to be a "good Christian." Salvation isn't found in how you vote. It's not determined by where you send your kids go to school. You can't buy it through giving to the church. You can't lose it through what you eat, drink or wear. False teachers will burden you with rules and guilt, stealing your freedom in Christ.

Pray for discernment today. Let God show the difference between human commands and his perfect will. Be set free from living up to people's expectations. Praise God for loving, forgiving, and giving you new life. If he has set you free, you're free indeed! (John 8:36).

Lord, guard us from those who trade grace for do's and don'ts. Let us fully trust in your salvation through Jesus.

Amen.

May 18

Our Prayer Pattern

"This, then, is how you should pray: "'Our Father in heaven, hallowed be your name, your kingdom come, your will be done, on earth as it is in heaven. Give us today our daily bread. And forgive us our debts, as we also have forgiven our debtors. And lead us not into temptation, but deliver us from the evil one.'" (Matthew 6:9-13)

Jesus came to make a way to the Father. In his love, he taught us to pray so we can draw near to him all the time.

Today, pray and worship the Lord. Name him as your heavenly Father. Tell him how he's perfect, holy, and true. Call on him to establish his kingdom on earth. Pray for the lost to be saved and the church to obey him in everything. Ask him to provide for your needs, trusting him to care for you. Confess your sins and failures. Ask for a merciful heart to love your enemies and forgive as God forgives you. Pray for protection from sin and strength to stand against evil.

Since Christ has torn down the barrier to God, pray all the time. Worship. Advance his kingdom. Ask for help. Be made clean and new. Make peace. Be safe and secure. Know his love more than ever before.

Lord, teach us to pray every day. Reveal your glory and love as we call on you.

Amen.

May 19

Trust and Tell

*If you declare with your mouth, "Jesus is Lord,"
and believe in your heart that God raised
him from the dead, you will be saved.* (Romans 10:9)

Every person must answer Christ's question, "Who do you say I am?" (Matt. 16:15). He's been named a prophet, a teacher, a miracle-worker, and a figure from history. These fall short of his true identity – the Son of the Most High God.

Salvation is found in what Jesus, the true Messiah, promised across the pages of Scripture. We believe in his name, his death on the cross for our sins, and his resurrection to life forever. We surrender our lives to his authority as King of kings and Lord of lords (Rev. 17:14). Through faith in Jesus Christ, our sins are forgiven. We receive eternal life with him forever.

Who do you say that Jesus is today? Is he your Lord? Is your hope for eternal life placed in his nail-scarred hands? Praise him today for his salvation. Find peace in knowing your future is secure. Share the good news of all he's done to rescue the lost. Pray for endurance to keep trusting in his love until you see him face to face.

Lord, thank you for saving us through Jesus. Give us a faith that cannot be shaken. Deepen our love and trust in you each day.

Amen.

May 20

The Mercy of Love

> Grace and peace to you from God our
> Father and the Lord Jesus Christ. (Ephesians 1:2)

Imagine if you brought God's grace and peace into every relationship. Grace offers forgiveness when others let you down. Grace shows mercy to the suffering and needy. Grace gives room for people to be themselves, with all their quirks and faults. Grace is given out of deep awareness of your own need for a Savior.

Peace makes a choice to leave the past in the past. Peace pursues reconciliation. Peace leaves no room for gossip, slander, and criticism that tears others down. Peace creates a welcoming place where others find rest. Peace releases the need for revenge, knowing God will make it right. Peace is found in Jesus' never-ending love.

Meet one another today with the gift of grace and peace. Forgive the past. Give help where it's needed. Comfort your pain. Draw close and listen. Then take God's grace and peace out into a world that desperately needs to know his love.

Lord, thank you for grace that forgives all our sins. Thank you for the mercy you show when we're struggling. Thank you for creating peace with God as we put our trust in Jesus. Teach us how to give grace and be at peace with everyone.

Amen.

May 21

Keeping Score

"If you love those who love you, what credit is that to you?
Even sinners love those who love them.
And if you do good to those who are good to you,
what credit is that to you? Even sinners do that." (Luke 6:32-33)

We can fall into a vicious cycle of waiting to feel loved before giving love to our spouse. We hold back gifts of time, attention, help, and affirmation until our partner has earned them. We use sexual intimacy as a "reward" for making us happy. We sign an unwritten contract that says, "I'll do good things for you if you do good things for me."

This is the opposite of how Jesus loves you. He died for us while we were still sinners. He served and healed the ones who later demanded his crucifixion. He loved the unlovely. He served the selfish. He taught the unteachable. He gave everything for the least deserving.

Ask God for his kind of unconditional love today. Take every opportunity to build each other up. Consider how your choices are helping or hurting your partner. Be willing to give up your plans and preferences out of love for one another. Take the initiative to do good and love in Jesus' name.

Lord, it takes courage and strength to give when we might not receive anything in return. Make us like Jesus so we can love without holding back.

Amen.

May 22

Free at Last

"Therefore, say to the Israelites: 'I am the Lord, and I will bring you out from under the yoke of the Egyptians. I will free you from being slaves to them, and I will redeem you with an outstretched arm and with mighty acts of judgment." (Exodus 6:6)

Do you feel like a slave today, trapped by others' selfish expectations? Are you stuck in a miserable workplace? Are you backed into a corner by creditors you can't repay? Is there no relief from sickness or pain? Does temptation drag you down again and again? You long for freedom but there's no help in sight.

Christ broke the power of sin when he died on the cross and rose to life again. Since you're adopted as God's children, you're given everything you need to overcome temptation. "So if the Son sets you free, you will be free indeed" (John 8:36).

You're also rescued from the burden of making everyone happy. "We are not trying to please people but God, who tests our hearts" (1 Thess. 2:4). Give your allegiance to Christ, living for him alone.

You don't have to fight your own battles: "He is my loving God and my fortress, my stronghold and my deliverer, my shield, in whom I take refuge, who subdues peoples under me (Ps. 144:2).

Call on God in prayer today. He loves you and will set you free.

Lord, restore our trust in you as you rescue us from sin and trouble.

Amen.

May 23

Get Ready!

"Therefore keep watch because you do not know when the owner of the house will come back – whether in the evening, or at midnight, or when the rooster crows, or at dawn. If he comes suddenly, do not let him find you sleeping." (Mark 13:35-36)

We know Jesus could return at any moment. Yet as the days and years go by, anticipation fades. We desire more of earth than heaven. We're easily satisfied by temporary things instead of craving eternal rewards. Sin doesn't seem as ugly, and God's holiness doesn't seem as beautiful.

Pray for a spiritual awakening today. Ask the Lord for a deep longing for him. Open the Word and rediscover its power and truth. Let the Lord examine your life to see if you've fallen into sin. Stay alert to recognize the enemy's schemes and lies. Surrender any relationship, goal, or possession that's become more precious than Jesus.

Help each other to stand firm in the faith. "Encourage one another daily, as long as it is called 'Today,' so that none of you may be hardened by sin's deceitfulness" (Heb. 3:13). Look for ways to be generous and serve the Lord together. Commit to pray, worship, and study the Word as a family. Help each other "keep watch" until he comes.

Lord, let us be faithful to love and obey until we see your face. Come, Lord Jesus.

Amen.

May 24

The Danger of Desire

> One evening David got up from his bed and walked around on the roof of the palace. From the roof he saw a woman bathing. The woman was very beautiful, and David sent someone to find out about her. (2 Samuel 11:2-3)

God fills this world with beauty and wonderful experiences to enjoy. He showers us with blessings, and he's pleased by our joy and gratitude. Problems arise when we covet what he's given to others, or we seek to please ourselves instead of him.

David had choices when he encountered another man's beautiful wife. He could avert his eyes and preserve her honor and dignity. He could thank God for giving his loyal soldier a lovely wife. He could ask the Lord to renew his love and devotion to the wives he already had. Instead, he surrendered to his emotions. He lusted, lied, and murdered a man to satisfy his own desires.

Are you reaching out to take someone else's gift? Are you craving a relationship, reward, or recognition outside of God's will at this time? Are you tempted to grab what you want instead of appreciating what you have?

God promises peace and contentment when you find your life in him. Lean into his goodness. He is enough to satisfy every longing of your hearts.

Lord, thank you for the hope, love, and peace you pour into our lives. Teach us to be grateful and content with all you give. Amen.

May 25

Living Life Together

> Rejoice with those who rejoice;
> mourn with those who mourn. (Romans 12:15)

*I*t can be hard to celebrate the blessings of others. An infertile couple stands by while their friends have children. A husband in a dead-end job sees his co-workers promoted. A one-income family stays home while their neighbors enjoy a vacation. Parents of a disabled child look on while other kids play and succeed at school. It's hard when someone's joy shines a light on our pain.

It's also a challenge to share others' grief. We don't know how to comfort their heart. We can't relate to the loss they've suffered. We have no idea how to help. Our efforts to encourage seem awkward and inadequate. It's tempting to avoid their struggle out of fear we'll make it worse.

The Word challenges you to share life with other believers. It's possible when you remember the goodness and love you've received. You can rejoice over others' blessings when you're grateful for your own. You can get close to someone's pain when you've received God's comfort. As you join together in the ups and downs of life, he'll make you one by his Spirit.

Lord, we want to love our brothers and sisters in Jesus. Fill us with joy when you do wonderful things for your people. Give us courage and mercy to enter into their pain.

Amen.

May 26

Waiting for Pain

> He took Peter, James and John along with him, and he began to be deeply distressed and troubled. "My soul is overwhelmed with sorrow to the point of death," he said to them. "Stay here and keep watch." Going a little farther, he fell to the ground and prayed that if possible the hour might pass from him. (Mark 14:33-35)

Jesus submitted himself to whatever God required, even a torturous death on the cross. But his obedient heart wasn't numb to emotion. He wanted his friends' support. He felt the horror of what was coming. He knew overwhelming grief and distress. He pleaded for God to make another way.

Is difficulty on the horizon of your life? Can you see the grief and pain heading toward you? Have you asked God to re-route your journey, but he's keeping you on this path? You know you won't make it through on your own. You're broken and beyond yourselves.

Today, "stay and keep watch" together. Hold each other as you share your fears. Look for hope in the Word. Pray when your loved one has run out of strength to speak.

Give God your feelings and ask him hard questions. Ask for faith to believe he's with you. Claim his promise to use your suffering for good in the end. Trust him to love you all the time.

Lord, we're overwhelmed. Give us your strength to make it through.

Amen.

May 27

Fragile Faith

> When Pharaoh let the people go, God did not lead them on the road through the Philistine country, though that was shorter. For God said, "If they face war, they might change their minds and return to Egypt." (Exodus 13:17)

When we're saved through faith in Jesus, we're set free from slavery to sin. Satan's power is overcome by the Holy Spirit. We begin a brand-new journey, following God wherever he leads.

Yet despite our freedom and life in God, enemies attack. Skeptical friends and family cast doubt on our faith. The enemy tempts us to sin and disobey God's Word. Hard circumstances test our confidence in God's love and power. We wonder if the Christian life is really worth the cost in the end.

God has compassion for our weakness. He hears every lie we're tempted to believe. He knows the struggle to stand firm in a world that hates Jesus. In his mercy, he allows us to bend but not break. He leads us down safer roads to avoid spiritual danger.

He keeps his promise to "keep you firm to the end, so that you will be blameless on the day of our Lord Jesus Christ. God is faithful, who has called you into fellowship with his Son, Jesus Christ our Lord" (1 Cor. 1:8-9).

Lord, thank you for protecting our faith and keeping us secure in you. We praise you for leading us every day.

Amen.

May 28

It's a Sure Thing

Now it is God who makes both us and you stand firm in Christ. He anointed us, set his seal of ownership on us, and put his Spirit in our hearts as a deposit, guaranteeing what is to come. (2 Corinthians 1:21-22)

Even in the joy of our salvation, doubts can trouble our minds. Does God really forgive and forget the past? If I keep sinning, will he reject me? Is there any chance I'm not really saved? Am I really becoming a new person as a Christian? His promises can seem too good to be true.

Security comes in knowing our salvation begins and ends in Christ. He chose us before the beginning of the world. His death on the cross was sufficient to cover every sin, whether past, present, or future. He promises to pick us up when we fall, keeping us on the path of faith. His love is unconditional – it's not earned by anything we've done – so we can't do anything to turn him away.

Find peace in knowing that once you belong to God, you're his forever. Trust in his faithfulness to keep working in your life. Enjoy the exciting hope of eternity forever with him. Let go of your fears and celebrate your identity as his child!

Lord, thank you for saving us and calling us your own. Give us confidence in your gift of the Spirit. Fill us with hope for eternity with you.

Amen.

May 29

The Blame Game

*Do not accuse anyone for no reason –
when they have done you no harm.* (Proverbs 3:30)

Stressful days and sleepless nights can wear you down. Emotions are raw, patience is thin, and tempers flare. The normal irritations of life begin to feel personal – you believe that nobody's on your side.

The Lord allows difficulties to invade your lives. He declares he's in control and promises to use everything for your good. The very thing you're resisting today could be the best thing of all to grow your faith. Rather than accusing others of doing harm, thank God for stretching you and proving himself faithful.

Are you on the offense today, stirring up conflict with those around you? Are you looking for a scapegoat for your problems? Does life feel unfair, as if the world is out to get you? Take a moment to consider who you might be falsely accusing.

Turn away from your anger; turn to God in prayer. Strive for peace with everyone. Let the Lord provide the help and justice you need in every situation.

Lord, help us to trust you have a purpose for hard times. Guard our hearts and words from accusing the innocent. Be our strength and help when we're treated unfairly.

Amen.

May 30

Get Away with God

Jesus often withdrew to lonely places and prayed. (Luke 5:16)

*I*s there room in our lives for solitude? It's difficult to find a quiet moment once the demands of work, family, and commitments take over the day. Even if there's a lull in the busyness, our minds keep racing through our worries and to-do list. We pick up our phone or turn on the TV, uncomfortable with silence.

Jesus knows how we feel. He was constantly surrounded by crowds hungry for healing and teaching. There was always one more question. One more sickness. One more problem. In his wisdom he created time and space to be alone with his Father. He knew he couldn't fully hear the voice of God with the voice of the world in his ears.

Create a "lonely place" for yourselves today. Carve out hours from your schedule to seek God's face. Rearrange your home to include a private, quiet corner to pray. Shield each other from the interruptions of children and phone calls during your prayer time. Experience the peace that comes from rest in the presence of God.

Lord, rescue us from our hectic pace. Draw us away to meet with you. Teach us the priceless value of faithfully seeking you in prayer.

Amen.

May 31

Fight on Your Knees

> I urge you, brothers and sisters, by our Lord
> Jesus Christ and by the love of the Spirit, to join me
> in my struggle by praying to God for me. (Romans 15:30)

We're stunned by the tragedy around us. Our friend suffers more than we can imagine. Loved ones know grief we've never had to face. People we respect are knocked down by injustice. Our words of comfort seem useless in the face of their pain. We don't know what to say or how to make a difference. We're afraid we'll hurt more than help.

Today, pray. Join in the struggle by taking their burden to God. Plead with him to hold them close. Call on him as healer, deliverer, and friend. Invite the Spirit's love to wrap around their broken hearts. Seek him for angelic protection and defense against the enemy. Ask for God's perfect will to be accomplished. Praise his name for displaying his glory in the midst of it all.

Most of all, pray that they "may have power, together with all the Lord's holy people, to grasp how wide and long and high and deep is the love of Christ" (Eph. 3:18). He's there, he's good, and he's enough.

Lord, meet our brothers and sisters in their suffering. Give us eyes to see their need so we can bring their burden to you. Show us how to love them like you do.

Amen.

June

June 1

The Message of Your Life

You show that you are a letter from Christ, the result of our ministry, written not with ink but with the Spirit of the living God, not on tablets of stone but on tablets of human hearts. (2 Corinthians 3:3)

When the Word of God – Jesus – lives in you, your life is his letter to everyone. Your compassion and mercy tell a beat-up world of his love. Your obedience to the Scriptures tells of a holy God. Your hope for tomorrow tells of eternal life and peace. Your forgiving spirit tells of the grace you've found in Jesus.

How is Christ writing on the pages of your heart today? Soak in the truth of his Word through diligent Bible study. Receive instruction through preaching and teaching. Pursue his wisdom by constant prayer and godly counsel. Grow in love by helping and serving others. Take every opportunity to hear God's voice and mature in your faith.

Remember whose lives you've "read", helping you to believe in God. Thank God for revealing himself through other believers so you could know him more.

Lord, write the letter of Christ on our hearts by your Spirit. Use us to show your love to everyone we know. Thank you for calling us to be your own.

Amen.

June 2

Watch Your Step

> Give careful thought to the paths for your feet and
> be steadfast in all your ways. Do not turn to the right
> or the left; keep your foot from evil. (Proverbs 4:26-27)

Our life's path is marked by the daily choices we make. Hard work and perseverance build our career. Kindness and honesty lead to healthy, close relationships. Integrity brings a strong reputation. Wisdom and mindful spending prosper our finances. Consistent discipline and attention help kids thrive. Faithful love lets our marriage grow closer.

Yet stepping into sin can lead to disaster. One lie leads to another to cover it up. An emotional attachment grows into an affair. Impulsive spending creates a mountain of debt. Giving in to a hot temper alienates friends and family. Cutting corners puts a job in jeopardy. Neglecting prayer, worship, and the Word weakens faith and hope in God.

Pray for strength to stay faithful to your loved ones and the Lord. Take a close look at your choices and consider where they'll lead. Keep your eyes on Jesus, trusting him to guide your steps. Walk in peace as you love the Lord with all your heart and soul (Deut. 13:3).

Lord, make us steady in every way. Give us wisdom to know which path to follow. Keep our feet from evil that will turn us away from you.

Amen.

June 3

Never Forgotten

> "But when all goes well with you, remember me and show me kindness; mention me to Pharaoh and get me out of this prison." The chief cupbearer, however, did not remember Joseph; he forgot him. (Genesis 40:14, 23)

It hurts to feel forgotten. Our boss gives the promotion to someone else. Our friends exclude us from the party. Our relatives fail to share the latest family joys or sorrows. Our house sits ignored by the real estate market. Our spouse chooses friends, work, or the kids over time with us. We feel trapped and alone in our situation, with no hope in sight.

No matter how neglected you feel, God sees you. He knows how you've given and served. He recognizes how life is unfair. He has a plan to show you kindness. He's with you now, preparing what he has for you tomorrow.

Just as God remembers you, pay attention to each other. Keep your promises to care and help. Don't leave your spouse behind to pursue your own happiness. Use the strength and blessings you've received to build up your loved one every day.

Pray and ask for God's help in your trouble. Ask him for greater love to stand by each other through it all. Trust him to remember you always.

Lord, we feel trapped in our circumstances. Help us find freedom, and show us how to 'remember' each other with love. Amen.

June 4

Seen, Heard, and Loved

And when they heard that the Lord was concerned about them and had seen their misery, they bowed down and worshiped. (Exodus 4:31)

The Lord is concerned about you today. He sees your tears over lost loved ones. He knows the weight of responsibility on your shoulders. He's aware of your fears for tomorrow. He hears every word of slander against you. He knows what it costs you to follow him.

Perhaps you feel forgotten today. You're doubting if your prayers are heard. You wonder if God has sympathy for your problems. Take heart – he sees everything and cares for you.

Pray once more about your pain. Believe that he knows every detail. Trust that he's working even now to get you through. He knows what's coming at the end. He promises to use each hard thing for your good since you love him. Thank him for standing by your side. Praise him for the perfect plans he's unfolding. Tell him how grateful you are for his love.

Share the hope of God with those who hurt around you. Offer reassurance that he sees and is concerned for them as well. Worship him together as he meets you in the struggle.

Lord, you know we're feeling low. Thank you for caring about us all the time. Give us faith to trust in your love.
Amen.

June 5

The Pitfall of Pride

> Live in harmony with one another. Do not be proud,
> but be willing to associate with people of
> low position. Do not be conceited. (Romans 12:16)

*H*ave you become snared by the trap of comparison? When filled with pride, we point fingers and criticize others who seem inferior. We feel angry and insecure when encountering those with greater success. Both pride and insecurity close the door to loving relationships with others.

Examine your family and social circle: does it include a variety of backgrounds, ages, and abilities? Examine your budget: does it allow for generosity to those in need? Examine your goals: are you pursuing status and comfort above everything else?

The world promotes the big and the beautiful. The Lord, however, gives honor to the humble servants among us. When you see others through his eyes, you recognize the worth of each person. Your pride is turned to praise as you see God's image displayed in everyone. He opens your hearts to love the world in his name.

Lord, forgive us for caring so much about our image. Make us willing to share your love with all people. Give us grace and fill our relationships with your peace.

Amen.

June 6

Waiting for Wisdom

> Desire without knowledge is not good – how much more will hasty feet miss the way! (Proverbs 19:2)

Everybody wants something. They hope to lose weight. Make more money. Find new friends. Drive a better car. Get their kids to behave. But good desires can lead to bad choices. If you make decisions too fast without seeking God's wisdom, you'll be worse off than before.

Today, slow down before you chase your desires. Research what's healthy before jumping into a fad diet. Be willing to work and save instead of looking for shortcuts. Have patience to invest in godly relationships that build you up. Shop carefully and save up for what you need. Take time to teach and train your kids instead of reacting in anger when they misbehave. Pray, ask for good advice, and wait for God to provide.

God knows your hopes and dreams. He loves you and cares about your needs, big and small. Remember his direction to "Get wisdom. Though it cost all you have, get understanding" (Prov. 4:7). Depend on his Word for truth. Love him more than anything else. "Take delight in the Lord, and he will give you the desires of your heart" (Ps. 37:4).

Lord, keep us from running ahead of you to get what we want. Let us love you as our greatest desire.

Amen.

June 7

A Parent's Joy

It gave me great joy when some believers came and testified about your faithfulness to the truth, telling how you continue to walk in it. I have no greater joy than to hear that my children are walking in the truth. (3 John 3-4)

If you're a parent, you're proud of your kids. You celebrate first steps, first days of school, and first paychecks. You're elated when they make the team or get a part in the play. You reward their good grades and achievements. Their success is a thrill to your heart.

Even greater joy is found when a child loves the Lord. When they know the Bible and do what it says. When they resist peer pressure. When they share the gospel with unbelieving friends. Their good character stands out in a crowd. Their rewards in heaven surpass any prize in the world.

Today, pray for the kids in your life. Cry out for their salvation. For courage to obey the Word and follow Jesus. For wisdom to know God's will for the future. For compassion and kindness to others. For protection from the evil one who wants to destroy their lives. Pray for God to grow them in love every day. It will be the greatest joy of your life to know they're walking in the truth.

Lord, we know the kids we love are precious to you. Call them to yourself, and give them strength to be faithful until you come.
Amen.

June 8

Willing but Weak

"Watch and pray so that you will not fall into temptation. The spirit is willing, but the flesh is weak." (Mark 14:38)

We want to obey the Lord. We want to be humble, generous, and kind. We want to walk in truth and integrity. We believe the Word and want to live by its wisdom. We love Jesus and want to be like him.

Yet no matter how pure our motives, we find ourselves struggling with temptation. We give in to anger. We take out our stress on our loved one. We stare too long at a suggestive picture. We forget the needs of those around us. We slip into pride and self-promotion. We exaggerate or tell a lie. The pull to please ourselves takes over, even while we want to please the Lord.

Today, watch and pray. Stay on alert to recognize temptation when it comes. Make a plan for how to resist and do the right thing. Talk to God about the ways you struggle. Admit how you're weak and ask for strength to overcome. Pray together for God's help to keep from falling. His love and power are enough to help you stand firm today.

Lord, our spirits are willing to obey, but our flesh is weak. Give us strength to resist temptation. Keep us "awake" so we can remain faithful to you.

Amen.

June 9

Unashamed

> Adam and his wife were both naked,
> and they felt no shame. (Genesis 2:25)

It's hard to imagine a world free from shame and embarrassment. We cringe at the reflection in the mirror as we see our physical flaws. Regrets and failures stain our memories and steal our confidence. It seems impossible to be fully "real" in our marriage – we're sure if our partner could see our true self, they'd push us away.

In Christ, we're fully known, accepted, and loved. We don't have to work for God's favor. We don't have to buy his affection. That same grace sets us free from shame in our marriage. We can forgive as Christ has forgiven us. We can "always hope, always protect, and always trust" in each other as God persistently works in our hearts and lives (1 Cor. 13:7).

Which part of yourself are you holding back from your loved one today? Which insecurities are keeping you from oneness and intimacy? How can you show greater acceptance and patience, honesty and love? Let God's grace set you free from shame and draw you closer together.

Lord, thank you for your perfect mercy and love. Teach us to show grace to each other. Tear down the walls that are keeping us from truth and oneness in our marriage.

Amen.

June 10

The Real Thing

> Religion that God our Father accepts as pure and faultless is this: to look after orphans and widows in their distress and to keep oneself from being polluted by the world. (James 1:27)

The world looks for peace and spiritual security through ritual, tradition, and ceremony. Tragedy occurs when people kill and slander each other in religion's name. Yet the Bible's true definition of religion is love for God and others.

Show your devotion to the Lord by living holy lives. Jesus tells us, "If you love me, keep my commands" (John 14:15). Rather than following a rule book or checking off the boxes of good behavior, he calls us to live out his Word in love. Your lives are set apart from the sin of the world as you obey him every day.

Obedience includes loving the weak and vulnerable among us. God's people are called to feed the poor, cherish the children, and honor the elderly. As we care for the marginalized and forgotten, the love of God is displayed for all to see.

Pursue love instead of empty religious activity today. Give the Lord your whole heart and life, and let him pour out his grace through you to the ones who need it most.

Lord, thank you for giving us Jesus to open the way to you. Keep us from settling for religious habits instead of the life of love you have in mind.

Amen.

June 11

Love the Unlovable

"But to you who are listening I say: Love your enemies, do good to those who hate you, bless those who curse you, pray for those who mistreat you." (Luke 6:27-28)

Your enemy isn't a soldier bearing down on you with a sword. It could be the neighbor mowing his lawn at 6 a.m. on a Saturday. Or the road-raging driver in the next lane. The sneaky co-worker taking credit for your project. That relative who puts you down at every family gathering. You find yourselves insulted, embarrassed, or mistreated by those who don't care.

Jesus challenges you to go against our instincts. You're to show love instead of lashing out. You're to pray, not punish. Offer care and concern, not cursing and criticism. You can take your desire for justice and revenge to God. In his perfect timing he'll make everything right. He'll give you his mercy and patience toward everyone.

Who is your enemy at this time? What is your wound? Find love, healing, and goodness through prayer today.

Lord, we lift up our enemy to you today. Bring salvation and blessing to their life. Give us strength to love like Jesus.
Amen.

June 12

King of Kings

> Let everyone be subject to the governing authorities, for there is no authority except that which God has established. The authorities that exist have been established by God. (Romans 13:1)

Politicians break our trust. Elections stir up ugly accusations and divide people from one another. Leaders fail to stand for those they're meant to serve. We fall into fear of losing our freedom and safety.

Today, remember who's really in control. God is on his throne. He's the one who puts earthly government in place. He uses the best and the worst to accomplish his perfect will. No human authority can surpass God's power and majesty: "'As surely as I live,' says the Lord, 'every knee will bow before me; every tongue will acknowledge God'" (Rom. 14:11).

Choose to pray instead of panic. Let "petitions, prayers, intercession and thanksgiving be made for all people – for kings and all those in authority, that we may live peaceful and quiet lives in all godliness and holiness" (1 Tim. 2:1-2). Trust in God as your true provider and protector. Believe you're in his hands.

Obey the Lord by obeying the law. Show respect for your leaders out of submission to God. Your peaceful life will show his goodness to everyone.

Lord, teach us how to honor the authorities you've put in place. Let us find our security and hope in you.

Amen.

June 13

There's Room for Everyone

> My brothers and sisters, believers in our glorious
> Lord Jesus Christ must not show favoritism. (James 2:1)

We know the sibling rivalry parents create when choosing a favorite child. In school, students resent the "teacher's pet" who can do no wrong. When friends shut us out to pursue other relationships, the loneliness hurts. When we're treated as second-best the wounds are deep. And if we're the favorite, we're under pressure to perform and meet expectations. Favoritism can only bring division and pain.

This is true in the church as well. God never values one person above another. In his eyes, we hold equal standing by our need for salvation from sin. He's the source of our gifts and abilities so no one can boast. He establishes all authority, so no one can say they deserve the top spot. His love is lavished equally upon all of us.

How are you giving and receiving love today? Do you feel lonely and left out or included? Are you reaching out or staying comfortable in your circle? Are you able to look past outer appearance to the inner value of each person in God's family?

Set aside favoritism in order to love. Walk away from gossip or criticism that divides you. Open your arms to welcome everyone in Jesus' name. In this way, you love like Jesus loves you.

Lord, thank you for giving your love to us all. Set us free to care for everyone in your name, without choosing favorites.

Amen.

your June 14 *marriage* ♡
God Is Enough

His divine power has given us everything we need for a godly life through our knowledge of him who called us by his own glory and goodness. (2 Peter 1:3)

As we journey through life with Christ, we can wonder what's missing. Where is the "abundant life" he promised? Why can't we seem to do "all things through Christ who strengthens me" (Phil. 4:13). We lose hope that our faith and obedience will ever grow and change.

In God's mercy he doesn't expect you to overcome sin on your own. He does the spiritual work of making you holy. His Spirit teaches you when you're slow to understand. His power gives you strength to help and serve others. His love and goodness overcome the selfishness and pride in your hearts.

His power is found in knowing him. Pray and listen for his voice. Read his Word to take in his thoughts and truth. Soak in the stories of faith in Scripture and other believers' testimonies – proof of God's power in people's lives. Follow the One who's called you. He'll take you deeper into himself and the life of faith he's promised.

Lord, restore our confidence in your great salvation. Let us trust you to provide everything we need for to love and obey with all our hearts.

Amen.

June 15

Free to Grow

> We who are strong ought to bear with the failings of the weak and not to please ourselves. (Romans 15:1)

No one is loveable – or likeable – all the time. Depression and anxiety can steal the joy from our home. Pregnancy and parenting create fatigue and stress. Personality differences, conflicting goals, and sinful choices strain our patience with each other. It's hard to wait for our spouse to heal from the past. We wonder if they'll ever overcome bad habits or grow in strength and maturity.

Even so, God calls us to love with humble hearts. We're to focus on our own weakness instead of each other's. We offer acceptance and affirmation. Constructive criticism is gentle and helpful. We forgive as we've been forgiven. We trust God to work things out in his perfect timing.

Give each other room to struggle today. Be supportive as you each wrestle with difficult emotions and circumstances. Have faith in God's promise that "he who began a good work in you will carry it on to completion until the day of Christ Jesus" (Phil. 1:6).

Lord, we know we're not perfect. It's hard to show patience and understanding all the time. Give us strength to love unconditionally, just as you love us.

Amen.

June 16

Anxious? Just Ask

> Do not be anxious about anything, but in every
> situation, by prayer and petition, with thanksgiving,
> present your requests to God. (Philippians 4:6)

Stress can saturate every aspect of life as a couple. Conversations revolve around work challenges, discipline issues with kids, financial pressures, and countless obstacles to our well-being. Anxiety can make us lash out or withdraw as we try to cope with life. The struggles we hope to face as a team become the very things that tear us apart.

God invites you to bring your worries to him. He's eager to carry those burdens that weigh you down and steal your joy. No concern is too trivial for him to notice or too overwhelming for him to handle. Freedom is found by trusting in his perfect strength and love.

Begin with prayer – express your feelings of exhaustion and strain. Confess the ways you've tried to stay in control and depend on your own strength. Ask him for exactly what you need. And finally, thank him for all the ways you've seen him provide in the past. Praise him for his faithfulness and how he'll take care of you tomorrow. Find peace in knowing he's with you all the time.

Lord, thank you for your promises to love and help us in every situation. Teach us to pray and depend on you.

Amen.

June 17

Stand Your Ground

Like a muddied spring or a polluted well are the righteous who give way to the wicked. (Proverbs 25:26)

As believers, your hearts want to obey the Lord in everything. You want to show integrity at work. You want to honor your parents. You want to faithfully manage what God's provided. You want to be a trustworthy friend. You want to teach your children right from wrong. You want to be devoted to each other. Yet as much as you want to do what's right, others work to break your good intentions.

Pray for strength to stay true to the Lord today. Stand firm if your boss tells you to cheat or cut corners. Show respect to your parents despite their difficult behavior. Tear up the credit card applications tempting you into debt. Walk away when you're invited to hear gossip. Discipline your children despite their complaining. Set firm boundaries to shield your marriage from pornography or inappropriate relationships. Respond to hate with love.

You might pay a high price for obeying God's Word. Be confident, knowing the Lord is with you. He'll give you courage, stand for you, and bring countless blessings and rewards in the end.

Lord, we love you and want to be faithful. Give us strength to stand up to evil and resist temptation.

Amen.

June 18

Read and Remember

Dear friends, this is now my second letter to you.
I have written both of them as reminders to stimulate
you to wholesome thinking. I want you to recall the words
spoken in the past by the holy prophets and the command
given by our Lord and Savior through your apostles. (2 Peter 3:1-2)

When you hold the Bible, you have a letter in your hands. God's words show the world through his eyes. He speaks truth to challenge the lies you're told. He tells the good news of life in Jesus, helping you find the way home.

The Bible holds God's promises across the ages – his plan to take this broken world and make it new. It tells how he's always good, wise, and in control. He assures you if you're his, he'll never let you go. He'll keep loving and working to make you like Jesus.

God's "letter" teaches right from wrong. When you're sick of the evil in the world, it's beautiful in its purity. It tells you how to love and obey your Father. It gives courage to keep going when your faith is beaten down. It reminds you that God is on his throne forever.

Meditate on the Word all the time. Let it do its work of transforming your mind and heart. Receive it as God's letter of love for you.

Lord, stir up a greater passion for your Word in our hearts. Let us live by all you say.

Amen.

June 19

One More Chance

> Then Peter came to Jesus and asked, "Lord, how many times shall I forgive my brother or sister who sins against me? Up to seven times?" (Matthew 18:21)

No matter how much you like your loved one, some of their behavior is hard to understand. They may be too careless or perfectionistic. They may chew too loudly or forget to answer your texts. They might keep you awake by snoring or stealing the covers. If you're not careful, your spouse's quirks and habits can start to feel like a personal offense. You assume they're self-centered and insensitive or they would change.

Give your partner grace today, and room to be themselves. Ask God for discernment to know if their actions are truly a sin against you or just a unique part of who they are. Remember the patience and understanding your partner has shown toward you. Work together to find creative ways to work through your frustrations.

You look forward to a lifetime of sharing every day with your loved one. Pursue peace. Forgive each other's faults. Pray for every kind of blessing in their life. Choose to love through it all.

Lord, fill our marriage with peace and acceptance. Give us tender hearts that are always ready to forgive.

Amen.

June 20

Trust When You're Tired

> Let us not become weary in doing good, for at the proper time we will reap a harvest if we do not give up. (Galatians 6:9)

Sometimes our efforts seem pointless. No matter how much we discipline and encourage our kids, they still rebel. We work hard and go the extra mile, but the job promotion goes to someone else. We're polite and cheerful with our mother-in-law, but she still finds plenty to criticize. We give and save our money, but debt still crushes our budget. We wonder if it's worth it to do the right thing.

Thankfully, your future is in God's hands. He recognizes your obedience when you feel invisible. He knows your desire to live by the Word and promises a reward in his perfect time. He encourages you – "do not give up" – when you're exhausted at the end of your rope.

Renew your hope in the harvest he has in store. Carry on in doing good as an offering of love to your Father. Trust him to see you and walk beside you every step of the way.

Lord, we're tired of doing the right thing with no reward in sight. Give us strength to stay faithful in obedience to you. Thank you for the promises we know you'll fulfill in our lives.
Amen.

June 21

Wounding Words

> Like a fluttering sparrow or a darting swallow,
> an undeserved curse does not come to rest. (Proverbs 26:2)

Gossip. Harsh criticism. False accusations. Put-downs. Cursing words can shred your confidence. Threats to your reputation steal your peace. Trust is gone as your "friends" show their true colors.

Take heart knowing God is for you today. He sees your clean conscience. He knows your deep commitment to your marriage. He recognizes your hard work. He watches you love others in his name. He cherishes your hopes for the future. He "takes great delight in you" and "rejoices over you with singing" (Zeph. 3:17).

Trust the Lord to stand for you today. Take each painful word to him in prayer. Ask him to replace the lies with truth. Have faith that he'll keep slander from doing permanent damage to your family. Call on him to silence your accusers. Rest in his protection and love.

Remember, "There is now no condemnation for those who are in Christ Jesus" (Rom. 8:1). When others are quick to accuse and tear you down, you're still right with God. No one can remove his grace or kindness. The cruel words of today will be overcome by his perfect love that never ends.

Lord, lies and accusations create so much pain. Heal us, stand up for us, and give us peace as we trust in you.

Amen.

June 22

Two Hearts, One Life

> But Ruth replied, "Don't urge me to leave you or to turn back from you. Where you go I will go, and where you stay I will stay. Your people will be my people and your God my God. (Ruth 1:16)

When you marry, you commit to journey through life together. You promise to stay faithful no matter what. You make choices as a team – where to work, live, and worship, how to grow your family, what to spend and give – and share the outcome of those decisions. You become part of each other's families. You study the Word, pray, and share your faith in God. Every part of your lives becomes intertwined.

Keep moving toward oneness today. Don't let busyness or distractions push each other away. Share experiences and make memories. Unite your hopes and dreams so what's good for one will bless the other. Do all you can to respect your in-laws and create unity in your families. Pursue God as a couple, participating in prayer, Bible study, and the life of the church. Keep "us" ahead of "me" in all you do.

Lord, unite our heart and minds as one. Show us where you want us to go. Let us worship you together all the days of our life.

Amen.

June 23

Loving Your Leaders

> Now we ask you, brothers and sisters, to acknowledge those who work hard among you, who care for you in the Lord and who admonish you. Hold them in the highest regard in love because of their work. (1 Thessalonians 5:12-13)

God provides spiritual guidance and accountability through our brothers and sisters in Christ. Pastors delve into the Word to help us understand the Scriptures more fully. Authors and speakers challenge us to live out our faith wholeheartedly. Other believers come alongside when we struggle with sin, discouragement, or difficulty. The benefits of God's family can become so familiar, we can take its gifts for granted.

Who has sacrificed their time and energy to teach you God's Word? When has the help of God's people brought light to your dark situation? How has the example and challenge of a fellow Christian led you to obedience? Make a list today of those the Lord has used to share his truth and love.

Consider how you can support your spiritual leaders today. Commit to pray for them as they minister. Do all you can to uphold their reputation and show respect. Offer a gift of thanks for all they've done for you. Praise God for them today.

Lord, thank you for loving us through the teaching and work of your servants. Let us encourage them as they serve in your name.

Amen.

June 24

Thinking Like Jesus

> May the God who gives endurance and encouragement give you the same attitude of mind toward each other that Christ Jesus had, so that with one mind and one voice you may glorify the God and Father of our Lord Jesus Christ. (Romans 15:5-6)

What does Jesus think about you? He calls you his prized possessions, chosen and loved. You're his new creations made righteous, innocent, and clean. You're fearfully and wonderfully made, in the image of God himself. You have the Holy Spirit living in you. You're adopted as his children. You're citizens of heaven – you belong to him forever.

It's hard to share the same attitude as Jesus toward one another. Yet by God's power, you can show his grace and love. You can praise him for making you special and joining you together. You can hold on to hope that your spouse is growing and changing. You can forgive the past and keep moving forward. Your faith can bind you together as you pray, worship, and believe.

Today, pray for endurance to love each other when it's hard. For the encouragement of seeing Jesus' character in one another. For unity in how you think. For a shared joy in following Jesus side by side. He'll make you one through his Spirit.

Lord, give us your attitude of love toward each other today. Let us praise your name with "one mind and one voice."

Amen.

June 25

No Strings Attached

> Make sure that nobody pays back wrong for wrong,
> but always strive to do what is good for each
> other and for everyone else. (1 Thessalonians 5:15)

Have you erected a scoreboard over the "field" of your home? Do you keep track of who spent the most money, had the most fun, or got the most done? Is your conversation filled with nagging, complaining, and criticism? When you feel let down or disappointed, bitterness can creep into your hearts and divide you from each other.

Tear down your scoreboard today. Ask God for grace to forgive each other's mistakes. Focus on your own weakness instead of your partner's. Put away any thoughts about getting what you deserve or what's fair. Stop waiting for your partner to bless you before you give to them in return.

Create a new list for your marriage – all the ways you can encourage, help, and honor one another each day. Strive to out-do one another in love. Give freely without expecting anything in return. In this way, the perfect love of God will fill your home.

Lord, forgive us for wanting to receive instead of give. Guard our hearts from anger or a desire to get even. Show us how to bless each other in every way.

Amen.

June 26

Enough Is Enough

> Better one handful with tranquility than two handfuls with toil and chasing after the wind. (Ecclesiastes 4:6)

Our culture tells us that bigger is better – to "go big or go home." We chase after a better job, a fatter paycheck, and a pricier neighborhood. We can push our kids to achieve all A's, first chair, and varsity status. It's a challenge to align our calendars and efforts with God's priorities. When we trade God's definition of blessing with the world's, we find ourselves discouraged and exhausted.

Before taking on another commitment or tackling another goal, ask yourself if you're chasing "wind" or wisdom. Are you feeding your pride or your soul? Will adding one more thing bring peace to your home or wear you down even more? Let the Lord guide your schedule, your heart, and your household.

Give your family the gift of rest today. Find freedom from striving for more. Discover God's love that brings true peace. In him you always have enough.

Lord, forgive us for seeking your gifts more than we seek you, the Giver. Teach us your way of peace – contentment and gratitude for all you've done. Help us to find your perfect rest as we commit our way to you.

Amen.

June 27

Fellowship in Christ

We proclaim to you what we have seen and heard, so that you also may have fellowship with us. And our fellowship is with the Father and with his Son, Jesus Christ. We write this to make our joy complete. (1 John 1:3-4)

Marriage holds the potential for beautiful intimacy, companionship, and a life of shared memories and purpose. In Christ we have the promise of even more – a deeper fellowship with God and each other through the Holy Spirit.

Sometimes your Christian life can feel too personal to share with anyone else. But your faith was designed to be lived as part of a larger whole – the church. Allowing your partner into the deeper places of your heart will bind you together. You'll help each other to know Christ more than ever before.

How are you sharing your spiritual lives today? Join together in prayer to experience God's answers as a couple. Keep each other up to date on what you learn from the Word. Share a favorite worship song you hear on the radio or at church. Ask each other for insight into challenging questions about faith or the Bible. Celebrate together when you see God's healing or salvation in the lives of others. Let your closeness with the Lord create a deeper connection between you as well.

Lord, may our fellowship with each other lead to a closer walk with you.

Amen.

June 28

Blessed Forever

Praise the LORD, my soul, and forget not all his benefits – who forgives all your sins and heals all your diseases, who redeems your life from the pit and crowns you with love and compassion. (Psalm 103:2-4)

Every believer has been lifted from the pit of sin and death by the Lord's loving hand. He knows that remembering his goodness will build our faith and confidence in Christ.

What are the benefits of God in your life today? How has mercy and salvation erased the shame you once carried? How has he restored your heart and body from abuse, depression, injury, or sickness? What is the pit that once held you captive – unbelief? Anger? Addiction? Pride? Greed? Fear? How are you living in freedom today?

Count the ways his love and compassion have altered your life. Which relationships have found peace and unity? How has your empathy and generosity grown for others? How are you longing for more of Christ and his Word?

Once we receive Christ's salvation and the gift of the Spirit, our entire self is transformed. "Therefore, if anyone is in Christ, the new creation has come: The old has gone, the new is here!" (2 Cor. 5:17). Spend some time today reflecting on his power in your life. Give him thanks in prayer for all he's done.

Lord, thank you for bringing us from death to life; despair to hope. Your love and compassion have changed us forever.
Amen.

June 29

God's Perfect Power

> "Ah, Sovereign LORD, you have made the heavens and the earth by your great power and outstretched arm. Nothing is too hard for you." (Jeremiah 32:17)

What are you facing today that's impossible? Perhaps it's a rebellious child who's wandering farther each day. Too many bills with too little money. Sickness or injury that just won't heal. A wall between you that won't come down. A dead-end job or no job at all. Infertility that's crushing your dream of a baby. At some point in life, you'll find yourselves tempted to give up.

Your hope is found in a powerful God who can overcome anything you face. You can release your tension and problems to him in prayer. You're set free from the strain of solving our own problems and finding all the answers. You never have to wonder if you're struggling alone – he's always close, always hears, and always loves.

Reach out to God together today. Ask him to strengthen the bond in your marriage and your trust in him. Let his Spirit and his Word build your confidence in his "great power and outstretched arm." Take heart, knowing that nothing is too hard for him!

Lord, we can't overcome this painful trouble without your help. Show us your power to love and rescue us as your children. Give us hope as we put our faith in you.

Amen.

June 30

Shaped by Love

> Yet you, LORD, are our Father. We are the clay, you are the potter; we are all the work of your hand. (Isaiah 64:8)

When you belong to God, he's working on you all the time. He's cleansing you, making you holy and flawless. He's shaping you for the good works he's prepared for you to do. He's making you stronger. He's putting you through pressure and fire to test your faith and make you mature.

Yet we struggle to give God control. We're tempted to talk back, saying, "Why did you make me like this?" (Romans 9:20) We want to be smart and attractive, creative and confident. We want more talent and skill. We want to choose how we're gifted to serve. We resist his will as he decides how we're "fearfully and wonderfully made."

Pray for humility to surrender to your Father today. Trust in his perfect wisdom. Go where he leads. Repent of your sin and stubbornness. Obey him in all things great and small. Believe his promise to finish the good work he's begun in your lives.

Lord, thank you for working in us to make us like Jesus. Give us faith to accept and obey your will. Have your way — we are yours.

Amen.

July

July 1

The Gift of Love

I always thank my God as I remember you in my prayers, because I hear about your love for all his holy people and your faith in the Lord Jesus. (Philemon 1:4-5)

Today, thank God for the gift of each other. Praise him for giving you a partner who believes in Jesus. Who encourages you to trust in hard times. Who wants to do God's will beside you every day. Who prays for you and your family. Who will share eternal life with you in the presence of God. Thank him for making you one in the Spirit.

Pray and thank God for your spouse's love. For the way they sacrifice their time and energy for your well-being. For the comfort and help they offer in your darkest days. For their faithfulness and affection, generosity and fun. For the way they believe in you when you've lost hope in yourself. You give and receive the love of God by loving each other in his name.

Make a habit of praying for each other each day. Let the Lord make you one as you thank him for your marriage. Depend on him to grow your faith as you seek him together. Your relationship will become a testimony to everyone of what God's love looks like.

Lord, make us diligent to pray for each other. Thank you for the love and faith we share in you.

Amen.

July 2

Two Are Better Than One

> Also, if two lie down together, they will keep warm.
> But how can one keep warm alone? (Ecclesiastes 4:11)

Are you feeling the cold winds blowing today of stress, conflict, or heartache? Your marriage is a blessing when you offer the warmth of our love and support. Yet your pain is compounded if your partner is absent or distant in your struggle.

How does life feel cold to you today? If you're experiencing rejection or loneliness, build in extra time for companionship together. Does your job feel like a dead-end, or insufficient to meet your needs? Praise each other's talents, strength, and hard work. Pray for God's provision of a rewarding career. Are you struggling through physical sickness or limitations? Serve each other and create room for rest. Have you lost a person, place, or possession that meant the world to you? Offer comfort and understanding through the grieving process.

Your relationship is a gift from God to keep you from suffering hard times alone. Turn your hearts and attention to one another in all you're going through. Praise God for the warmth you can share in every situation.

Lord, thank you for giving us encouragement and love through our marriage. Keep us close to you and each other in hard times. Amen.

July 3

Our Savior, Our King

"The Son is the radiance of God's glory and the exact representation of his being, sustaining all things by his powerful word. After he had provided purification for sins, he sat down at the right hand of the Majesty in heaven." (Hebrews 1:3)

When we think of Jesus, we picture the Baby in a manger. The Provider who gave fish and bread to the crowds. The Healer who touched the sick and broken. The Teacher who explained God's Word. The Miracle Worker who calmed the storm and raised the dead. He was the Messiah the world was waiting for.

Today, worship Jesus as the image of God himself. He's your Creator who sustains your life. He died as the holy, perfect sacrifice for your sin. He rules forever as King of kings and Lord of lords.

"Splendor and majesty are before him;
strength and glory are in his sanctuary.
Ascribe to the Lord, all you families of nations,
ascribe to the Lord glory and strength.
Ascribe to the Lord the glory due his name;
bring an offering and come into his courts.
Worship the Lord in the splendor of his holiness;
tremble before him, all the earth.
Say among the nations, "The Lord reigns" (Ps. 96:6-10).

Lord, thank you for revealing your glory in Jesus. May we worship you forever.

Amen.

July 4

No Longer Slaves

"I am the LORD your God, who brought you out of Egypt so that you would no longer be slaves to the Egyptians; I broke the bars of your yoke and enabled you to walk with heads held high." (Leviticus 26:13)

When we receive Christ as our Savior, "the old has gone, the new is here!" (2 Cor. 5:17). We're made clean, set free from slavery to sin. We're given a new identity as children of God. The shame of failure, sin, and destructive habits is washed away.

Are you walking with your heads held high today? Perhaps the disgrace of the past is stealing your confidence. The pain of regret is wiping out the joy of your salvation. You feel marked by what you've done, rather than joyfully free in God's grace.

Pray for faith to believe you're truly forgiven. Take hold of God's Word as it declares you righteous. Accepted. Transformed. Reconciled. Confident. Blameless. Reject the enemy's lie that you're past the reach of God's mercy. Praise Jesus for bearing the full penalty of your sin, releasing you from guilt and fear.

Celebrate, since "in him and through faith in him we may approach God with freedom and confidence" (Eph. 3:12). Amen!

Lord, set us free from the shame of the past. Give us faith to trust in your love and salvation. Remind us who we are in you. Amen.

July 5

Jesus Understands

For we do not have a high priest who is unable to empathize with our weaknesses, but we have one who has been tempted in every way, just as we are – yet he did not sin. (Hebrews 4:15)

Jesus knows how hard it is to live in this world. He knows the physical strain of our busy days. The stress of balancing our budget. The worry we feel for our children. The pull of greed and lust. The tension between pleasing our partner and ourselves. The disappointment of lost opportunities. The cruelty by those who should have loved us most. Jesus came and lived among us, so he experienced every kind of suffering we'll ever face.

Take your troubles to God in prayer today. Tell him how you're tempted. Name your fears and frustrations. Confess how you've fallen, and receive his forgiveness. Ask for his power to resist the enemy. Place your hurts and burdens in his hands.

Trust in Jesus' heart for you – his empathy and compassion for your struggle. Let his Word teach you what to do. Encourage each other to keep pressing on. "Do not be overcome by evil, but overcome evil with good" (Rom. 12:21).

Lord, you've walked in our shoes so you know what we face. Thank you for your compassion for our weakness. Give us strength to do what's right today.

Amen.

July 6

Excuses, Excuses

If we claim to be without sin, we deceive ourselves and the truth is not in us. If we confess our sins, he is faithful and just and will forgive us our sins and purify us from all unrighteousness. (1 John 1:8-9)

We're good at making excuses for our sin. I had a bad day so I lost my temper. I ran out of time to keep my promise. Everybody else was doing it. They don't deserve a second chance. It was a one-time thing. Nobody will find out. At least I'm not as bad as they are. We compare ourselves to others, instead the holiness of Jesus shown in the Word.

Are you giving yourself permission to sin today? Pray and ask God to show you the truth of what's in your heart and life. Confess the sins he uncovers. Trust him to forgive and make you clean. Pray for strength to obey without compromise.

Encourage each other to do what's right. Look to the Word as your standard for right and wrong. Pray for each other to walk in the light with a clear conscience. Have joy knowing you're living in the truth.

Lord, we fool ourselves into thinking we're innocent. Thank you for your grace that lets us begin again.

Amen.

July 7

Strong and Satisfied

The LORD will guide you always; he will satisfy your needs in a sun-scorched land and will strengthen your frame. You will be like a well-watered garden, like a spring whose waters never fail. (Isaiah 58:11)

It can feel hard to keep up with your own life. The calendar is packed with appointments and plans. The needs of your family never let up. Your boss keeps piling on the work. Decisions, bills, and "what-ifs" are draining your strength. You don't have all the answers and you're burning out.

Jesus sees how much you carry on your shoulders today. He offers living water to refresh your soul. He takes your problems out of your hands, promising to lead the way through. He knows your needs and is ready to provide. It's no secret you're tired and ready to quit – he wants to build you up with strength to keep going.

Let the Lord satisfy your thirst today. Pray for help. Ask for guidance. Tell him what you need. Read the Word and let its promises restore your hope for tomorrow. Trust in God's love that never lets you go. The One who brings rain in the desert will give you life and joy.

Lord, we are desperate for your living water. Give us wisdom and strength through your Spirit. Let us trust in you all the time.

Amen.

July 8

A Promise to Hold on To

But in keeping with his promise we are looking forward to a new heaven and a new earth, where righteousness dwells. (2 Peter 3:13)

You can look at the past with all its regrets. You remember your shameful choices and embarrassing mistakes. Hindsight tells how you failed to be strong, smart, and brave. You grieve what's been lost. You wish to go back and do it over again.

You can also be consumed with the here and now. You're chasing your goals as hard as you can. You're overwhelmed by so many responsibilities. You're just trying to make it, one day at a time.

We're called to look forward to the day of the Lord. We'll be transformed – set free from sin and temptation. We'll be healthy and whole. We'll have perfect peace, surrounded by God's family. Every longing and disappointment will be satisfied in Jesus. Justice will reign. We'll live forever in the presence of our Father.

"So then, dear friends, since you are looking forward to this, make every effort to be found spotless, blameless and at peace with him" (2 Pet. 3:14). Let go of the past as a new creation in Jesus. Be wise in the present, preparing to see his face. Walk in obedience. Put your hope in God instead of your circumstances. Have joy, knowing he's coming soon.

Lord, let us live holy and godly lives as we look forward to your coming.

Amen.

July 9

Steady Together

Jesus said to his disciples: "Things that cause people to stumble are bound to come, but woe to anyone through whom they come. It would be better for them to be thrown into the sea with a millstone tied around their neck than to cause one of these little ones to stumble." (Luke 17:1-2)

As we share the closeness of married life, we affect each other's attitudes and choices. Our eating habits tend to fall in line. We support similar political views and social causes. Our social circles blend into one. We laugh at the same jokes and enjoy the same entertainment. As "I" becomes "we", it's important to remember the influence we hold over one another.

Today you have a choice: will you bring temptation or encouragement to your partner? Will you "spur one another on to love and good deeds"? (Heb. 10:24). Or will you cause each other to stumble into fear, anger, lust, selfishness, or pride.

Choose to be a spiritual blessing to your loved one. Pray together. Commit to obey the Lord in every way. Search the Scriptures to know what to do. Turn away from sin and walk in the light. Find hope and strength by following Christ together.

Lord, keep us from tempting each other to sin. Fill our home with faith and love. Make us holy as you are holy.

Amen.

July 10

Made by Love

So God created mankind in his own image, in the image of God he created them; male and female he created them. (Genesis 1:27)

Imagine the transformation in your marriage if you viewed one another as image-bearers of God! The Lord chose to display his attributes through mankind – the final masterpiece of all he created.

How do you see the Lord's image displayed in one another today? Value each other's intelligence and creativity. Your compassion and mercy. Beauty and strength. Justice and integrity. Discernment and wisdom. Kindness and love. Despite your imperfections, the fingerprints of God are wonderful to see.

Take a moment to pray and thank God for the unique creation of your spouse. Name the qualities you value most – the ones that remind you of Jesus. Ask for a greater appreciation for who they are. Pray for eyes to see past their weaknesses and celebrate their strengths.

Trust that God has made you "very good" and delights in who you are (Gen. 1:31). He's ready to show himself to a lost world as his character is revealed through your lives.

Lord, help us understand what it means to be made in your image. Let us cherish one another as your priceless creation. May we know you better as we grow closer to each other.
Amen.

July 11

Gentle Like Jesus

> Husbands, love your wives and do
> not be harsh with them. (Colossians 3:19)

Husband, your wife is not a child in need of discipline. She's not an employee performing her duties. She's not a slave, serving in silence. She's not an object for your pleasure. She's not a student needing your teaching. She's a wife who needs your love.

Be careful with your loved one's heart today. Have patience when she makes mistakes. Show courtesy and respect all the time. Treasure her as God's creation – a helper made just for you (Gen. 2:18). Provide for her needs. Protect her from harm. Cherish her body. Value her wisdom and insight. Recognize her efforts to make a home for your family. Pray for her every day.

You show the world the love of Jesus every time you serve and care for your wife. Let his light shine in you as you love without holding back. Ask the Spirit to do his work, giving you the fruit of gentleness and self-control. In him, you'll become a man she can trust with her life.

Lord, teach me to be gentle and compassionate toward my wife. I want to love her like you love me.

Amen.

July 12

The School of Love

> Now about your love for one another we do not need to write to you, for you yourselves have been taught by God to love each other. (1 Thessalonians 4:9)

You want to love each other but don't know how. Perhaps your parents were cold and distant all your life. Maybe they gave up on marriage and walked away. Your friends are constantly angry and disappointed by their partner. Couples who seemed strong are breaking their vows, one after the other. No book or psychologist holds all the answers. You feel lost and alone as you try to figure it out.

Be encouraged, because you have the Spirit as your marriage counselor. The One who loves perfectly offers all you need to love each other. The Word tells exactly what to do:

Love is patient, love is kind. It does not envy, it does not boast, it is not proud. It does not dishonor others, it is not self-seeking, it is not easily angered, it keeps no record of wrongs. Love does not delight in evil but rejoices with the truth. It always protects, always trusts, always hopes, always perseveres. Love never fails (1 Cor. 13:4-8).

God paints the picture of what love is, and gives power through the Spirit to do it. Learn from him and let him make your marriage beautiful.

Lord, thank you for teaching us how to love each other. Bind us together by your Spirit.

Amen.

July 13

Call for Help

"And will not God bring about justice for his chosen ones, who cry out to him day and night? Will he keep putting them off? I tell you, he will see that they get justice, and quickly." (Luke 18:7-8)

It's not fair when you're cheated, abused, or betrayed. When you work hard and others get the credit. When you pour all you've got into a goal and it comes to nothing. When you invest love and attention in a friend who rejects you in the end. When you're falsely accused, unfairly punished, or let down by broken promises. Your grievance is painful and leaves you raw.

If you find yourself beaten down by injustice today, cry out to God to make it right. Call on him to uphold your reputation. Let him comfort and heal your wounds. Seek his will, trusting he'll kindle new goals and dreams for tomorrow. Know him as your friend that never leaves your side. Depend on him as your mighty deliverer to protect and save you from trouble.

Draw near to God and each other as you suffer unfairness today. Trust the Lord to bring justice and help. Believe he's on your side, fighting for you, his chosen ones.

Lord, overcome our trouble with your justice today. Shield us from harm and repair what's broken. Restore our hope for tomorrow.

Amen.

July 14

The Way, the Truth, and the Life

We all, like sheep, have gone astray, each of us has turned to our own way; and the Lord has laid on him the iniquity of us all. (Isaiah 53:6)

Everyone is looking for someone or something to follow. People chase money and success. Popularity and romance. Comfort and entertainment. Meaning and significance. As they pursue their own desires, they turn their backs on God.

Jesus took the punishment for the world's wandering. He offers himself as the Good Shepherd, willing to lead each person to life in God. Each person is left with a choice: to go their own way or follow Christ.

Who is leading you today? Who's the loudest voice in your ear? Who's pressuring you to conform to their opinions? Who's promising satisfaction apart from God? Who's telling you how to fit in? Who's advising you which way to go? Today, listen to your Shepherd. Read his Word to know right from wrong. Pursue his love so you can love others. Take on the humility of Christ. Be content with all he's given. Follow Jesus as he promises, "I am the light of the world. Whoever follows me will never walk in darkness, but will have the light of life" (John 8:12).

Lord, teach us to follow wherever you lead. We want to love and obey you in every way, all the time.

Amen.

July 15

Our Father's Love

See what great love the Father has lavished on us, that we should be called children of God! And that is what we are! (1 John 3:1)

One of the greatest gifts we receive from God is a new identity as his children. Our earthly father may be an abuser, a criminal, or a liar. Yet our heavenly Father is gentle, holy, and true. Our biological mother may have hurt us through cruelty and rejection. But our God is kind, merciful, and accepting. Destructive behaviors that persist in families for generations are broken by God's love.

Today, you are an adopted child of God. He declares, "Can a mother forget the baby at her breast and have no compassion on the child she has borne? Though she may forget, I will not forget you!" (Isa. 49:15). Your name is written forever in his book of life, a guarantee of eternity with him. He'll wipe away your tears from the pain of the past. He gives safety, belonging, and love forever.

Remember whose you are. Take hold of your new identity in Jesus. Live with joy in his peace and love. Keep your eyes fixed on the future to come, when your Father brings you home.

Lord, you know the grief and pain we experienced as children of broken parents. Heal our wounds, and let us know you as our true Father.

Amen.

July 16

The Best Treasure of All

Then Peter said, "Silver or gold I do not have, but what I do have I give you. In the name of Jesus Christ of Nazareth, walk." (Acts 3:6)

The sick look to doctors and natural remedies for healing. The lonely visit online-dating sites and social events to find a special someone. The hungry search for a paycheck or a handout. The bored and disillusioned look for adventure. Money, success, and pleasure falsely promise to satisfy the human heart.

You're surrounded by lost and broken people. They're asking for relief. They need hope for tomorrow. They're frustrated, as their search for happiness leaves them empty. They're wounded by betrayal. They don't know where they're going, or why. They carry secret guilt and shame.

You've already found all you need in Jesus. You hold the "good news of peace through Jesus Christ, who is Lord of all" (Acts 10:36). You can't rescue everyone from their circumstances, but you can give what you have – the life-giving message of the gospel. You can share the hope of salvation. You can tell of God's healing, deliverance, and strength in your life. You can share the treasure that lasts forever.

Lord, let us be willing to share the love you've given to us. Show us how to tell the good news of Jesus.

Amen.

July 17

Not Me!

> But Moses said, "Pardon your servant, Lord.
> Please send someone else." (Exodus 4:13)

Sometimes our assignment from God feels impossible. We're sure he picked the wrong ones for the job. We're asked to love the unlovable. Work beyond our strength or talents. Bring help to a hopeless situation. Stretch our budget to give even more. Move outside of what's comfortable or familiar. Stand on truth that's unpopular with the world. The task demands more than we've got – we want to quit before we start.

Where does God want you to go today? How do you feel unqualified or "not enough"? What excuses are keeping you from saying 'yes' to what he's calling you to do? Our confidence is lost when we focus on our weakness instead of his power.

Confess your fears and doubts to God in prayer. Ask for faith to believe he'll give you everything necessary to do his will. Trust him to provide courage, wisdom, and strength when it's needed most. Surrender your lives to his control, saying, "Here am I. Send me!" (Isa. 6:8).

Lord, forgive us for putting our faith in ourselves instead of you. Give us courage to obey what you ask us to do. Show your love and power in our lives.

Amen.

July 18

Open Heart, Open Home

> Do not forget to show hospitality to strangers,
> for by so doing some people have shown hospitality
> to angels without knowing it. (Hebrews 13:2)

Hospitality is defined as showing generosity and making others feel welcome. It's part of God's plan for you to "love your neighbor as yourself" (Mark 12:31). In sharing your blessings, attention, and personal space, you make God's love tangible to everyone.

Reach out to create a new relationship today. Share a meal, meet a need, and open your home. Consider who's lonely around you, and extend the gift of friendship. Invite others into conversation as you go about your day – take every opportunity to listen to their troubles and build them up.

Ask God for courage to lower your defenses and invite people into your life. Let him take you outside your comfortable circle to interact with people from all walks of life. Pray for a generous attitude that's eager to share. Build margin in your busy schedule to leave room for people. Prepare to see God do amazing things as you show hospitality – the love of God – to those that need him.

Lord, teach us how to welcome others in your name. Show us who needs a friend or a helping hand. Take our home, our resources, and our time and use them for your glory.

Amen.

July 19

All or Nothing

This is how we know what love is: Jesus Christ
laid down his life for us. And we ought to lay down
our lives for our brothers and sisters. (1 John 3:16)

If Jesus had only come to teach, heal, and comfort, we'd call him a kind person. He'd be a moral example, a wise prophet, or an intriguing historical figure. But Jesus did more: he gave up his heavenly glory to suffer and die on a cross. He gave up everything to save us and he loves us forever.

In your marriage, love is more than sentiment or good deeds. It means giving up your very selves. You no longer pursue goals at the expense of your partner. You adjust your priorities and habits for their well-being. You give up your independence to remain by their side. Your time, money, and strength is spent caring and giving to your loved one for life.

Selfishness and pride are the enemies of love. Jesus gave up his rights, choosing to give and serve instead. May we love like him – willing to lay down everything in devotion to God, his people, and our family.

Lord, teach us how to lay down our lives for each other and for you. Thank you for the sacrifice of Jesus, who shows us what love really is.

Amen.

July 20

Our Best Defense

Some trust in chariots and some in horses,
but we trust in the name of the LORD our God. (Psalm 20:7)

Each person is fighting a battle today. To achieve a goal or dream. To overcome an injury or health concern. To reconcile a broken relationship. To finish an overwhelming to-do list. To raise a stubborn child. To cope with pain from the past. To manage hard emotions. To resist temptation. We know we can't win on our own, so we look for help we can count on.

Where do you place your trust today? Are you putting hope in education or technology? In money or a good reputation? In professionals who claim to know all the answers? In hard work and a strong will? In pleasure and possessions? So many people and things promise victory. Yet the Lord your God is the best hope of all.

Take your battle to God in prayer today. Ask him for strength to keep fighting. Seek him for wisdom to know what to do. Let him provide godly advice and help. Depend on him for healing and rescue. Count on him to give what you need. Put your trust in his name.

Lord, victory is only found in you. Give us faith to believe you're with us in the fight. Thank you for your power and love that never fail.

Amen.

July 21

Singing Through Suffering

> After they had been severely flogged, they were thrown into prison, and the jailer was commanded to guard them carefully. About midnight Paul and Silas were praying and singing hymns to God, and the other prisoners were listening to them. (Acts 16:23, 25)

A beautiful part of marriage is knowing you don't have to struggle alone. When troubles knock you down, you can cry out to God together. As a couple you can remember his good gifts and praise his name. You share the blessings and the pain that life will bring, and experience God's faithfulness side by side.

Your response to suffering sends a powerful message to your unbelieving friends, family, and co-workers. When you choose trust over doubt, contentment over complaining, and hope over despair, faith is on display. When God's love gives joy in times of pain, his glory is revealed. When you invite God into your deepest sorrow, you're declaring we're never alone.

How is God meeting you in your circumstances today? Come together to pray and give thanks. Lean on him together to meet your needs. Share his faithful goodness with everyone. Be encouraged, knowing that this temporary trial can bring hope to many.

Lord, thank you for your love that meets us in our pain. Help us to trust you and praise you at all times. Use our trials to testify of Jesus' love.

Amen.

July 22

Grace to Get Along

> Better a dry crust with peace and quiet than a
> house full of feasting, with strife. (Proverbs 17:1)

Your family pays the price if you try to have it all. Chasing success at any cost leaves a wake of stress, fatigue, and fractured relationships. Material gain and achievement are a hollow substitute for love and closeness in your home.

Consider your priorities today. How has quality time been traded for busyness? Which goals and desires are dominating your thoughts? Who are you trying to impress or please the most outside of your household? Are life's demands creating tension between you? Do your loved ones know how much they mean to you?

Take your goals and schedules to God in prayer. Ask him for wisdom to know which steps to take. Let him renew your devotion to your family. Thank him for your blessings and seek contentment with what you have. Seek the servant-heart of Christ that puts people above plans. Pursue peace and unity at home with your whole heart.

Lord, it's hard to feel close and enjoy one another as we run in different directions. Teach us to put our relationship first above life's demands. Let us cherish each other more than anything the world might offer.

Amen.

July 23

Promises in the Pain

Dear friends, do not be surprised at the fiery ordeal that has come on you to test you, as though something strange were happening to you. But rejoice inasmuch as you participate in the sufferings of Christ, so that you may be overjoyed when his glory is revealed. (1 Peter 4:12-13)

When we believe in Jesus, his love and blessings pour into our lives. We're given grace and forgiveness. Peace with God. Freedom from sin. The Holy Spirit. Protection and strength. An inheritance in heaven. He meets our needs. He writes the Word on our hearts. He gives us a purpose and plan. Love and joy transform our lives forever.

As you enjoy his countless benefits, you're surprised when faith is hard. Friends accuse you of a holier-than-thou attitude. Family talks about you behind your backs. Your company is frustrated by your integrity. Your neighbors assume you're a hypocrite. The sins you left behind still call your name. You wrestle with questions – how to vote, how to train your kids, how to spend your money – as you determine to do what's right. Living for God is harder than living for yourself.

When it costs to follow Jesus, be glad. When you're hurt in the heat of battle, rejoice! You're suffering with Christ – it proves your salvation is real. You're passing the test. You're blessed by the Spirit. You'll "be overjoyed when his glory is revealed" (1 Pet. 2:13) in the end.

Lord, give us joy when we suffer for your name.
Amen.

July 24

A Vow for Life

> The angel of the Lord went up from Gilgal to Bokim and said, "I brought you up out of Egypt and led you into the land I swore to give to your ancestors. I said, 'I will never break my covenant with you.'" (Judges 2:1)

We follow a covenant-keeping God. When he makes a promise, he sees it through to the end. This is why God takes the marriage covenant so seriously and "hates divorce" (Mal. 2:16). Marriage is not just a promise between husband and wife, but a covenant with the Lord himself. Just as he is keeping his promise to love us with an everlasting love, we're to love our spouse faithfully all the days of our life.

God created marriage as a beautiful picture of devotion to his beloved, the church. Every day we choose to keep our marriage vow affirms the kind of love offered to us through Christ. On hard days where our spouse seems unlovable and our commitment is hanging by a thread, we can find strength in our promise-keeping God.

Take a moment to reaffirm your vows to love, honor, and serve one another for life. Praise God for his love that never ends and the hope of eternity with him.

Lord, you keep every one of your promises. Thank you for demonstrating your everlasting love in the bond of our marriage. Give us the strength to faithfully keep our covenant until we see you face to face.

Amen.

July 25

Grace or Gossip?

Whoever would foster love covers over an offense, but whoever repeats the matter separates close friends. (Proverbs 17:9)

As you share life together in your marriage, it is inevitable that you'll let each other down. You'll disregard a promise. You'll lose your temper. You'll be selfish and insensitive. You'll break things, lose things, and forget things. Over and over, you'll depend on one another's patience and understanding heart.

Keeping a list of past failures builds a wall of resentment. Complaining to friends and family about your spouse breaks trust. Sarcasm and mocking words tear apart the love and unity you long for.

The gift of grace builds your love. Leaving the past in the past sets you free from bitterness. Second chances offer hope for tomorrow. Respect and privacy between you creates peace and security. The humility of "I'm sorry" meets the kindness of "I forgive you", and love grows deep.

Offer the gift of mercy today. Silence your accusations. Speak words of honor and blessing to build each other up. Keep your mistakes and failures between you and the Lord. Choose to love no matter what.

Lord, fill our marriage with your grace. Teach us to forgive as you've forgiven us. Let our words show respect and kindness. Keep us close and grow our love.

Amen.

July 26

Not Your Own

> Do you not know that your bodies are temples of the
> Holy Spirit, who is in you, whom you have received from God?
> You are not your own; you were bought at a price.
> Therefore honor God with your bodies. (1 Corinthians 6:19-20)

God loves your mind, spirit, personality, and your physical body. You were created in his image. You were "fearfully and wonderfully made" (Ps. 139:14). The Lord knit you together in your mother's womb and he knows every detail about you (Ps. 139:13). In his great love he purchased you with Jesus' blood on the cross. He lives within you now, and he'll glorify your body in the future.

With all of these truths in mind, we're to honor God with our bodies. We won't degrade or despise what he's made. We'll never use God's possession for sexual sin. We'll provide nourishment and rest for ourselves to stay strong. We'll dress modestly and appropriately wherever we go. We'll pursue healing when we're sick. We'll unite in intimacy with our spouse as we belong to God and one another. Our identity as God's child is made known through our physical body.

Lord, thank you for creating our bodies and filling us with your Holy Spirit. Let us obey you in purity and wisdom, giving you authority over our lives.

Amen.

July 27

Strength in Surrender

Humble yourselves, therefore, under God's mighty hand, that he may lift you up in due time. Cast all your anxiety on him because he cares for you. (1 Peter 5:6-7)

In our pride, we attempt to be the author of our lives. We work to control our circumstances. We think, *If I can just be smarter, try harder, and keep pushing through, I can make it all work out.* We deny that God ordains each day we live. We forget his compassion that sees our trouble. We're arrogant, thinking we can solve our problems without him.

Today, admit you can't handle what you're facing. Pray for comfort. Ask for help. Seek his Word for wisdom and understanding. Tell God your fears and frustrations. Let him carry your burdens as you trust him like a child. Encourage each other to give up complaining and arguing as you wait for him to work. Receive his perfect peace as you believe his promise to care for you.

God is strong enough for you today. His timing is perfect. His love for you has no limit. Give him all your worries today.

Lord, forgive us for trying to rely on our own strength. We need your help. Give us faith to believe you'll take care of us. Amen.

July 28

A Work in Progress

He who began a good work in you will carry it on to completion until the day of Christ Jesus. (Philippians 1:6)

"He's never going to change." "There she goes again." "When is he going to figure it out?" "I'm so tired of waiting for her to 'get it.'"

The love in your marriage can be crushed by disappointment. You see your partner break their promises, betray their values, and struggle with immaturity. Expectations sink lower and tempers rise higher as you face their weakness again and again. It feels impossible to keep hoping they'll grow and change.

Yet, you serve a God who never gives up. He promises that when you receive his salvation, he works to make you new. His process of teaching, purifying, and building your faith never ends in this life.

Ask God for a fresh filling of hope today. Take your concerns and fears for your spouse to him in prayer. Have faith in his promise to keep making you like Jesus. Set aside your own desire to push and fix – let God do his work, his way, in his time. He is faithful and will amaze you with all he's going to do.

Lord, thank you for transforming us to be like Christ. Give us patience and faith to believe you'll keep working in each other.
Amen.

July 29

Love and Live

> But a man who commits adultery has no sense;
> whoever does so destroys himself. (Proverbs 6:32)

As God created Adam, the first husband, he knew "It is not good for the man to be alone" (Gen. 2:18). A wife is a gift from God to provide help, encouragement, and love for life. When a husband risks his marriage by pursuing an affair, he sabotages his well-being. He risks his happiness, his reputation, and the security of his children. Years of memories and dreams for the future are thrown away. Giving in to adultery leads to pain and regret.

Pray for wisdom to understand the priceless value of your marriage. Remember your vows and recommit to keeping them. Eliminate any sources of temptation to betray your partner. Keep your eyes fixed on each other – pour your energy, attention, and love into your relationship.

Look around at the couples you know whose bond is breaking. Have courage to remind them of God's Word. Pray for them to hold on to each other no matter what. Let your faithful marriage stand as proof that the Lord's ways are wonderful and good.

Lord, keep us from betraying our marriage at any cost. Give us joy and faithful love as we build our life together. Thank you for loving us enough to warn us of the dangers of sin.

Amen.

July 30

The Joy of Intimacy

But since sexual immorality is occurring, each man should have sexual relations with his own wife, and each woman with her own husband. The husband should fulfill his marital duty to his wife, and likewise the wife to her husband. (1 Corinthians 7:2-3)

The intimacy you share is a gift from God. It creates an unbreakable bond as you become "one flesh." It provides a way to express and receive one another's love. It sets your relationship apart from any other. It's a physical, emotional, and spiritual blessing. It increases the joy in your marriage. It shields you from the temptation of lust and sexual sin. It pleases the Lord as you live by his design.

Is anything hindering you from coming together? Is your marriage bed a place of distance, hurt, or sin? Bring your relationship to God in prayer. Ask him to break down the barriers between you. Pray for courage to overcome your insecurities. Confess if you've been manipulative or selfish. Do whatever it takes to keep pornography or lust from polluting your life. Make your love a priority – take time to connect and enjoy one another.

Today, offer yourselves to God and each other. Let his love fill your marriage and make you one.

Lord, bind us together in body and spirit. Keep us pure and free to love one another without holding back.

Amen.

July 31

Coping in Tough Times

Rejoice always, pray continually, give thanks in all circumstances; for this is God's will for you in Christ Jesus. (1 Thessalonians 5:16-18)

Even in the strongest relationship, you experience seasons of feeling alone. Your partner might be preoccupied and withdrawn, anxious or depressed. A demanding job, health issue, or family crisis can push you apart. It's painful to feel disconnected, especially when you feel excluded from their struggle.

Take comfort by knowing that even when your marriage isn't close, the Lord is always here. Take your feelings of sadness and frustration to him in prayer. Thank him for keeping your marriage together even when it's hard. Praise him for his power to break down any walls between you. Ask him to bring peace in the stress and healing where you're wounded. Call on him to reach your spouse's heart, even when you can't. Thank him for this season of loneliness, trusting he's using it to grow your faith and reveal his love.

You can praise, pray, and trust your God no matter what you're struggling with today. Find hope in him to bring you together again.

Lord, thank you for being with us in our marriage. Bind us together in your love today.

Amen.

August

August 1

It's Not All About Me

Do nothing out of selfish ambition or vain conceit. Rather, in humility value others above yourselves, not looking to your own interests but each of you to the interests of the others. (Philippians 2:3-4)

Life is busy! Jobs, family responsibilities, errands, church commitments … Calendars fill up quickly without room to catch your breath. It's easy to take a "divide and conquer" approach instead of pulling together to tackle what's at hand. You can lose sight of caring for each other as you focus on your own to-do list.

Take a moment to share your personal goals and priorities. Discover how they fit together, or how you feel alone and unsupported. Discuss which of your tasks could be shared or traded. Most of all, express interest and concern for what's important to each other.

Ask God for a humble heart to put each other first. Let him set you free from the need to have your own way. Discover the intimacy and joy that come from laying down your lives for one another.

Lord, forgive us for serving ourselves instead of each other. Give us humble hearts to show respect and support at all times. Make us like Jesus, who was willing to give up everything to make us your own.

Amen.

August 2

The Gift of Friendship

> A friend loves at all times, and a brother is
> born for a time of adversity. (Proverbs 17:17)

When God brought you together, he knew the problems you would face. He created your marriage as a safe place in frightening times. It gives companionship when you're lonely. Forgiveness when you fail. Encouragement when you feel defeated. An ally when enemies come against you. Acceptance when you're put down or rejected. Help when you can't make it on your own. Your spouse is a gift from God in times of trouble.

Today, commit to each other as friends. Build each other up. Help out and lighten one another's load. Share laughter and fun. Keep each other's secrets. Stay faithful and loyal in every situation. Show unconditional love.

Remember your bond in Christ. Pray together about the good and the bad in your lives. Thank God for how he's working in your circumstances. Encourage each other to trust in the Word. Praise him for building your marriage and filling it with love.

God truly did make you for each other. Embrace each other as lovers, friends, and brother and sister in Christ today.

Lord, thank you for our marriage. Let us be true friends, no matter what happens. Join our hearts together by your Spirit. Amen.

August 3

Faith to Follow

> From this time many of his disciples turned back and no longer followed him. "You do not want to leave too, do you?" Jesus asked the Twelve. (John 6:66-67)

Many are attracted to Christianity. They hear the Word. They desire peace and joy. They want God's grace. They wish to be part of his family. Yet despite his countless blessings, they turn from following Jesus.

Hard teaching can make us discouraged. God's moral law can be hard to accept. We struggle to know the Word. We're not sure which teachers to trust. We're tempted to give up on Bible study, silencing God's voice in our lives.

Suffering can make us stumble. We wonder if God's love is real. We doubt his power and strength. We feel like he's far away when we need him. We don't believe he's good when circumstances are bad.

Fear can make us fall away. We're afraid of rejection. The cost to follow Jesus feels too high. We're intimidated by evil, though nothing "will be able to separate us from the love of God that is in Christ Jesus our Lord" (Rom. 8:39).

Today, pray for unbreakable faith in Jesus. "So do not throw away your confidence; it will be richly rewarded. You need to persevere so that when you have done the will of God, you will receive what he has promised" (Heb. 10:35-36).

Lord, we want to follow you without turning back. Let us remain in you.

Amen.

August 4

Evil Enemies

And pray that we may be delivered from wicked and evil people, for not everyone has faith. But the Lord is faithful, and he will strengthen you and protect you from the evil one. (2 Thessalonians 3:2-3)

Satan wants to destroy believers' faith and every godly marriage. We sense his destructive influence everywhere we turn. Sexual temptation makes us question our vow of faithfulness. Negative church members discourage us from serving. Easy credit and persuasive salespeople sabotage our wise financial planning. Sarcastic, critical in-laws tempt us to put down our loved one. The enemy's accusations make us doubt God's love and our salvation.

Pray for deliverance from every threat to your trust in God. Ask for wisdom to set boundaries around your marriage. Eliminate any influences that could undermine your obedience to the Word and devotion to each other. Allow God to strengthen you, so the enemy's schemes are powerless against your family.

"The name of the Lord is a fortified tower; the righteous run to it and are safe" (Prov. 18:10). Run to God today to find safety and protection from every kind of evil. His love will hold you secure.

Lord, you know how the enemy is attacking our faith and our household. Protect us and give us strength to stand firm.
Amen.

August 5

Perfect Promises

> Yet he did not waver through unbelief regarding the promise of God, but was strengthened in his faith and gave glory to God, being fully persuaded that God had power to do what he had promised. (Romans 4:20-21)

Does God's love seem too good to be true? Is total forgiveness, eternity in heaven, and abundant life only for those who seem to have it all together? Your doubts, failures, and temptations can shake your trust in God's promises.

If you're "wavering through unbelief" today, remember the One you worship. His love offered Jesus to cover your sins. His power raised Jesus from the dead and is working in you this very moment. He gives healing, wisdom, and life forever to each of his children. If you've put your faith in God, he will never let you go.

Give glory to God – pray and thank him for bringing you this far. Praise his name for the help and rescue he's given. Ask for greater faith to trust in his promises. Take each of your doubts and fears and lay them at his feet, choosing to believe his Word. "He gives strength to the weary and increases the power of the weak" (Isa. 40:29). Find joy in his strength today!

Lord, when our struggles in life and our battle with sin seem hopeless, our faith in you is shaken. Give us strength by your power and perfect love that never ends.

Amen.

August 6

Help, Not Harm

> But Joseph said to them, "Don't be afraid. Am I in the place of God? You intended to harm me, but God intended it for good to accomplish what is now being done, the saving of many lives." (Genesis 50:19-20)

In the middle of stress and struggles, it's hard to believe God has a purpose for the pain. His love and affection are hard to receive when we're hurt by others. We doubt he's in control when we're blindsided by tragedy and loss. Yet out of his power and love he always brings goodness in the end.

Friends and loved ones let us down, yet God is faithful through it all. Goals and dreams are crushed, yet he gives us a hope and a future. Death and crisis separate us from all we hold dear, yet God is our anchor in the storm. He'll use every trial to build our faith and prove he's truly enough.

How are you suffering today? Take heart by knowing that even in this, the Lord has not forgotten you. Peace and joy will return to your life. You'll look back on this season with a thankful heart for all the good he had planned. Trust in God and keep the faith – his salvation is coming.

Lord, we feel wounded and alone. This struggle feels unfair, with no answer is in sight. Show us your faithful love that will bring good from this pain.

Amen.

August 7

Staying Strong

*Many are the foes who persecute me,
but I have not turned from your statutes.* (Psalm 119:157)

Not everyone will like your devotion to God. They'll think you're uptight, missing out on a good time. They'll criticize your parenting as too strict or old-fashioned. They'll accuse you of wasting your money by giving. They'll be angry if you choose church over other activities. They'll wonder why you don't laugh at crude jokes or join in the gossip. The pressure is on to give up and fit in.

Be encouraged – God knows the price you pay to follow him. He's walked in your shoes, being put down and left out. He's heard the mocking remarks and accusations. He's felt the sting of slander and rejection. The ones against you today are against the One you serve.

Pray together for encouragement from God. "For just as we share abundantly in the sufferings of Christ, so also our comfort abounds through Christ" (2 Cor. 1:5). He's standing with you in the pain. He's preparing rewards for all it costs you to obey right now. He offers strength to keep believing and living for him.

Lord, people think we're fools for loving you. Keep us faithful to your Word all the time.

Amen.

August 8

Parenting Partners

Discipline your children, and they will give you peace;
they will bring you the delights you desire. (Proverbs 29:17)

It's hard to see eye-to-eye on handling kids' behavior. One of you may come from a strict, "because I said so" kind of upbringing while the other's was permissive and relaxed. Disagreements over everything from bedtime to screen time, homework to healthy habits, can ruin the peace in your marriage. Sharing your expectations and discipline of your children is key to unity in parenting.

Kids respond best to consistent discipline. Your lessons will bear the most fruit when taught by both parents. Take some time today to discuss the behaviors and values you're seeking to teach your children. Work toward agreement on the rewards and consequences for their choices. Strive to reconcile the conflicts that have been dividing your household.

Intentional love and training will bless your children. Parenting as a team builds their trust and binds you together as a couple. In turn, you'll benefit from respectful, obedient kids who know what's right. Find the joy and peace that come from raising your children according to God's Word.

Lord, thank you for loving us as your children. Let us discipline our kids in unity and love as we seek to follow you as a family.
Amen.

August 9

Ups and Downs

> There is a time for everything, and a season for every activity under the heavens. (Ecclesiastes 3:1)

Marriage calls you to journey through life's ups and downs together. In birth and death, laughter and sorrow, close friendship and painful conflict, you share times of joy and struggle.

What is the season you find yourselves in today? Are you building a career or taking steps toward retirement? Are you planning for little ones, wrestling through teenage years, or releasing adults to follow their dreams? Are you enjoying old friends and connections or finding your way in a new community? Whether it's a season of receiving joy or grieving loss, your committed marriage can be a blessed constant through it all.

Praise God today for his faithfulness and love that never changes. Look back over seasons past to remember how far you've come. Share how you see the Lord moving in your life today, and get excited about your hopes for the future. Let him bind you together as you face each new day.

Lord, thank you for keeping us together and close to you in every situation. Help us to trust you as we walk through life's seasons. Let us embrace all you have for us, knowing your timing and your will are perfect.

Amen.

August 10

New Thoughts, New Life

> The mind governed by the flesh is death, but the mind governed by the Spirit is life and peace. (Romans 8:6)

Our thoughts and attitudes drive our actions. Our battle with sin is fought in the mind. Whatever we depend on for truth, information, and advice will influence our belief in God.

Turn to the Word and prayer to make sense of your world. Choose faith over fear. Seek purity and devoted love over the gratification of sexual sin. Show generosity and trust in the Provider over greed for money. Discover significance as a child of God rather than others' definition of success.

The world's cravings and sin lead to death. There's no hope of eternity with God, no grace in broken relationships, and no satisfaction for the heart. A mind transformed by the Spirit through the Word finds life and peace. There's joy in knowing our true Father. You find belonging and love in the family of God. You're set free from guilt and shame, and the destructive power of sin in your life.

Choose carefully whose voice you listen to today. Look to God to find the life and peace you long for.

Lord, govern our minds by your Spirit. Keep us faithful, give us wisdom, and let us live forever in your peace.
Amen.

August 11

Cleaning House

> But now you must also rid yourselves of all such things as these: anger, rage, malice, slander, and filthy language from your lips. (Colossians 3:8)

We can do a lot of damage with our mouth. We shred one another's confidence. We set people up to look foolish. We lie and manipulate to get our way. We accuse and blame. We bulldoze others with our anger. We get mad and get even. We're ugly and offensive. Our words deny the love and life we've found in Jesus.

Today, remember that the old you is dead. You've been raised with Christ – your life is now hidden with him. You can throw away your filthy clothes and put on compassion, kindness, humility, gentleness and patience (Col. 3:12). You're no longer harsh and mean. You tell the truth. You build people up. You create safety and peace. You're pure and clean. Your loving words are proof you're alive in Christ.

Lord, forgive us for the mean and hateful things we've said. We've hurt each other and silenced your love with our words. Teach us to get rid of our old selves' habits and sins. You've made us alive and set us free forever.

Amen.

August 12

Does He Care?

*A furious squall came up, and the waves broke over the boat,
so that it was nearly swamped. Jesus was in the stern,
sleeping on a cushion. The disciples woke him and said to him,
"Teacher, don't you care if we drown?"* (Mark 4:37-38)

As you work and try to move forward in life, setbacks and problems can overwhelm you. Financial crises can wipe out your savings. Health issues leave you tired and broken. Difficult relationships fill your days with stress and conflict. Children fail and rebel. You feel as if you're drowning with no relief in sight. In these times of desperation, your hearts can cry out to God like the disciples: "Don't you care if we drown?"

Jesus does care about everything you're going through. Today's hard circumstances will become a chapter in the story of God's goodness in your life. Pray for help. Trust him to respond. Place your future in his hands and patiently wait for his rescue.

"The righteous cry out, and the Lord hears them;
he delivers them from all their troubles.
The Lord is close to the brokenhearted
and saves those who are crushed in spirit.
The righteous person may have many troubles,
but the Lord delivers him from them all" (Ps. 34:17-19).

Lord, we're drowning in the storm today. Deliver us from trouble by your mighty, loving power. Help us to trust you.

Amen.

August 13

The Gift of Kids

> Children are a heritage from the LORD,
> offspring a reward from him. (Psalm 127:3)

We know the Bible says children are a blessing. But sleepless nights, testing behavior, and the daily demands of parenting can feel more like a burden. We lose confidence that our efforts to teach and train are paying off. We're not always sure we can meet their needs. We worry that no matter how much we do, it won't be enough.

Take a fresh look at your child today. Which qualities display the image of God? What aspects of their personality are a refreshing contrast to your own? Which strengths are building and growing? Which weaknesses deserve compassion and help?

Spend some time thanking God for your child today. Celebrate their individuality as his own special creation. Ask for a renewal of joy in your work as a parent. Pray for wisdom to know how to raise them in Christ. Let him breathe fresh hope for the future into your family.

Lord, thank you for the gift of parenthood – a priceless gift from you. Give us grace to faithfully serve, teach, and love our child for your name's sake. Create a legacy of faith in our family for generations to come.

Amen.

August 14

Sweet Talking

> Gracious words are a honeycomb, sweet to the
> soul and healing to the bones. (Proverbs 16:24)

One of the most valuable gifts we share with our spouse is free – the blessing of our words. Compliments boost spirits. Affirmation builds confidence. Tenderness creates a safe place for intimacy. Honesty and truth sustain trust. Humor fills our home with smiles. Words of comfort and empathy soothe our suffering. Confession and forgiveness protect our hearts. Prayers grow faith in God. Words of grace give life to our loved one and our marriage.

Today, speak generous words of blessing over your partner. Share something you admire in their character. Offer thanks for a recent act of help or kindness. Express how you're proud of their talents and hard work. Let them know you see the burdens they bear, and support them fully in it. Name the ways you see each other becoming more like Jesus.

Pray and ask God to fill your conversations with grace. Let his love and healing flow through your words each day. Enjoy the "sweetness" of soul-satisfying words.

Lord, bring your grace into our marriage as we show love through what we say. Teach us to comfort, encourage, and heal each other's hearts.

Amen.

August 15

Always Enough

Keep your lives free from the love of money and be
content with what you have, because God has said,
"Never will I leave you; never will I forsake you." (Hebrews 13:5)

We've heard the television preachers say that with enough faith, prosperity can be ours. They teach us that material wealth is a sign of God's favor. Many embrace the lie that if we make God happy, he'll give us everything we want.

This false teaching will leave you brokenhearted in your struggles. You'll wonder if God is punishing you for small faith. You'll think he's turned his back because you're not good enough. You'll wonder if somehow you could pray harder or believe him for more, all your dreams would come true.

God gives his peace by telling you to walk away from craving more. He offers freedom from the slavery of loving money. He gives you himself as your greatest treasure – nothing on earth can compare.

God wants to be more to you than a heavenly banker, meeting your worldly desires. He wants you to love him fully and find he's all you need. Money may come and go, but his love remains forever.

Lord, guard our hearts from doubting you when money is tight. Let us love you more than the gifts you provide. Thank you for loving us faithfully, forever.

Amen.

August 16

Too Good to Be True

> Abraham fell facedown; he laughed and said to himself, "Will a son be born to a man a hundred years old? Will Sarah bear a child at the age of ninety?" (Genesis 17:17)

Are you facing the impossible today? Perhaps infertility is crushing the dream of a child. Piles of bills mean a lifetime of debt. Unemployment drags on while everyone else finds success. Broken relationships seem beyond repair. The shame of the past says you'll never change. Our trust in God is buried under the weight of worry and doubt.

Yet we serve a God who is bigger than our problems. We can pray, "Ah, Sovereign LORD, you have made the heavens and the earth by your great power and outstretched arm. Nothing is too hard for you" (Jer. 32:17). Nothing we can imagine or hope for is too difficult for our Father.

Take your dreams and disappointments to God today. Ask for faith to trust in his promises to care for you. Depend on his strength to walk through the darkest valley. Find comfort knowing he'll never leave you alone. Believe again that "weeping may stay for the night, but rejoicing comes in the morning" (Ps. 30:5). Put your future in his hands.

Lord, forgive us for doubting and laughing off your promises. Give us patience to wait for you and faith to believe in your Word. Teach us to trust you in everything.

Amen.

August 17

Never Alone

My friends and companions avoid me because of my wounds; my neighbors stay far away. (Psalm 38:11)

Our pain can drive others away. They can't relate to the grief of infertility or miscarriage. They don't know how to support us through financial hardship. They're offended by our sins and mistakes. They're ill-equipped to encourage us through depression or disease. They don't know what to say or do, so they pull away in silence.

When friends, co-workers, and relatives keep a distance from your trouble, the Lord draws near. He is close to the brokenhearted (Ps. 34:18). He shows his strength on your behalf (Ps. 86:16). He carries you close to his heart (Isa. 40:11). He's your ever-present help in trouble (Ps. 46:1). No amount of suffering or failure can keep God's love away.

Reach out to God when you're lonely in your struggle. Trust him to stay close. Believe he hears your prayers for comfort and help. Lean on him as your perfect, faithful Friend.

Lord, thank you for your constant love. Give us faith to trust you're with us in our pain. Bring your strength and peace to us today.

Amen.

August 18

Take a Break

> The apostles gathered around Jesus and reported to him all they had done and taught. Then, because so many people were coming and going that they did not even have a chance to eat, he said to them, "Come with me by yourselves to a quiet place and get some rest." (Mark 6:30-31)

When you're hard-working and generous, you're the one who people depend on. You become the boss's go-to employee. Your family counts on your help and care. Your church and community rely on your capable hands. You give and serve without thinking of yourself.

Jesus knows that despite our best intentions, our strength has limits. We can wear down emotionally as we carry others' burdens. Our energy is drained without taking time to recharge. Just as the Lord offered rest to his apostles, he offers it to you today.

Plan some time to step away from life's demands. Meet with Jesus at "a quiet place and get some rest." Read the Word and pray so he can refresh your spirit. Take a nap, enjoy God's creation outdoors, and 'unplug'. Reconnect with each other over an unhurried meal. Remember once more the joy of God's love and your marriage.

Lord, thank you for allowing us to give and serve in your name. Give us wisdom to know when to stop and rest. Be our strength and peace all the time.

Amen.

August 19

Open Eyes, Open Hearts

> Rescue those being led away to death; hold back those staggering toward slaughter. If you say, "But we knew nothing about this," does not he who weighs the heart perceive it? Does not he who guards your life know it? Will he not repay everyone according to what they have done? (Proverbs 24:11-12)

The young mother directed to an abortion clinic. The orphan with no place to go. The victim enslaved to prostitution. The elderly neglected in a nursing home. The neighbors lost without Jesus' salvation. The college student swayed to deny the Creator. While we live in freedom and the hope of eternity, the world is wounded and lost without Christ.

We can't pretend the trauma isn't there. We can't hoard God's love for ourselves. We can't enjoy our gifts without giving them away. Today, offer yourselves to God to be his hands of rescue. Bend your knees to pray for the broken. Release the attachment to your money, time, and personal space so they can be shared. Crack open the door of your hearts so you can feel others' pain as your own. Be willing to open your eyes and see.

Whatever God asks you to give for his suffering ones, he'll repay even more. Invite the dying into the life you have in Christ.

Lord, show us how to rescue the ones you want to save. Teach us to give. Open our hearts to love in your name.

Amen.

August 20

If Only …

The rabble with them began to crave other food, and again the Israelites started wailing and said, "If only we had meat to eat! We remember the fish we ate in Egypt at no cost – also the cucumbers, melons, leeks, onions and garlic. But now we have lost our appetite; we never see anything but this manna!" (Numbers 11:4-6)

When God's gifts come into our lives day after day, we can take them for granted. The excitement of a new home gives way to criticism of small rooms and outdated style. Our car seems dull compared to the new models driving past. Last year's warm coat holds less appeal than the attractive one in the catalog. Food in our pantry doesn't satisfy like the chef's creations we see on TV. Grumbling replaces gratitude. Complaining kills contentment.

Have you lost your appetite for what God's provided? Take time to count your blessings today. List the ways he meets your physical needs. Consider the value of precious friends and family. Remember his gift of work and the strength to do it. Thank him for creation's beauty and recreation you enjoy.

Pray and ask God to renew your gratitude for all he's given. Fill your conversation with thanks each day.

Lord, you've given more good things than we could ever count. Teach us to be thankful.

Amen.

August 21

Inside Out

> "You are like whitewashed tombs, which look beautiful on the outside but on the inside are full of the bones of the dead and everything unclean. In the same way, on the outside you appear to people as righteous but on the inside you are full of hypocrisy and wickedness." (Matthew 23:27-28)

We're good at cleaning up our act. We know how to smile and look like we've got it together. Yet no matter how spiritual we seem on the outside, God looks at our heart.

Let grace transform your image today. Admit if you're doubting – God's truth will meet you in the questions. Share your fears and sadness so he can comfort and help. Confess your sins and failures so he can make you clean. A show of religion won't bring you peace. Playing by the rules won't earn God's favor. Bring him the sacrifice of a broken spirit; "a broken and contrite heart you, God, will not despise" (Ps. 51:17).

Give up any effort to impress the people around you. Please the Lord through a sincere desire to know and follow him. Rest in Jesus' work on the cross instead of trying so hard to be perfect on your own. Turn from empty religion to the intimate love of your Father in heaven.

Lord, keep us from faking our faith in you. Teach us to be humble, trusting in you alone for our life and salvation.
Amen.

August 22

Honor Your Elders

"Stand up in the presence of the aged, show respect for the elderly and revere your God. I am the Lord." (Leviticus 19:32)

Our culture embraces the young and beautiful, yet has little use for the elderly. Despite their wisdom and experience, seniors are overlooked and forgotten. We refuse to slow down to their pace. We think we have nothing in common. We have little compassion for their physical limitations. We forget their precious value to the Lord.

Commit to cherishing the elderly today. Offer help to your older neighbors. Serve the seniors in your church. Visit relatives who are lonely and confined to their home. Invite them to give advice, reminisce, and share their troubles. Offer the gift of a listening ear and thoughtful care.

Stand up for older loved ones who can't help themselves. Advocate for their medical and financial needs. Pay attention to their physical needs – keeping a clean, safe home and preparing nourishing food can be a challenge every day. Look for help if their needs are beyond what you can provide. Care and serve in the name of Jesus who loves them.

Lord, thank you that as we get older, we're dear to you. Help us to care for those around us. May we honor you as we respect the ones you love.

Amen.

August 23

God Provides

And my God will meet all your needs according to the riches of his glory in Christ Jesus. (Philippians 4:19)

Jesus is the source of God's riches. He holds "all the treasures of wisdom and knowledge" (Col. 2:3). He owns "the cattle on a thousand hills" (Ps. 50:10). He gives "every spiritual blessing" (Eph. 1:3). He doesn't let the righteous go hungry (Prov. 10:3). Yet with all his promises, we wonder if God is willing and able to take care of us.

Take your needs to the Lord in prayer today. Name your worries. Ask him to fix what's broken. Ask him to provide your daily bread. Claim his power to overcome temptation. Cry out to him to ease your loneliness and disappointment. Ask for insight to understand his Word. Let him carry the burdens weighing you down.

He didn't say he would meet some of your needs and ignore the rest. Answer his call to trust him with your life. Believe he knows every detail of your situation. He's eager to give and show his love. He knows every need before you ask him, so pray and ask. Be ready to praise his name as he cares for you.

Lord, we don't have the resources, emotional strength, or wisdom we need for our life. Please provide all we're lacking today. Thank you for loving us completely. In Jesus name. Amen.

August 24

Safe in His Arms

But I have calmed and quieted myself, I am like a weaned child with its mother; like a weaned child I am content. (Psalm 131:2)

An attentive mother knows her baby is hungry by his cries. She responds to her daughter's shiver with a warm blanket. She tenderly tucks her son into bed as she sees his heavy eyes. She senses her child's needs before a word is spoken. Her little one is secure as she's faithfully loved each day.

Your God gives the same kind of peace to you, his children. You can be calm in every situation as you trust him to meet your needs. You can be quiet instead of angry or scared, knowing he's standing on your side. You can be fully content because he gives good things to the ones he loves.

You're called to "receive the kingdom of God like a little child," trusting, believing, and depending on your perfect Father (Luke 18:17). Today, name the needs and troubles causing concern in your life. Bring each one to the Lord in prayer. Receive his peace as you trust him to care for you in every way.

Lord, we want to receive you and your goodness with childlike faith. Forgive us for doubting how much you care. Thank you for giving us peace as you watch over us and meet our needs.
Amen.

August 25

Work and Wait

> The plans of the diligent lead to profit as
> surely as haste leads to poverty. (Proverbs 21:5)

It's hard to keep on working when there's no end in sight. It's tempting to look for a quick fix to the problem we're striving to overcome. We want a shortcut to success – an escape from the slow, persistent effort to reach our goal. A fad diet, a lottery ticket, a credit card, or a cheap fix just set us back instead of moving us forward.

What are the plans you're pursuing today? What is holding you back from reaching the finish line? How are you tempted to quit or settle for less? Take your hopes and goals to God in prayer. Ask him for endurance to keep going. Seek patience and perseverance by his Spirit, trusting he'll be with you to the end. Praise him for the freedom and joy that's ahead when you realize his will for your life.

Hold on to his promise that "his divine power has given us everything we need for a godly life through our knowledge of him who called us by his own glory and goodness" (2 Pet. 1:3). In Christ, you can accomplish all he's called you to do.

Lord, give us strength to keep on working even when we're tired. Help us to accomplish your good plans with wisdom, endurance, and faith.

Amen.

August 26

When Faith Falters

> "'If you can'?" said Jesus. "Everything is possible for one who believes." Immediately the boy's father exclaimed, "I do believe; help me overcome my unbelief!" (Mark 9:23-24)

In times of desperation, God is our only hope. Yet we wonder if he truly hears our prayers. We believe in his great power but wonder if he'll use it for us. We trust in his love but hesitate to ask for big things. His promises to carry our burdens and deliver us from evil can seem too good to be true.

The Lord is patient with your doubts. He knows your faith can be shaken. His love is a free gift that you're not required to earn. At the same time you're asking for help, you can ask for deeper trust to believe he'll do it.

Call out to God in prayer today. Give him your deepest fears, longings, and struggles. Ask for stronger faith in his goodness and power. Invite him into every part of your life – be ready to see him work beyond your wildest expectations. Praise his name for his mercy and love that never ends.

Lord, we need your strength and help today. Give hope to believe you're with us. Build up our faith when we doubt your promises. Thank you for all you're going to do.

Amen.

August 27

Give Him Everything

But the angel of the Lord called out to him from heaven, "Abraham! Abraham!" "Here I am," he replied. "Do not lay a hand on the boy," he said. "Do not do anything to him. Now I know that you fear God, because you have not withheld from me your son, your only son." (Genesis 22:11-12)

God promises in Psalm 37:4 that he'll give us the desires of our heart when we trust in him. We stand in awe and gratitude for our beautiful family. The career that rewards our talent and effort. The friends who give priceless companionship through the years. Healing, blessings, significance – God pours out his love and goodness beyond what we imagine.

Our faith is tested by our response to God's generosity. Do we keep his gifts for ourselves? Are we terrified of losing what we've gained? Is our worth and happiness dependent on a person or possession? Would our life lose hope and meaning if a blessing was taken away? Abraham's trust and obedience were proved by his willingness to give his only son back to God.

What is your greatest treasure today? Offer it freely back to the Source, our Lord. Praise his name for every blessing, but let him be your greatest desire. Nothing he will ever give can surpass the gift of Jesus himself.

Lord, thank you for your goodness that is too great to measure. Let us trust you with our blessings and love you most of all. Amen.

August 28

Overcome Together

Brothers and sisters, if someone is caught in a sin, you who live by the Spirit should restore that person gently. But watch yourselves, or you also may be tempted. (Galatians 6:1)

In marriage, our lives are an open book. We know each other's mistakes and weaknesses. We know when our partner is struggling to obey the Lord. We share in the difficult consequences of each other's sin.

As believers you're not just husband and wife, but brother and sister in Christ as well. In your relationship you can offer encouragement to seek God's will together. You can offer mercy and forgiveness in Jesus' name. You can challenge each other to greater obedience. You can pray for strength when you see your partner tempted to fall. You can provide accountability to do the right thing, even when it's difficult.

Humble your heart today to accept your spouse's counsel. Be willing to admit your mistakes and ask for help to change. Pray together for strength to obey the Lord in everything.

Lord, give us courage to confront the sin in our life. Show us how to encourage each other in obedience to you. Let us live in faithfulness and truth by your Spirit.

Amen.

August 29

Blessing and Cursing

With the tongue we praise our Lord and Father, and with it
we curse human beings, who have been made in
God's likeness. Out of the same mouth come praise and cursing.
My brothers and sisters, this should not be. (James 3:9-10)

The Lord knows that our speech reveals a divided heart. We speak tender words of affection, then lash out in anger when our loved one lets us down. We worship and express our love for God, yet slander and judge those who he's created. We thank him for our happiness and prosperity, but complain and argue when he allows us to suffer. Our words act as a window to reveal who we really are inside.

Ask the Lord for a pure heart of love today. Pray for the fruit of the Spirit – love, joy, peace, patience, kindness, goodness, faithfulness, and self-control – to fill your lives. Trust in his transforming work, as he's always faithful to make you new.

Pray for ears to hear yourself when you're tearing others down. Seek restoration when your words have damaged a relationship. Take every opportunity to encourage and affirm those around you. Praise God all the time, from a heart and mouth that are devoted to him.

Lord, forgive us for the sinful words we say. Work in our minds and attitudes so we speak what's true and right. Thank you for the words of love you speak into our lives.

Amen.

August 30

Joy and Sorrow

> A cheerful heart is good medicine, but a crushed spirit dries up the bones. (Proverbs 17:22)

The troubles of life can crush your spirit. Financial strain and job stress leave you depleted of energy. Conflict with friends and relatives robs you of peace. Physical sickness and pain drains your strength. Grief and loss leave you empty inside. Depression and anxiety make joy and hope impossible to find. It's hard to face another day.

Is your loved one discouraged today? Offer them the healing medicine of a cheerful heart. Meet their sorrow with warmth and kindness. Express thanks for the daily blessings God provides. Comfort rather than criticize their struggle. Let your peace and trust in God's faithful help give you joy to share.

Seek the Lord together for contentment in all circumstances. Let his strength give you courage to face whatever comes. Allow his healing love to soothe your hurt. Believe his promise to use everything for good in the end. Allow him to breathe new life into your dry, tired hearts. In him, joy is possible in all things.

Lord, help us to look to you for joy and peace no matter what happens. Give us a cheerful attitude, and make us ready to encourage one another in hard times.

Amen.

August 31

Finding Our Feet

> When I said, "My foot is slipping," your unfailing love, Lord, supported me. When anxiety was great within me, your consolation brought me joy. (Psalm 94:18-19)

No matter how hard we try, it can all come crashing down. We put in overtime but still get fired. We follow the doctor's advice but our condition gets worse. We love and help our child, but they rebel and shut us out. We work with the creditors but still face bankruptcy. We visit counselors but our marriage hangs on by a thread. As we stand on the brink of disaster, the stress is overwhelming.

Through it all, God's love doesn't change. He's always ready to hear your prayers. His wisdom and truth are there for the asking. His strength gives hope when you're ready to give up. He holds you close with comfort and compassion when you feel alone. With God, you can have joy in the darkest night.

Do you feel you're beyond hope today? Are you slipping into despair, ready to quit? Call on the Lord for his loving support. Receive his comfort and unconditional love. Trust that he's with you and will stay until the end.

Lord, even when everything falls apart, you never change. Thank you for your unfailing love. Quiet our fears as we trust you to take care of us in every way.

Amen.

September

September 1

The Peace of Surrender

"Six days you shall labor, but on the seventh day you shall rest; even during the plowing season and harvest you must rest." (Exodus 34:21)

God's command to Israel to rest on the Sabbath wasn't about just taking a break. He knew they would be tired and worn out from their labor. He knew they should set aside time to worship. He knew they needed quiet hours with their families. But he also knew the human heart – its pride, self-reliance, and drive to get ahead. The seventh day of rest forced each one to remember the true source of everything they needed – God himself.

Are you wearing yourself out trying to solve all your problems? Are you afraid to let down your guard in case trouble comes? Is everyone counting on you? Are you carrying the weight of your family's needs on your shoulders? Today, remember who cares for you. Trust in God as your provider. Rest – emotionally, mentally, and physically – by putting your life in his hands.

Give your needs and burdens to God today. Pray for faith to believe he'll care for you. Let him lead you into his rest.

Lord, we've been working so hard to get it all done. We're tired from trying to take your place as our provider. Let us depend on you and find true rest.

Amen.

September 2

The Trap of Self-Sufficiency

> Jesus looked around and said to his disciples, "How hard it is for the rich to enter the kingdom of God!" (Mark 10:23)

God knows how easily our hearts are divided. It's tempting to love this world more than the One who made it. We depend on our own strength and resources instead of our Provider. We build prosperity instead of God's kingdom. We live to please ourselves instead of our Father.

Whether you're rich or struggling to make ends meet, money competes for your heart. God doesn't want you to love what can't love you back. Today, thank him for his gifts. Let him examine your hearts to see if he's in first place. Talk about your goals and dreams for the future – are they focused on your own gain or his purposes? Look for ways to share your blessings with others in his name. Surrender every dollar, possession, and achievement to his control.

God gave his Word and Spirit, and invites you to pray. He's strong enough to guard your hearts and keep you faithful. He can satisfy you completely like nothing else. Encourage each other to seek him first.

Lord, guard our hearts from the love of money. We want to love you most of all as part of your kingdom forever.
Amen.

September 3

Love and Obey

> "If you love me, keep my commands. And I will ask the Father, and he will give you another advocate to help you and be with you forever – the Spirit of truth." (John 14:15-17)

It's hard to obey all the time. We're tempted to bend the truth. We fall into worry and doubt. We choose to please ourselves instead of giving as we should. We're jealous, ungrateful, and proud. We wrestle with sin despite our love for Jesus. We want to prove our devotion by doing his will, but we're weak and fall short every day.

God doesn't leave you to struggle alone. He gives the Spirit to make you strong in faith. He helps you understand the Word and writes it on your hearts. He renews your minds so you can think like Jesus. He transforms the desires of your hearts so you love to do what's right. He sets you free from the slavery of sin.

Pray and ask for more love and strength to obey. Thank him for the Spirit who helps you all the time. Have hope, believing that "he who began a good work in you will carry it on to completion until the day of Christ Jesus" (Phil. 1:6).

Lord, we want to love and obey you in every way. Help us by the power of your Spirit.

Amen.

September 4

The Gift of a Wife

> In this same way, husbands ought to love their wives
> as their own bodies. He who loves his wife loves himself.
> After all, no one ever hated their own body, but they
> feed and care for their body, just as Christ does the
> church – for we are members of his body. (Ephesians 5:28-30)

Husband, your wife is a gift from God. Her calling is to respect, encourage, and support you every day. She's to care for your family, build up your home, and help you prosper. She's to promote your success and protect your good name. She's to love you with all she's got. She's the greatest blessing you'll know in this life.

Your love is what makes her calling a joy. But she'll struggle if you leave her tired and alone. She'll grow discouraged if you put her down. She'll pull away if you're harsh and critical. She'll want to give up if she's ignored and unappreciated. If you hurt her, you'll hurt yourself.

Today, love your wife. Treat her as your equal. Care for her heart. Respect her mind. Protect and honor her body. Provide for her needs and support her dreams. Let her know she's your treasure from God.

Lord, thank you for your gift of marriage. Teach us to love and serve one another like Jesus.

Amen.

September 5

Chosen and Cherished

But you are a chosen people, a royal priesthood, a holy nation, God's special possession, that you may declare the praises of him who called you out of darkness into his wonderful light. (1 Peter 2:9)

You may be rejected by your family. Passed over by employers. Left out instead of welcomed in. Yet God says you're hand-picked to be his very own. "For he chose us in him before the creation of the world to be holy and blameless in his sight" (Eph. 1:4). He created you, called you, and has plans for you for now and forever.

You're God's special treasures today. He loves you so much, he gave Jesus to save your lives. He gave his Spirit to comfort and guide you. He built his church so you have a family to belong to. He provided his Word, with all the wisdom and truth you need for this life. He cares for you and never leaves your side.

You're no longer marked by your sins and failures. You're clean and new. You're children of light, free from the darkness. Shame and fear are gone. No one can accuse you anymore. You're free to love and live for him without holding back.

Pray and thank God for his love. Shine his light in the darkness as you praise his name today.

Lord, give us faith to believe we're chosen and special to you. Thank you for calling us into your light.

Amen.

September 6

Grateful Giving

> Honor the LORD with your wealth, with the firstfruits of all your crops; then your barns will be filled to overflowing, and your vats will brim over with new wine. (Proverbs 3:9-10)

As we grow in our faith, our understanding of God's generosity grows too. Each blessing and every cent is a gift of provision from his hand. Our first response to all we receive should be praise and gratitude to God.

He asks us to honor him with our money and possessions. As we enjoy his generosity we also give to others. We support our church and ministers of God's Word. Our hearts respond to those in need with eagerness to help. We hold on loosely to all we have, understanding that God is the owner of it all.

Nothing we share escapes God's notice. He's so pleased when we give, he pours out an even greater abundance. We can never surpass his generosity!

Today, give thanks for the little or lot you possess. Open your eyes to the needs around you and give in Jesus' name. Anticipate with joy the ways the Lord will provide and bless your home.

Lord, give us grateful hearts for all you do. You know our needs and are the source of all we have. Teach us to honor you as we share your good gifts.

Amen.

September 7

The Generous Heart

> Each of you should give what you have decided in your heart to give, not reluctantly or under compulsion, for God loves a cheerful giver. (2 Corinthians 9:7)

When starting out together, we look forward to giving to each other for life. We imagine helping, encouraging, and supporting our loved one in every way we can. But over time, the joy of giving can fade. We feel unappreciated. We focus on our own needs and wants. We wonder if it's worth the sacrifice to bless our spouse.

Today, decide once more to give from the heart. Lighten each other's load. Share positive, uplifting words. Freely offer your time and a listening ear. Buy a thoughtful gift. Look for creative ways to say "I love you." Anticipate each other's needs and help before a word is spoken.

God knows if you give from the heart, or only out of guilt or duty. He loves when you're glad to bless each other. Pray for a fresh desire to serve. Ask for a generous spirit. Depend on him to show what your loved one needs the most.

Lord, forgive us for holding back in giving to each other. Make us eager to show our love in every way. Give us generous hearts like yours.

Amen.

September 8

The Parent Principle

"Honor your father and mother" – which is the first commandment with a promise – "so that it may go well with you and that you may enjoy long life on the earth." (Ephesians 6:2-3)

Our relationship with parents changes once we've said "I do." They move from a position of authority to one of influence in our lives. Couples provide for themselves instead of depending on parents for every need. Two separate households are created with different traditions, habits, and goals to pursue.

This transition isn't always easy. It can be difficult for parents to release their children to full independence. It can be hard for couples to create an identity as a new family. It takes wisdom to set healthy boundaries – to obey God's instruction to leave your parents' home and be united to one another (Matt. 19:5).

As you create your own household, strive to honor your parents. Be patient and understanding if you feel resistance to letting you go. Communicate your boundaries with love and kindness. Respect their advice as you make decisions. Express appreciation for their generosity and interest in your life. Pray for your parents. Be willing to meet their needs in difficult times. In honoring your father and mother you'll honor the Lord as well.

Lord, teach us to honor our parents as we build our own family. Show us how to help and love them in obedience to you. Amen.

September 9

Getting Along

> How good and pleasant it is when God's
> people live together in unity! (Psalm 133:1)

Conflict is stressful and steals the joy from your home. Bickering, complaining, and critical words tear intimacy apart. Harsh tempers and stubborn hearts break down trust. There's nothing "good and pleasant" about constant fighting in your marriage.

The only solution to division is humility and prayer. Unity requires listening to the other's point of view. It means giving up the desire to win and have your way. It focuses on the strengths and precious value of your partner. It admits where you're wrong and need to change. It chooses the way of love and self-sacrifice.

Pray for peace between you today. Confess how you've put yourselves first. Ask for wisdom in difficult decisions. Seek the Lord's help to understand your partner's way of thinking. Thank God for the gift of your spouse in your life.

Let the love of Jesus breathe peace into your relationship. He'll give you strength to forgive the past and cherish one another in the future. Your unity will demonstrate the love of God to a lost and hurting world.

Lord, make us one by your Spirit. Bind our hearts together and show us how to love like Jesus in every situation.
Amen.

September 10

Trusting in Trials

When they hurled their insults at him, he did not retaliate; when he suffered, he made no threats. Instead, he entrusted himself to him who judges justly. (1 Peter 2:23)

Jesus let us know that since the world hates him, it will hate us too. We'll suffer all kinds of accusations – that we're legalistic, narrow-minded, and judgmental. That we're ignorant and old-fashioned. That we're brainwashed or backward in our thinking. We'll be a target for mocking in the media. We'll be left out at work. We'll be lonely in our own families as they criticize our choices.

Through all of this, we're called to love. We keep quiet in the face of ugly words. We lift others up while they're tearing us down. We set aside any right to take revenge, trusting God's justice will stand in the end. We take our fears to the One who watches over us. We bring every wound to our Healer. We follow the example of Jesus who showed mercy to those who nailed him to the cross.

Place yourselves in God's hands today. Find hope, knowing he'll reward you for all you suffer for his name.

Lord, you're our safe place in the storm of hatred against your people. Give us courage and peace as we trust in you.

Amen.

September 11

Grumbling or Gratitude

> Do everything without grumbling or arguing, so that you may become blameless and pure, "children of God without fault in a warped and crooked generation." (Philippians 2:14-15)

Grumbling and arguing come naturally for all of us. We complain when we can't have what we want. We argue and demand our own way. These habits and attitudes can take over our marriage and family. It may seem too hard to do everything without grumbling or arguing. But God gives the example of Jesus who gave up his rights, served others, and willingly died on the cross (Phil. 2:6-8). He'll give us what we need to obey.

You're given a choice: to love and obey selflessly like Jesus, or to complain and argue out of a desire to please yourselves. When you choose a willing, cheerful attitude to surrender and sacrifice, you stand out from the crowd. You pick up the torch of God's light and shine it in the world. Your identity as Christ-followers is confirmed by the grace of your words.

Serve each other with gladness today. Confront opposition with a peaceable heart. Embrace God's will for this day – whether full of joys or challenges – and display his love to everyone.

Lord, forgive us for resisting each other and you. Fill our mouths with words of gratitude and peace. Let us display your holiness to a lost and broken world.

Amen.

September 12

Our True Treasure

"But store up for yourselves treasures in heaven, where moths and vermin do not destroy, and where thieves do not break in and steal. For where your treasure is, there your heart will be also." (Matthew 6:20-21)

We spend money and energy protecting what's ours. Insurance policies, safe-deposit boxes, and retirement funds are efforts to keep what we acquire in this life. Yet there's no perfect defense against loss or disaster – nothing in this world is truly secure.

In God's goodness he provides treasures that last forever. His storehouses in heaven are eternally protected. Money that's hoarded is easily lost, yet generous giving yields a rich reward. Whatever you give in this life – your time, resources, energy, and prayer – is saved up by our Father to be lavished upon our life in heaven.

You can strive to fill your house and bank account during your years on this earth. Or you can love, serve, and give abundantly in Jesus' name. You can focus on what you're leaving behind or the glorious gifts to come. The only treasure worth seeking is the reward from your Father. Let him fill your storehouse to overflowing!

Lord, keep our eyes fixed on eternity with you instead of this world. Teach us the truth that whatever we give, we ultimately receive from your hand. Thank you for your treasures.

Amen.

September 13

A Wife's Worship

> Wives, submit yourselves to your own husbands as you do to the Lord. For the husband is the head of the wife as Christ is the head of the church, his body, of which he is the Savior. Now as the church submits to Christ, so also wives should submit to their husbands in everything. (Ephesians 5:22-24)

God knows you love him. He sees your heart that wants to obey. Your marriage provides a place to serve and worship his name.

Submit to the Lord by respecting your husband. Willingly honor his God-assigned role as leader in your home. Keep anger and criticism out of your conversation. Give him room for his own ideas and opinions. Look for the good in him and name it out loud. Pray for his struggles. Don't do anything to hurt his reputation. Be someone he can count on for support. Have patience when he fails, giving the grace you've been given yourself.

Your husband may not always deserve your respect. His decisions may backfire. His emotions will override his judgment. He'll be selfish and sinful. But you're called to build him up, not tear him down. By surrendering yourself to let him lead, you show how believers trust and submit to Jesus.

God loves you – you're not to be a doormat, victim, or slave. Your submission is freely given in his name. Pray for strength to honor your husband today.

Lord, fill our marriage with love, honor, and obedience to you.

Amen.

September 14

Love without Limits

And God is able to bless you abundantly, so that in all things at all times, having all that you need, you will abound in every good work. (2 Corinthians 9:8)

It's not always easy to give to your spouse. You become stressed. Busy. Self-absorbed. Daily irritations and arguments come between you. You feel so distant and tired, you don't know what to do. Be encouraged – God is able to provide all you need to love each other well.

With God's help, "abound in every good work" for each other today. Pray and ask God for time to listen and care. Ask for strength to manage the house as a team. Speak words of hope and encouragement. Bless each other with affirmation and "I love you's." Pray for each other's struggles. Show compassion and patience when you fail. Share loving intimacy together. Show courtesy and respect. Take every opportunity to do good and build each other up.

Tell each other what you need right now. Take those needs to God in prayer. Ask him to break down any obstacles to your love. Let him refresh your commitment to bless each other in every way, all the time. Thank him for the gift that marriage can be.

Lord, forgive us for failing to help and serve each other. Fill us with strength and grace so we can love without holding back. Amen.

September 15

Back in the Fold

For "you were like sheep going astray," but now you have returned to the Shepherd and Overseer of your souls. (1 Peter 2:25)

Remember how you wandered before Jesus led your life? You thought money could buy happiness. You believed you'd matter if people liked you. You tried to feed your soul by feeding your cravings. You expected intelligence and education to give all the wisdom you needed. You looked to family, friends, and romance to fill up your heart. You attempted to ease your guilt by doing good things. Whatever path you took led you further from God's love.

Praise your Shepherd today for leading you home. Thank him for his mercy and acceptance. Name the ways he's taken care of you. Remember how he's set you free. Commit to follow wherever he leads. Pray for deeper understanding of his Word and will for your life. Trust in his love that will never let you go.

"My sheep listen to my voice; I know them, and they follow me. I give them eternal life, and they shall never perish; no one will snatch them out of my hand" (John 10:27-28).

Lord, thank you for finding us when we were lost. Let us follow you faithfully and love you forever.

Amen.

September 16

The Heritage of Faith

> The righteous lead blameless lives; blessed
> are their children after them. (Proverbs 20:7)

Kids are observant – they know who we really are. They have a front-row seat to view our habits, priorities, and relationships. We're teaching by example every time we handle conflict, cope with failure, and express our emotions. When we live in obedience to God, we're showing them how to love and serve him in their own lives.

Bless your children by following God wholeheartedly. Let them see your faith is real by how you obey his Word. Invite them to pray with you so they can witness God's faithful answers. Serve others so they can recognize love in action. Let praise and gratitude fill your conversation so they know the Lord as your provider. As you trust in him year by year, your children will see what it means to follow Christ.

There's no greater gift than the message of salvation. Our children are forever blessed when we tell them of Jesus and give him our lives.

Lord, our children are watching – let us obey you in everything. Use our faithful devotion to you as a witness to our family. Let them see how real you are as you lead us day by day. Amen.

September 17

Only God

> Those who cling to worthless idols turn away from God's love for them. (Jonah 2:8)

We hold on tight to what we love. We grab hold of what makes us feel secure. Significant. Satisfied. What's in our hands proves what's in our hearts.

Receive God's love as your provider instead of holding on to success and money. Praise him for the gift of children, receiving their affection as a blessing from him. Put away the mirror and focus on the beauty of Christ. Find contentment in the Giver, not what he's given.

Loosen your grip on anything that's become more precious than God himself. Tear down the idols that compete for your attention and loyalty. Flee temptation. Step away from those who put down your faith. Give up the craving to have more and more in this world.

Turn toward the love of God today. Remember his perfect worth that earns our praise. Trust him to meet every need in your life. Satisfy your soul with his good Word, worship, and prayer. Remember how he captured your heart in the beginning – how he proved himself as Savior and Friend. Fix your eyes on God and make him the center of everything.

Lord, forgive us for loving things that can never truly satisfy. Make us faithful in our love for you, as you are always devoted to us. Let us praise your name alone, forever.

Amen.

September 18

Running the Race

> "Therefore, since we are surrounded by such a great cloud of witnesses, let us throw off everything that hinders and the sin that so easily entangles. And let us run with perseverance the race marked out for us, fixing our eyes on Jesus, the pioneer and perfecter of faith." (Hebrews 12:1-2)

In times of struggle, doubt, or temptation, it's encouraging to remember believers who have gone before us. Heroes of the faith such as Noah, Abraham, Sarah, and Moses kept pressing on and trusting God despite their challenging circumstances.

We need a "witnesses" for our marriage, too – couples who fought for their relationship through hard times that threatened to split them apart. When we wonder if our love will survive, another couple's perseverance can give us courage to keep going. We find hope that someday our marriage may stand as an example for another struggling husband and wife.

The race is marked out for you – to love one another well until God calls you home. Throw off bitterness, doubt, and sin that are hindering your progress today. Remember Jesus, whose perfect love never fails. Find strength in him to keep your promises and grow as one.

Lord, give us a deeper faith in you, and renew our hope in one another. Provide us with examples of godly marriage. Teach us to love each other more fully each day.

Amen.

September 19

Hope in the Heartache

Yet this I call to mind and therefore I have hope:
Because of the Lord's great love we are not consumed,
for his compassions never fail. (Lamentations 3:21-22)

You've suffered together. You've let each other down. You've been overwhelmed by trouble. You've hurt each other's hearts. Yet you're still here today, standing together through it all.

God is compassionate toward you and your marriage. He loves you too much to leave you alone. He offers his strength when you've got nothing left. He helps you forgive the past and find hope for the future. He builds you up to keep your vows, keep the faith, and keep moving forward.

The enemy says your spouse doesn't deserve your love. The world says to cut and run, pursuing your own happiness. The Lord says stay and fight. Stand up against threats to your relationship. Refuse to give up on each other. Follow his wisdom to know what to do. Trust him to give you the love and grace you need to stay together. He holds all you need to make it through.

Lord, we don't want to lose hope in you or each other. Help us to trust in your mercy. Let us love each other as you've loved us.
Amen.

September 20

The Scent of Sacrifice

> Follow God's example, therefore, as dearly loved children and walk in the way of love, just as Christ loved us and gave himself up for us as a fragrant offering and sacrifice to God. (Ephesians 5:1-2)

Love demands sacrifice, requiring us to love whether it's deserved or not. Thankfully, our great God provided us with the ultimate example of love – he offered his one and only Son to die for us while we were still sinners. Are we willing to "walk in the way of love" for our spouse?

Be encouraged, knowing the love you give to each other is an act of worship and obedience to God. Your kind, uplifting words reflect his mercy to you. Your generosity flows from the blessings from his hand. Your humility and patience are an echo of the servant-heart of Christ. When you lay down your lives for one another, you're surrendering yourselves more completely to the Lord.

Consider how you can love each other today. Are there words of comfort and forgiveness to be spoken? Is there help to be given? Is there time, money, or gifts to be shared? Are there hopes and dreams to be supported? Love one another without holding back, and rejoice in delighting God's heart.

Lord, thank you for your lavish love that knows no limit. Teach us to walk in the way of love, and let our marriage be a fragrant offering to you.

Amen.

September 21

Never Too Late

> While Jesus was still speaking, some people came from the house of Jairus, the synagogue leader. "Your daughter is dead," they said. "Why bother the teacher anymore?" Overhearing what they said, Jesus told him, "Don't be afraid; just believe." (Mark 5:35-37)

In the face of disappointment, we can believe our chances for blessing are over. The job opportunity passes us by. Another pregnancy test reads negative. Our offer on a house is rejected. The insurance company puts our medical issues on hold. Our hopes for the future are crushed. It seems too late for God to meet our needs.

Yet our God rules the universe. He's not limited by time or place. His resources are infinite, and his power is great. Put your trust in him. Believe that his plans for you are perfect. Keep calling out to him in prayer with the burdens on your heart.

When others tell you to just give up, "Don't be afraid; just believe" (v. 37). Praise God for how he'll use every trial to strengthen your faith and display his love in your lives. Remember his true promises to give you a hope and a future. In the difficulty you face, Jesus will have the last word!

Lord, as our God of hope, fill us with all joy and peace as we trust in you, so that we may overflow with hope by the power of the Holy Spirit (Rom. 15:13).

Amen.

September 22

Sweet Sincerity

An honest answer is like a kiss on the lips. (Proverbs 24:26)

Honesty is a gift to your loved one. Your spouse can trust you to own your mistakes. They feel respected, knowing you won't manipulate to get your way. They're not worried you're cheating in secret. They're proud of your integrity as you mean what you say. They feel close to you as thoughts and feelings are kept in the open. Living in truth allows you to be one.

Today, show your love through honesty. Share what's on your minds. Admit how you've been wrong or failed. Open up about secret fears and frustrations. Be transparent about where you go, who you see, and what you're doing. Keep your promises. Be real so you can know each other through and through.

Pray together with honest hearts today. Confess your sins and receive forgiveness. Share your deepest hurts and find healing. Bring God your secret doubts and disappointments so he can build you up. Tell him how you need his help, trusting him to provide. Love him by inviting him into every part of your life.

Lord, we want to be honest instead of hiding our thoughts, feelings, and actions. Teach us to be truthful all the time.
Amen.

September 23

Love in Action

Suppose a brother or a sister is without clothes and daily food. If one of you says to them, "Go in peace; keep warm and well fed," but does nothing about their physical needs, what good is it? In the same way, faith by itself, if it is not accompanied by action, is dead. (James 2:15-17)

Sometimes words are just words. Homemade chicken soup can say more than a "get well soon." "I miss you" means more when followed by an invitation to dinner. "Have a nice day" becomes real when our needs are met and burdens are shared. Our sentiments are proved true by tangible gifts of time, energy, and resources.

God wants your faith to show. Take visible steps of obedience to his inner direction. Reach out to neighbors beyond just a friendly wave. Spend your money to relieve poverty and suffering. Interrupt your schedule to comfort a grieving friend. Set aside time for Bible study and prayer. Work to reconcile broken relationships. Surrender your lives to God's control.

Put your faith in action today. Respond to God's prompting to volunteer, give, or reach out. Dig deeper in the Word. Pray for the lost. Demonstrate your trust in God's love for you by loving someone else.

Lord, let our faith be more than words. Show us how to put our beliefs into action. Lead us to those that need help today. Amen.

September 24

We're in This Together

Because of the service by which you have proved yourselves, others will praise God for the obedience that accompanies your confession of the gospel of Christ, and for your generosity in sharing with them and with everyone else. (2 Corinthians 9:13)

When you serve each other you're obeying God. When you show love with words and actions, you're loving the Lord as well. When you give generously to one another, you bring praise to Jesus' name. When you care for your spouse with all your heart, you lead them to thank God for you.

Today, prove your love for God by loving each other. Speak words of encouragement. Put down your phone and the remote to give undivided attention. Carry each other's burdens. Pitch in without being asked. Be affectionate. Follow through on a promise. Choose to say "yes" instead of arguing.

Tell everyone how blessed you are. Put each other first. Love without holding back, so the world can see the heart of God through your marriage.

Lord, we want to obey you by loving each other. Teach us to lay down our lives for each other, as you gave yourself up for us. Let our marriage bring praise to your name.

Amen.

September 25

He Knows Your Needs

"So do not worry, saying, 'What shall we eat?' or 'What shall we drink?' or 'What shall we wear?' For the pagans run after all these things, and your heavenly Father knows that you need them." (Matthew 6:31-32)

The simple act of feeding and clothing ourselves is confusing and complicated. Organic, GMO, or conventional? Low-carb or low-fat? Wheat or gluten-free? The strain of making healthy choices on a sensible budget is stressful. For many, providing three basic meals per day is out of reach.

We also feel pressure to "dress for success" and keep an adequate wardrobe in our closet. Clothing our family from season to season is costly and challenging.

Taking care of these basic needs for your household can consume your attention. You can fall into worry, or complain you don't have enough. The Lord offers freedom from the struggle by promising to care for every need.

Bring your worries and questions to God in prayer. Ask him for guidance in making the right choices for your family. Share your specific needs and burdens, and ask him to provide. Nothing is too small or difficult to bring to him in prayer.

Be encouraged, knowing God is fully aware of every need in your life. Release your worries and allow contentment to fill your soul.

Lord, we need your help to keep meals on the table and clothing in our closet. Thank you for loving us and knowing every detail. Help us to trust in your promises.

Amen.

September 26

A Sling or a Sword

> So David triumphed over the Philistine with a sling and a stone; without a sword in his hand he struck down the Philistine and killed him. (1 Samuel 17:50)

*Y*our enemies want to bring you down. They'll step on you to get ahead. They'll attack your reputation to build up their own name. They'll take what's yours. They'll deny your faith and belittle the Lord Jesus. They'll intimidate you to make you feel small. You can cower in fear or trust in the power of God for victory.

You don't need wealth to overcome your enemy. You don't need invincible strength. Degrees and awards won't plead your cause. Popularity won't take you far. Your hope is found in the God who loves you. He is your rock, your fortress, and your deliverer (Ps. 18:2). "The LORD will fight for you; you need only to be still" (Exod. 14:14).

Put your battle in God's hands today. Believe in his power. Be confident he's on your side. Be courageous, knowing he's with you all the time. Trust in his strength instead of your own. "All those gathered here will know that it is not by sword or spear that the Lord saves; for the battle is the Lord's" (1 Sam. 17:47).

Lord, we are weak but you are strong. Show your power and love as you fight for us today.

Amen.

September 27

The Good News

> For the message of the cross is foolishness to those who are perishing, but to us who are being saved it is the power of God. (1 Corinthians 1:18)

The Gospel is nonsense to those who don't believe. You'll be discouraged and frustrated if you expect unsaved friends and family to celebrate your salvation. How can they praise a God they don't depend on? How can they rejoice in your freedom if they don't understand their slavery to sin? How can they encourage obedience to God's Word if they deny its truth? Your choices, beliefs, and eternal hope are confusing and even offensive to those who are lost.

You recognize the life-giving, transforming power of the cross in your lives. You know the miracle of rescue from death. You hold the message of the gospel. Have compassion on your relatives, friends, and co-workers who are "perishing" today. Respond to their criticism with kindness. Receive their pridefulness with humility. Meet their despair with the hope only found in Christ. Stand firm in the truth when they tempt you to sin. Offer love to everyone as God has loved you.

Pray and thank God for saving you through his power. Celebrate the life that's found in the good news of the cross today.

Lord, thank you for rescuing us from our unbelief in Jesus. Let us be your message-bearers to those who are perishing.
Amen.

September 28

Our Heavenly Home

Instead, they were longing for a better country – a heavenly one.
Therefore God is not ashamed to be called their God,
for he has prepared a city for them. (Hebrews 11:16)

You share an address with the one you love. Even if obligations keep you apart for a while, your true home is under the same roof. It would crush your marriage if one built a separate life somewhere else.

In the same way, God loves you and wants to be with you forever. He's preparing a place in his house even now. It's a beautiful paradise with no pain, sadness, or death. It's always day, shining with God's glory. It holds your inheritance he's promised for following Jesus. It's where you belong as his child.

Even with the promise of what's to come, we get attached to this world. We're easily satisfied by what we can touch and see with our eyes. Troubles and busyness consume our attention. Today, pray for a fresh longing for the "better country." Hold your life loosely, since "our citizenship is in heaven. And we eagerly await a Savior from there, the Lord Jesus Christ, who, by the power that enables him to bring everything under his control, will transform our lowly bodies so that they will be like his glorious body" (Phil. 3:20-21).

Live like you're leaving – obey God, share the gospel, and wait eagerly for Jesus to come.

Lord, let us always remember our true home is with you. Amen.

September 29

Glory Came Down

> The Word became flesh and made his dwelling among us.
> We have seen his glory, the glory of the one and only Son,
> who came from the Father, full of grace and truth. (John 1:14)

Jesus was here. He grew up under his parents' roof and learned the family business. He ate fish on the beach with his friends. He talked to people about what scripture had to say. He celebrated holidays. He liked little kids. He cried when people died. He got mad at cheaters who abused their power. He was loved and hated. He was one of us.

But he was so much more – he was God's full revelation of himself. He cast out demons. He turned water into wine. He commanded the waves to be still. He healed the sick and raised the dead. He conquered the power of sin. He revealed his glory and ascended to his Father in heaven. He was, and is, and is to come.

Because of his humanity he knows our temptations and struggles. Because he's the living, eternal, holy Son of God, he takes away the sin of the world. He reconciled us to the Father. He gives us life forever.

What can we do but worship? Love him. Obey his Word. Give him your life today.

Lord, thank you for Jesus. He is our truth and our life.
Amen.

September 30

Your One and Only

> Like a lily among thorns is my darling among the young women. Like an apple tree among the trees of the forest is my beloved among the young men. (Song of Songs 2:2-3)

You long to be cherished as your spouse's one and only love. You want to fully capture their heart and devotion. Yet the wear and tear of life can cloud your perspective. Affection gives way to irritation. Compliments are buried by criticism. Romance is lost to busyness. You don't feel unique or special any more.

Praise God for your loved one today. Remember what sets them apart from everyone else. Appreciate their strengths that complement your weaknesses. Affirm their character and abilities. Share why you're proud of who they are. Renew your conviction that your partner is a gift from God, just for you.

Pray and ask the Lord to set you free from the trap of comparison. Release any secret desires for someone more attractive, successful, or exciting. Let him breathe fresh life into your relationship. He'll give you grace to deepen your love again.

Lord, our marriage is a treasure from you. Give us eyes to see what's wonderful in each other. Renew our delight in one another today.

Amen.

October

October 1

Winning in Weakness

> God chose the foolish things of the world to shame the wise; God chose the weak things of the world to shame the strong. (1 Corinthians 1:27)

We don't find salvation because we're smarter than everyone else. We don't have hope for tomorrow because we're brave or optimistic. We don't stand firm against temptation because we're morally superior. Our faith and strength come from God.

We're living proof that God loves the unlovely. He heals what's too broken to mend. He gives wisdom when we're foolish. He forgives the ugliest of sins, to prove his love has no limit. For those working so hard to win God over, this kind of grace is hard to understand.

Praise God for choosing you today. You know we're not adopted because we're extra-special. We're not the most attractive, talented, or good. You're saved because he gave you Jesus with a love too great to comprehend. He deserves all the glory for what he's done.

Share your story of God's rescue. How he met you in your sin and made you new. How he gave you strength when you were falling apart. How his truth has never let you down. Let your life tell the "wise" and the "strong" who they really need.

Lord, thank you for choosing us to be yours. Your wisdom, strength, and love have made all the difference.

Amen.

October 2

Saved and Sealed

When you believed, you were marked in him with a seal, the promised Holy Spirit, who is a deposit guaranteeing our inheritance until the redemption of those who are God's possession – to the praise of his glory. (Ephesians 1:13-14)

Everyone who believes in Jesus is given the Holy Spirit. He's your seal – your deposit – so your future with God is guaranteed. No one can snatch you from his hand (John 10:29).

Are you insecure, wondering if God might change his mind about you? Shame over sin can shake your trust in his forgiveness. Friends and family think your faith is "just a phase" that will pass. Skeptics cast doubt over the truth of the Word. The world sinks deeper into darkness, and you wonder if God really has a plan.

Nothing will break God's hold on you. Your reward is waiting in heaven. Your room is being prepared in your Father's house. The final payment has been made for your sin. Your names are written in the book of life. You have the Holy Spirit even now, to give you hope.

Thank God today for his salvation and the promise of the Spirit. Have faith, the "confidence in what we hope for and assurance about what we do not see" (Heb. 11:1).

Lord, thank you for making us yours forever. Give us faith to wait with hope for what you have in store.

Amen.

October 3

Sin Hurts

*Streams of tears flow from my eyes,
for your law is not obeyed.* (Psalm 119:136)

As believers, we love the Bible. It gives us wisdom for every step. It spurs us on to greater love for others. It's an anchor of truth in a world of confusion. It gives knowledge, corrects us when we're wrong, and trains us in righteousness. It is the very Word of God himself.

It's hard when we see the Word rejected. Friends suffer broken lives as sin does its work. Loved ones lose their way by denying God's wisdom. Communities fall into poverty and violence by ignoring God's ways. The way to peace and joy is forgotten.

Today, pray for friends who don't know the Lord. Ask him to open their eyes to see him clearly. Pray for family who wandered from the faith. Ask God to bring them back to himself. Pray for neighbors and co-workers who refuse the Word. Ask him to open their hearts and minds to the truth. Pray for your community to look to God for rescue. Ask for wisdom for city, state, and national leaders. Pray for an outpouring of the Spirit to turn people's hearts toward Jesus.

Lord, it hurts to see others turn their backs on you. Let your Word go out and bring many to saving faith in Jesus.
Amen.

October 4

Seek and Believe

Without faith it is impossible to please God, because anyone who comes to him must believe that he exists and that he rewards those who earnestly seek him. (Hebrews 11:6)

Faith in God is far more than a religious system or set of traditions. Faith trusts that God is real. It expects him to hear you when you pray. It anticipates his help when you cry out to him in trouble. It sees his glory displayed in the creation he made. It recognizes that he speaks, by trusting in his Word. Faith is so confident in the reality of God that it transforms you, inside and out.

Is your faith moving you to earnestly seek God today? Trust him to provide for your needs. Expect him to heal the wounds of the past. Depend on him to bring peace in the conflict and stress you suffer. Praise him for the beauty and order he's created in the natural world.

Dig deep into Scripture for answers to your soul's fears and questions. When you reach out to him in belief, he delights in you. He's eager to reward your steps of faith.

Lord, give us authentic faith in you. Let us seek you for help, truth, and love at all times.

Amen.

October 5

Put Words in Action

Dear children, let us not love with words or
speech but with actions and in truth. (1 John 3:18)

*I*t's exhilarating to fall in love. We gaze into each other's eyes over a candlelight dinner. We walk hand-in-hand on the beach. We exchange heartfelt gifts, talk late into the night, and want to be together every moment. We can't say enough to express our love.

Over time, the intensity of romance will fade. Passionate words give way to love in action. You'll manage the household while your spouse has the flu. You'll share the bills, errands, and household chores. You'll invest your time and energy to parent children, serve others, and build a career. You willingly give your loyalty, help, and support through everything that comes your way.

Tender, loving words do your hearts good. But self-sacrifice, honesty, and faithfulness do even more. Are your words proven by action today? What does your partner do that makes you feel loved the most? How can you serve in new ways to deepen the love between you?

Jesus showed his love by laying his life down for us all. Love like him, willing to give yourselves up for each other today.

Lord, thank you for the joy of romance. Teach us to love even more by serving, giving, and walking in your truth.

Amen.

October 6

The Open Door

*In him and through faith in him we may approach
God with freedom and confidence.* (Ephesians 3:12)

God tells us to pray all the time. He reassures us, saying, "Ask and it will be given to you; seek and you will find; knock and the door will be opened to you. For everyone who asks receives; the one who seeks finds; and to the one who knocks, the door will be opened" (Matt. 7:7-8). Yet fears and doubts can hold us back. Is anything keeping you from praying today?

Don't let sin or shame keep you from the Lord. Through Jesus, there's no condemnation. He makes you clean. You can "draw near to God with a sincere heart and with the full assurance that faith brings" (Heb. 10:22).

Don't let doubt or worry silence you. "This is the confidence we have in approaching God: that if we ask anything according to his will, he hears us" (1 John 5:14). He'll never turn his back on you. His power and love are more than enough to care for you. Put your needs and troubles in his hands.

Don't let inexperience hinder your prayers. The Bible shows the way. The Spirit intercedes when you don't have the words. Bring your sincere heart and know he will listen.

Approach God with faith, freedom, and confidence today.

Lord, teach us to pray. We want to know you, depend on you, and love you more every day.

Amen.

October 7

The Word of Life

Your compassion, Lord, is great; preserve my
life according to your laws. (Psalm 119:156)

Everything rests on the Word of God. "They are not just idle words for you – they are your life" (Deut. 32:47). The Bible gives wisdom for every situation. Whether eating or sleeping, working or making plans, it guides our steps.

It tells how to raise our children. How to show love and honor in our marriage. How to manage money. How to cope with stress and temptation. How to relate to authority. How to participate in church. When we do what the Bible says, our lives align with God's good and perfect will.

Today, consider how much influence the Bible has in your household. Is it your number-one source of knowledge and wisdom for life? Pray and ask God for more of his Word. Memorize verses together. Pray psalms together. Read it first when you face a challenge or decision. Listen to biblical teaching. Allow the Lord to bless your lives as you make the Bible the center of your home.

Lord, your Word gives us life. Use your truth to teach, counsel, and grow our faith. Let us be obedient to you in every way.
Amen.

October 8

Trusting and Loving

This is his command: to believe in the name of his Son, Jesus Christ, and to love one another as he commanded us. (1 John 3:23)

What is God's will for your marriage? Believe in Christ and love one another. The two go hand in hand, binding you together in love and faith.

Belief without love is empty religion. It's intellectual agreement with the Bible that's cold and empty without the love of Jesus. It opens the door to legalism, self-righteousness, and pride.

Love without belief is limited and superficial. It's motivated by emotion, and lacks the depth and power only found in Jesus. Without belief, your love for self will overtake your love for your spouse. Your strength to forgive, serve, and sacrifice for each other will crumble without a foundation of truth.

As you receive the love of God through believing in Jesus, share that love with one another. Forgive as you've been fogiven. Give as you've received from the Father. Surrender yourself for the good of your spouse, as Jesus gave his life for you. Let him fill your marriage with his perfect love today.

Lord, help us to trust in you more fully. Let us know Jesus deeply through your Word. Show us how to love each other as you love us.

Amen.

October 9

Phony Faith

> Now I am writing to you that you must not associate with anyone who claims to be a brother or sister but is sexually immoral or greedy, an idolater or slanderer, a drunkard or swindler. Do not even eat with such people. (1 Corinthians 5:11)

One of the greatest dangers to faith and obedience is a spiritual hypocrite. A person more devoted to sin than to Christ can damage your devotion to God. Their influence makes you lose confidence in Scripture – wrong seems right, God's ways seem old-fashioned, and faith seems foolish.

The truth is, "Every good tree bears good fruit, but a bad tree bears bad fruit. A good tree cannot bear bad fruit, and a bad tree cannot bear good fruit" (Matt. 17:17-18). A sincere believer will show the fruit of the Spirit: self-control instead of immorality and addiction. Patience and contentment instead of greed for more. Goodness instead of lying and cheating. Kindness instead of revenge and tearing others down. A love for God that surpasses everything else. Fruitful believers will encourage you to follow the Lord wholeheartedly.

Name those who are building up your faith today. Who encourages you to trust and obey God in everything? Praise God for placing them in your life. Ask for wisdom to know who will bless or hinder your commitment to Christ.

Lord, give us strength to stay faithful to you. Surround us with true believers who encourage us to love you more and more. Amen.

October 10

Christlike Character

Make it your ambition to lead a quiet life: You should mind your own business and work with your hands, just as we told you, so that your daily life may win the respect of outsiders and so that you will not be dependent on anybody. (1 Thessalonians 4:11-12)

In our celebrity culture, everybody wants to be a star. We want the stage and microphone. We strive for influence and authority. We crave success and status in the world. "Average" isn't good enough – we want to stand out and be noticed.

In the busyness of chasing after more, you can forget to value a quiet life. By showing up and working hard, you're a witness to God's faithfulness. In using your abilities to serve others, you're doing what he created you to do. When you mind your own business and tend to your affairs, you're living in humility like Jesus. You're making God's name great instead of your own.

Make it your ambition to live a life of peace and quiet obedience. Depend on God to direct your steps. The simple tasks that seem so unimportant are where your faith and character are shown. Be content, trusting God to show himself in all you do.

Lord, teach us humility to be satisfied right here, right now. Let us seek to please you instead of impressing others. Make us faithful and obedient in all you've given us to do today.
Amen.

October 11

A Thirsty Soul

> As the deer pants for streams of water, so my soul pants for you, my God. (Psalm 42:1)

Water is necessary for every living thing. Without water, a deer is unable to care for its young, flee from predators, resist disease, and ultimately survive. Denying its thirst means suffering and death.

Do you recognize your own desperate need for God? Just as your physical bodies require water to function, the well-being of your souls depends on God himself. He is the satisfaction of every need and desire. He is the source of your hopes and dreams as you live out your purpose each day. He is the peacemaker who heals broken relationships. He is your defense when you're attacked on every side. He is your healer when you're sick and depressed. He is your victory when battling temptation. He is your salvation – your hope of eternal life.

Ask God to awaken your thirst for him. Let him be your source of strength and healing today. Drink deeply of his Word and let him refresh your soul.

Lord, thank you for the life we find in you. Fill our souls with desperate longing for more of you. Let us seek you with all our hearts.

Amen.

October 12

Are You All In?

> Love the LORD your God with all your heart and with all your soul and with all your strength. (Deuteronomy 6:5)

We're called to love the Lord with our whole heart, soul, and strength. Yet we find other people and things compete for our devotion. Our affection runs deeper for our spouse and children. Our passion to build a career takes first place. Our craving for material comfort or social status consumes our attention. We're divided in our loves – devotion to God begins to fade.

Examine your life today. Has anything become a substitute for God in your life? Where do you find your identity and deepest satisfaction? Who are you most eager to please? Are you sad to miss time in worship and prayer? Have you given up intimacy with God for a superficial form of religion?

Remember the One who first loved you. Pray and thank him for his salvation. Meditate on Scriptures describing his awesome power, mercy, and wisdom. Ask him to rekindle your love so he holds your whole heart.

Lord, we want to love you with all our heart, soul, and strength. May we love you more than your gifts. Become our greatest desire.

Amen.

October 13

Never Forget

Remember that at that time you were separate from Christ, excluded from citizenship in Israel and foreigners to the covenants of the promise, without hope and without God in the world. (Ephesians 2:12)

A nourishing meal tastes best to a starving child. A warm, cozy home is the most inviting on a cold dark night. A familiar face feels like our best friend in a crowd of strangers. A wide open sky is most beautiful to a prisoner. Our joys are deeper when they come after pain.

Remembering God's love in the past is key to loving him today. Think back to your lives before you knew him. The doubts and fear of the future. The guilt you couldn't wash away. The sins that trapped you no matter how you tried to break free. The confusion as to what was real and true. The isolation, facing eternity alone.

Let those memories renew your love for Jesus. In him, you have hope. You're forgiven and clean. You've found a place to belong in his family. You have a faithful God to care for you and guide your way. You have a beautiful future that will never end. You're loved forever.

Lord, never let us forget who we were without you. Thank you for loving us and making us yours.

Amen.

October 14

Down But Not Out

> Why, my soul, are you downcast? Why so disturbed within me? Put your hope in God, for I will yet praise him, my Savior and my God. (Psalm 42:11)

Sometimes emotions take on a life of their own. We can't talk ourselves into a cheerful attitude. Pessimism clouds our perspective. We feel lost in darkness with no way out.

When depression weighs you down, you can't see past tomorrow. It's hard to face the day and pretend you're anything but miserable. Anxiety keeps you clenched, just waiting for the next crisis. You can't rest, you lose your focus, and you disconnect from others. You feel invisible, like no one can feel your pain.

In God's love he opens a door to life and joy. He promises to meet you in your suffering. He offers rescue and protection when you're scared. He lets a glimmer of hope break through the darkness – a reassurance of the daylight to come.

Take your emotions to God today in prayer. Ask for hope, freedom, and healing. Let his truth wash away the enemy's lies you're believing today. You are seen, heard, and loved by the One who created you. He is with you every moment. A new day is coming, full of joy and praise for all he's done.

Lord, renew our hope in you. Take our fears and depression and replace them with peace and joy. Help us to believe you'll fill the darkness with your light.

Amen.

October 15

Our Sure Thing

> Jesus Christ is the same yesterday
> and today and forever. (Hebrews 13:8)

In time, the person you marry is no longer the same person you married! Hairlines recede. Weight fluctuates. Dreams and goals give way to other plans. Anxiety, optimism, and attitudes rise and fall. Stress and aging take a toll on the "perfect" person you fell in love with. Your mate can't provide the happiness or security you hoped for in the beginning.

God knows this, and never intended a human relationship to take the place of Jesus in your life. When you grow tired, his power and strength never fail. When you lose patience and struggle to forgive, his mercy never ends. When your talents and intelligence can't get the job done, he holds all wisdom and knowledge. When your needs are impossible to meet on your own, he is your loving provider.

The peace and joy in your home will suffer from sin and pain you battle in this life. Take comfort in knowing God's love never changes. Lean on Jesus for strength and hope you can never give each other. Find freedom by releasing one another from pressure to be who only Christ can be – your source of love and hope forever.

Lord, thank you for being the same for all time. Teach us to rest in your never-ending love and care.

Amen.

October 16

Sealed By the Spirit

> Do not grieve the Holy Spirit of God, with whom you were sealed for the day of redemption. (Ephesians 4:30)

After the wedding, you live like you're married. You share your name, your bed, and your love. You wear a ring – a symbol to everyone that you belong to each other for life. If one of you is unfaithful or leaves to go their own way, the other is deeply hurt and wounded.

In the same way, when you believed in Jesus Christ you were given new life in God. You share his name – Christian – and follow him where he leads. You received the Holy Spirit as his seal, marking you as his forever. If you choose to sin and go your own way, you grieve the Spirit of God.

Today, remember whose you are. Live like you belong to God. Put away your old self – the angry, bitter, sinful person you used to be. Choose to "put on the new self, created to be like God in true righteousness and holiness" (Eph. 4:24). "Be completely humble and gentle; be patient, bearing with one another in love. Be kind and compassionate to one another, forgiving each other, just as in Christ God forgave you" (Eph. 4:2, 32). Give joy to the Spirit by your love.

Lord, thank you for calling us your own forever. Let us please you by our love instead of grieving your Spirit.

Amen.

October 17

Run to Win

Run in such a way as to get the prize. Everyone who competes in the games goes into strict training. They do it to get a crown that will not last, but we do it to get a crown that will last forever. Therefore I do not run like someone running aimlessly; I do not fight like a boxer beating the air. (1 Corinthians 9:24-26)

When you belong to Christ, you live with purpose. You're preparing and looking ahead to the day you'll meet your Savior face to face. You're in training to know him more deeply, believe more fully, and serve him more faithfully.

It takes intentional effort to run this race. Study the Bible diligently for training in righteousness. Put on the armor of God to stand firm when the enemy attacks. Pray, calling on God for wisdom to know which way to go. Learn from wise teachers and follow their example of godliness. Run away from temptation – anything that could make you stumble and take your eyes off Jesus.

How are you running your race today? Are there stumbling blocks of sin in your path? Are you tired and needing encouragement? Put your hope in the Lord, who will renew your strength. Keep your eyes on the prize!

Lord, thank you for the hope of eternity with you. Keep us strong in faith, and keep our eyes on you.

Amen.

October 18

The Destruction of Deceit

Like a club or a sword or a sharp arrow is one who
gives false testimony against a neighbor. (Proverbs 25:18)

A lie in our mouth is like a weapon in our hand. One word of gossip can batter a friendship. Slander can ruin a reputation. Perjury can steal a person's freedom. Cheating can destroy a business. Covering the truth breaks trust and tears a marriage apart.

You're called by God to show integrity in every situation. His grace gives you freedom to admit your mistakes. His strength enables you to keep your promises. His provision allows you to pay what you owe. His love is an example of sincerity and goodwill to everyone. His Word and Spirit work to make you people of truth.

Open up your hidden places to God's light today. Speak words of blessing to everyone in your life. Play fair; keep your word. Be trustworthy in all you do and say. In this way, you protect and honor the ones you love. God's faithfulness and truth is demonstrated to everyone in your life.

Lord, keep us from hurting our family, friends, and community with lies and broken promises. Teach us to walk in your truth as we live by your Word.

Amen.

October 19

Silent Prayers

In the same way, the Spirit helps us in our weakness.
We do not know what we ought to pray for, but the Spirit
himself intercedes for us through wordless groans. (Romans 8:26)

Under the weight of suffering, we can barely breathe. Fear and panic freeze us in our tracks. Confusion and doubt leave us lost for words. Our hearts long to reach out for God, but we have no strength to pray.

The Lord shows mercy when you're too weak to form a prayer. He knows when you need guidance, comfort, or truth. In his great love, he anticipates your needs before you even ask him (Matt. 6:8). You can sit in his presence without a word, trusting he knows your heart and mind.

Take comfort in knowing that God is for you today. He sees your troubles. He knows your despair. He is faithful when you have nothing left to give. Let him meet you in the struggle. Have faith that he's speaking your name when you can't say a word. The God of heaven is living, loving, and working in your life even now.

Lord, we don't know what to say. Thank you for loving us even when our prayers are weak. Lift us up and give us your strength.

Amen.

October 20

Together Again

> Brothers and sisters, we do not want you to be uninformed about those who sleep in death, so that you do not grieve like the rest of mankind, who have no hope. For we believe that Jesus died and rose again, and so we believe that God will bring with Jesus those who have fallen asleep in him. (1 Thessalonians 4:13-14)

The most painful word is *goodbye*. Our hearts are broken when loved ones pass away. We know we'll see fellow believers again in the future, but the wait feels much too long. Grief can overwhelm our hope as we struggle to let them go.

God gently reminds us to keep our eyes on eternity. The joy of Jesus' return will include a beautiful reunion with those we've lost. We're set free from the despair of the world, since we know God's precious promise to bring us together again.

Who are you missing today? Let the Lord comfort your pain and restore your hope. Embrace your memories and praise God for all you shared in life. Thank him for bringing your loved one home to enjoy his presence. Ask him to sustain you and show you his purpose until you meet again.

Lord, it hurts to lose the ones we love. Give us comfort as we look forward to seeing them at your glorious return. Fill us with joy as we anticipate our future with you.

Amen.

October 21

The Offering of Worship

Through Jesus, therefore, let us continually offer to God a sacrifice of praise – the fruit of lips that openly profess his name. (Hebrews 13:15)

When we look at our life through human eyes, it's hard to see God's presence and power. We believe that safety, security, and success are in our own hands. We take credit for our blessings and feel shame for our weakness. We forget that God is in control as the author of our lives.

You're called as believers to a life of praise. Praising God is simply declaring the truth about who he is. Lay down your fears by declaring his power to save you. Sacrifice your hopes and dreams by embracing his good and perfect will. Give up your sins and secrets so you can praise the Lord in your inmost being (Ps. 103:1). Fill your mouth with words of honor and glory to God, even when fear and fatigue pull at your emotions.

What is keeping you from praising God today? Open his Word and remember the wonderful One you serve. Tell him why you love him, need him, and believe in him today.

Lord, accept our praise and worship today. Fill our hearts with wonder at your awesome power and love. Give us courage to profess your name in this world.

Amen.

October 22

Pursuing Peace

"In your anger do not sin": Do not let the sun go down while you are still angry, and do not give the devil a foothold. (Ephesians 4:26-27)

Our days don't always go as planned. People disappoint our expectations. Obstacles and interruptions hold us back. Pain and trouble knock on our door, and anger rises to answer. In the heat of the moment we find ourselves tearing down the one we love the most.

Has anger been triggered between you today? Think through the words and behaviors moved by emotion rather than God's Spirit. Are hurts from the past still raw in the present? Resentment and bitterness can easily take hold and tear apart the fabric of your marriage.

Seek peace before the day is over. Ask the Lord to examine your heart, revealing any sin coming between you. Confess your wrongs to one another; commit to begin again. Offer sincere forgiveness, and resist the enemy that seeks to divide you. Allow God's peace to fill your mind, spirit, and relationship.

Lord, teach us to show self-control when we're angry. Let love cover the sins of the past so we can begin again. Shield us from the enemy, and bring your peace to our home.

Amen.

October 23

Love and Liberty

When you sin against them in this way and wound their weak conscience, you sin against Christ. Therefore, if what I eat causes my brother or sister to fall into sin, I will never eat meat again, so that I will not cause them to fall. (1 Corinthians 8:12-13)

The Lord gave us his Word, the Holy Spirit, and our conscience to help us discern right from wrong. As believers, we're accountable to God as we follow our conscience. What's right for one may be wrong for another, since "whatever does not proceed from faith is sin" (Rom. 14:23). Our background, knowledge of the Bible, and maturity in faith will influence our moral decisions.

Show love and respect to your spouse by honoring their conscience. If you differ in your values, be willing to restrict your freedom for their sake. Don't pressure them to deny their conscience and tempt them to sin. In love, encourage them to obey the Lord from their heart.

Is your marriage suffering conflict or misunderstanding as you seek to follow your conscience? Talk about how you desire to obey the Lord, and how to support each other along the way. Choose love over liberty today.

Lord, we want to obey you in everything. Teach us to honor one another as we each follow our conscience.

Amen.

October 24

Slaves Set Free

> Remember that you were slaves in Egypt and that the Lord your God brought you out of there with a mighty hand and an outstretched arm. (Deuteronomy 5:15)

The key to obeying the Lord today is remembering his deliverance in the past. How has he freed you from addiction? Replaced your dishonesty with truth? Melted your anger with his patience? Covered your depression with joy? Won victory over the enemy? Transformed your fear and insecurity with courage? Knit your hearts together when sin drove you apart? He saved you, he is making you more like Jesus, and will bring you home to be with him forever.

We're sure to "drift away" from our faith when we forget "so great a salvation" (Heb. 2:1, 3). Take time to praise God for how far he's taken you. Celebrate how you've been healed and set free. Thank him for his peace and hope in every situation. Rejoice in the future in glory with him forever. Ask him to continue leading your life and teaching you his ways.

Remember your "slavery". And remember your mighty God who reached down to save you by his great love. In him you're free indeed!

Lord, thank you for setting us free from the destruction of sin. You've given us a hope and a future. Keep us close to you as we treasure so great a salvation.

Amen.

October 25

Better Together

As iron sharpens iron, so one person sharpens another. (Proverbs 27:17)

We're attracted to our partner's strengths – at first! But over time those strengths can rub against our weaknesses. They challenge the habits and faults we tolerate in ourselves. We're forced to take a fresh look at who we are and who we ought to be.

Your spouse's quiet patience stands in contrast to your own quick temper. Diligence and organization stand apart from a haphazard approach to life. Easygoing spontaneity draws you away from your need for control. Eager generosity loosens your grip on your finances. The character of your spouse becomes God's tool to build your faith and make you more like Jesus.

What do you admire about your partner today? Which qualities set an example for your life? Open your hearts to one another's influence. Be willing to change and grow. Pray for a teachable spirit to learn from your spouse. Allow the Lord to reveal himself in the ways they love, serve, and live like him.

Lord, thank you for our marriage. It shapes our minds, hearts, and actions. Give us humility to honor each other's strengths and abilities. Show us how to encourage one another in following you.

Amen.

October 26

Seek and Find

> "You will seek me and find me when you seek me with all your heart. I will be found by you," declares the Lord, "and will bring you back from captivity." (Jeremiah 29:13-14)

There's a difference between searching for God and just hoping he'll show up when you need him. Seeking him with all your heart means praying all the time. Digging deep into the Word for wisdom. Reaching out for prayer and encouragement from other believers. Looking for signs of his presence in every situation. Wanting to do his will more than anything else.

Are you moved to pursue the Lord today? What do you need him to do for you? What questions need answers? Which doubts need reassurance? Which sins need forgiveness? What chains need breaking? What broken places need healing? Which praises and thanks are you eager to express? Don't give up – if you look with your whole heart, he's sure to be found.

God isn't hiding out on you today. He's ready to pour all his love into your life. Are you ready to give all of your heart to him?

Lord, we don't want to live without you. Let us find you, know you more fully, and remain in you forever.

Amen.

October 27

Wonderful Words

Do not let any unwholesome talk come out of your mouths, but only what is helpful for building others up according to their needs, that it may benefit those who listen. (Ephesians 4:29)

God displayed his unlimited power through his words. He spoke, and the earth and all life were created. At a word, demons fled and the blind were healed. His wise teaching silenced his enemies and led sinners to believe. In the beginning was the Word, and the Word was with God, and the Word was God (1 John 1:1).

As a man and woman created in his image, your words are powerful too. You can bring the help and hope of encouragement. You can speak truth to bring the wandering home to Jesus. With your mouths you can confess sin and offer forgiveness, bringing peace to broken relationships. Your words can express the love of God to all who need him.

How are your words strengthening your marriage today? Commit to build each other up and do good – not harm – with what's spoken in your home. Let your conversations echo God himself as you speak his truth to one another. Praise his name together today.

Lord, thank you for the gift of words. Let our conversation be guided by your Spirit, bringing blessing into each other's lives. Teach us to speak in love and truth like Jesus.

Amen.

October 28

The Justice of Jesus

> I have seen something else under the sun: The race is not to the swift or the battle to the strong, nor does food come to the wise or wealth to the brilliant or favor to the learned; but time and chance happen to them all. (Ecclesiastes 9:11)

Life isn't fair. Some build a family legacy for generations, while other couples grieve through miscarriage. A hard worker goes bankrupt while a cheat grows wealthy. The innocent go to prison as the violent go free. A healthy athlete dies of disease. A loyal friend is betrayed. Corruption goes unchallenged. We're anxious for God to come and put things right.

Do you feel let down today? Your expected reward never comes. The help you give is unappreciated. Your patience doesn't bring what's hoped for. You wonder if it's worth it to trust God and do the right thing.

Be encouraged – Jesus knows all about injustice. Evil men accused him and nailed him to the cross. He bore the punishment for sins he didn't commit. He knows every hurt, lie, and betrayal you suffer. "In his great mercy he has given us new birth into a living hope through the resurrection of Jesus Christ from the dead, and into an inheritance that can never perish, spoil or fade (1 Pet. 1:3-4). Wait patiently for him today.

Lord, give us faith in your justice. We trust you're with us and love us all the time.

Amen.

October 29

When the Grass Is Greener

"You shall not covet your neighbor's wife. You shall not set your desire on your neighbor's house or land, his male or female servant, his ox or donkey, or anything that belongs to your neighbor." (Deuteronomy 5:21)

It's tempting to stare over the fence at our neighbor's immaculate landscaping and expensive new car. We smile politely as they describe their latest promotion, vacation plans, and child's perfect report card. Their wallets are bigger and their worries are smaller – we just don't measure up.

Nothing steals joy and gratitude like comparing ourselves to those around us. We can feel like God let us down by denying what we deserve. Instead of appreciating today's provision of food, work, and strength, we resent the blessings he's chosen to share with others. We forget the countless ways he's poured his goodness into our lives.

Spend some time making a list of his gifts. What needs has he met this week? Which relationships are mending? How have yesterday's hopes and dreams come true? Which weaknesses is he helping you overcome? How has he strengthened your marriage? Pray together and thank him for all he's done.

Lord, give us eyes to see your gifts, and fill our hearts with thankfulness for your love.

Amen.

October 30

I'm Yours

The wife does not have authority over her own body but yields it to her husband. In the same way, the husband does not have authority over his own body but yields it to his wife. (1 Corinthians 7:4)

Our culture is offended by any threat to our rights over our bodies. Protecting the unborn gives way to a woman's "right" to terminate pregnancy for any reason. Debates rage over legalizing drug use and the "right to die." Anything goes when it comes to modesty, sexuality, or expression. After all, it's our body, isn't it?

Scripture reminds us that we are not our own. We were bought with a price – Jesus' blood on the cross (1 Cor. 6:20). The bond of our marriage stands as a symbol of the church's union with Christ. With our bodies we express love and create oneness with our spouse.

Let the Lord hold authority over your bodies. As you submit to him, surrender yourselves to each other. Identify any barriers keeping you from sharing yourselves freely. Confess your sins and offer forgiveness so insecurity and hard feelings can melt away. Adjust your schedules to put each other first. Let God create love, trust, and oneness between you today.

Lord, teach us to love one another by sharing ourselves without holding back.

Amen.

October 31

Patient Partners

> Be completely humble and gentle; be patient,
> bearing with one another in love. (Ephesians 4:2)

No two people grow at the same pace or in the same ways. We're hindered by unique limitations. When we receive salvation, God begins shaping us to be more like Jesus. But it's not a smooth journey and we face setbacks along the way.

Are you losing patience with your spouse's struggles today? Perhaps your frustration with their faults is blinding you to their strengths. Maybe their issues are overshadowing your own. It's tempting to lash out in anger or secretly give up hope they'll ever change.

God's answer is to remember that we all have sinned and fall short of God's glory (Rom. 3:23). We all need salvation from our sins. Each of us has areas of immaturity. You can move from feeling superior to standing shoulder-to-shoulder as you grow.

Don't give up on each other in your discouragement. Confront each struggle side by side. Offer grace in the gift of another chance today.

Lord, it's hard to hold on to hope when we fail again and again. Give us your patience and compassion. Restore our faith in your promise to finish your good work in our lives.

Amen.

November

November 1

Share and Share Alike

All the believers were together and had everything in common. They sold property and possessions to give to anyone who had need. (Acts 2:44-45)

How far would you go for a brother or sister in Christ? When we commit to follow Jesus, our lives are no longer our own. We put "mine" out of our vocabulary. We place all we have in God's hands for him to use as he chooses. We show hospitality and respond to the needs around us. We stand ready and eager to give our time, energy, and resources to the family of God.

Pray today for a willing heart to give and share. Ask God to show you how to serve him best. Find joy in loving the body of Christ. Set an example to other believers by your empathy and generosity.

Remember how the Lord has provided in the past through his church. Praise him today for the power of community. Ask him to care for you through the loving hands of others who put their trust in Jesus.

Lord, thank you for building your church to stand as one. Teach us to give generously to one another without holding back. Use our love for each other to shine as a light in this dark world.

Amen.

November 2

What Love Looks Like

"My command is this: Love each other as I have loved you." (John 15:12)

Over time, romantic feelings fade. Life's troubles and distractions put distance between us. How do we find our way back to the love we once knew? Follow the perfect example of Jesus.

- Forgive the past. "You, Lord, are forgiving and good, abounding in love to all who call to you" (Ps. 86:5).
- Renew your commitment. "For great is his love toward us, and the faithfulness of the Lord endures forever" (Ps. 117:2).
- Value each other. "He will take great delight in you; in his love he will no longer rebuke you, but will rejoice over you with singing" (Zeph. 3:17).
- Help and serve. "For even the Son of Man did not come to be served, but to serve, and to give his life as a ransom for many" (Mark 10:45).
- Pray for each other. "Christ Jesus who died – more than that, who was raised to life – is at the right hand of God and is also interceding for us" (Rom. 8:34).

Jesus chose you to be his own, rescued you from sin and death, and will be with you forever. He will transform your hearts and minds so you can love like him. Let his love fill your marriage today.

Lord, thank you for a love that is too great to comprehend. Give us a deep, unconditional love for each other. Make us one in Jesus today.

Amen.

November 3

A Purity Promise

"I made a covenant with my eyes not to look lustfully at a young woman." (Job 31:1)

It takes more than wishful thinking to escape the trap of lust. It's an act of the will – a deliberate choice – to resist sexual temptation. Make a "covenant with your eyes" to keep your heart, mind, and body pure for each other.

Examine your choices of entertainment and media. Consider if the images you're viewing will lead you to sin. Put wise safeguards in place to avoid the trap of pornography.

Examine the intimacy in your marriage. Set aside time to connect and enjoy one another. Make your marriage bed an open, secure place of purity and love.

Examine your daily habits. Do you take a second look at provocative billboards, internet ads, or magazine covers? Does your imagination dwell on an attractive co-worker? Does your conversation honor others and reflect God's standard for sex?

Examine your sources of spiritual encouragement. Who could hold you accountable when you're tempted? Who could give wise advice as you pursue obedience to God?

Commit today to turn your eyes away from anything leading to sin. Instead, fix your eyes on Jesus: "My eyes are ever on the LORD, for only he will release my feet from the snare" (Ps. 25:15). Cherish and keep yourselves for one another, for life.

Lord, thank you for the affection and intimacy in our marriage. Set us free from temptation to lust and make us one. Amen.

November 4

The Ultimate Power

Do not put your trust in princes, in human beings, who cannot save. When their spirit departs, they return to the ground; on that very day their plans come to nothing. Blessed are those whose help is the God of Jacob, whose hope is in the Lord their God. (Psalm 146:3-5)

A president can't save your soul. A queen can't promise a life of peace and safety. A powerful army can't fight to keep a marriage together. No matter how your leaders plan and strategize, they can't control what's to come.

Leaders come and go, but the Lord reigns forever. Put your hope in him today. He holds the authority to calm any storm. He provides for your needs and protects you from danger. He holds your life and breath in his hands. He's perfect and holy, worthy of your praise.

The power of God "raised Christ from the dead and seated him at his right hand in the heavenly realms, far above all rule and authority, power and dominion, and every name that is invoked, not only in the present age but also in the one to come" (Eph. 1:20-21). Believe in him, depend on him, and obey him in everything.

Lord, you are God and we are not. Guard our hearts from trusting in people instead of you. Thank you for your love and power.

Amen.

November 5

Lift Up Your Leaders

> I urge, then, first of all, that petitions, prayers, intercession and thanksgiving be made for all people – for kings and all those in authority, that we may live peaceful and quiet lives in all godliness and holiness. (1 Timothy 2:1-2)

It's tempting to grow angry when politicians break their promises. They value their image over integrity. They reject the truth of God, pursuing power and popularity. They break our trust and lose our confidence in their leadership. The future of our country and community becomes fearful and uncertain.

The Word reassures us with the knowledge that God is in control. The government rests on his shoulders. All authority exists and is established by God (Rom. 13:1). No earthly power can rise above his throne.

We're instructed to pray for those in authority. Lift each leader up to God, pleading for wisdom and salvation. Ask for intelligent decisions to relieve suffering, provide safety, and prosper your land. Seek him for deeper faith to trust in his plans even when your leaders fail.

Stand as a peacemaker today. Choose words of blessing instead of slander. Choose to trust when you're afraid of what's to come. Fight on your knees in prayer for justice and honor. Take heart, knowing that Christ has overcome the world! (John 16:33).

Lord, give us trusting hearts to believe you're in control. Help our leaders to know and submit to you. Heal our land today. Amen.

November 6

Stand in Strength

Finally, be strong in the Lord and in his mighty power. (Ephesians 6:10)

You're in a battle every day. The "powers of this dark world" and the "spiritual forces of evil" are bent on wrecking your souls, your family, and your faith. No matter how invincible you feel, you can't win the fight on your own.

Be careful which weapons you choose today. Psychiatry can't give you a heart of love for your spouse. Financial success won't insulate you from worry. Bloggers and experts won't soothe your child's nightmares. Politicians can't guarantee the peace they promise. Legalistic rules can't deliver us from temptation. Our best efforts to find wisdom, security, and goodness are nothing without God's power.

Put on the armor of God today. When evil comes – and it will – you'll be able to stand firm. Hold on to the truth of the Bible. Believe in the gospel. Put your faith in God as your King and Deliverer. Pursue peace with everyone. Turn away from sin to holiness. Know your identity as God's chosen child.

Pray in the Spirit about everything in your life. Remain in God, and the enemy will have a formidable foe he'll never overcome.

Lord, we need your power and strength to stand against evil in these dark days. Be our Source of truth, faith, and love.
Amen.

November 7

The Best is Yet to Come

For our light and momentary troubles are achieving for us an eternal glory that far outweighs them all. So we fix our eyes not on what is seen, but on what is unseen, since what is seen is temporary, but what is unseen is eternal. (2 Corinthians 4:17-18)

When we suffer for Jesus' name, "his life is revealed in our mortal body" (2 Cor. 4:11). He shows his strength when we're weak. He reveals his wisdom when we don't know what to do. He demonstrates his mercy when we're kind to our enemies. His name is made great when our faith stands firm in trouble. His light shines when we sacrifice for the lost and suffering. His power is displayed in our fight against evil.

Today, there's a cost to follow Jesus. Be encouraged knowing God is preparing eternal comfort for every tear you cry. He'll pour out his goodness for everything you give away. He'll raise you up when others tear you down. He'll make you righteous as you stand firm against temptation. He'll bring justice for every threat against you. Keep your eyes on Jesus. The glory to come will overshadow every moment of pain in the present.

Lord, our troubles feel long and heavy. Keep our eyes on eternity and the beautiful, glorious joy to come.

Amen.

November 8

Transformation

Do not conform to the pattern of this world, but be transformed by the renewing of your mind. Then you will be able to test and approve what God's will is – his good, pleasing and perfect will. (Romans 12:2)

The world is determined to squeeze us into its mold. Success, material possessions, and good looks are the prizes to be won. Our dreams and goals become focused on achieving an image for others to admire. We work and strive but never find the satisfaction that's promised.

God sets you free from the pressure to please other people. He gives you a new identity as his son and daughter. Your hopes for the future are altered as you seek to make God's name great, rather than your own. He becomes the author of your life's story.

Whose expectations are weighing you down today? Are you exhausted from trying to please people, or joyful as you pursue God's wonderful plans for your life? Reach out to the Lord in prayer. Surrender your work, your relationships, and your money to his control. Study his Word diligently to find wisdom in knowing each step to take. Praise God for all he has in store as you discover his good, pleasing, and perfect will.

Lord, thank you for renewing our minds through your Word. Teach us your will, so we can serve you with joy and love every day of our lives.

Amen.

November 9

Our Overcomer

"In this world you will have trouble. But take heart!
I have overcome the world." (John 16:33)

As we fight on the battlefield of life, we can feel doomed to defeat. We face debts we cannot pay. Accusations with no defense. Hard hearts refusing to forgive our mistakes. Sickness and injuries that fail to heal. Barriers to success that we can't break through. Confusion and doubt that seem to have no answers. We're tempted to grab the white flag of surrender and simply give up.

Find strength in knowing that "the Lord will fight for you; you need only to be still" (Exod. 14:14).

Put down your 'sword' of self-effort and pick up God's Word. Remember his promise to be your Defender and Deliverer. The same God who conquered sin and death can overcome the trouble you're facing today. Take every battle to God in prayer and trust in him to answer. Take heart – he is with you.

Lord, we're too tired to fight this battle any more. We give our struggle to you today. Restore our hope as we trust you to overcome whatever we face.

Amen.

November 10

God's Very Good Creation

God saw all that he had made, and it was very good. (Genesis 1:31)

If God is the source, it's "very good." He created the beauty of the natural world. He inspired his holy Word. He designed the oneness of marriage and the blessing of children. He built his church that will endure forever. He gives each believer a Spirit-powered gift to bless the family of God. His works are wonderful, we know it full well (Ps. 139:14).

Today, remember the Lord made your loved one. Pray and thank him for the ways your spouse is "very good." The aspects of their personality that make you smile. Their attractive appearance that still makes your heart beat faster. Their unique talents and abilities you're proud of. Their willingness to give and serve by putting others first. Their patience with your imperfections. The ways they're becoming more like Jesus, overcoming sins of the past. Their love and faithfulness to keep their vows for life.

Thank God together for the gift of your marriage. Pray for grace to see the good in one another. Love each other as gifts from him.

Lord, thank you for all you've created. May we always praise you for our marriage.

Amen.

November 11

Why Me?

"Pardon me, my lord," Gideon replied, "but if the Lord is with us, why has all this happened to us? Where are all his wonders that our ancestors told us about when they said, 'Did not the Lord bring us up out of Egypt?'" (Judges 6:13)

*P*ain and struggle bring the question, "Why?" Human reason says if God is good, we'll never suffer. We'll always win over our enemies. We'll be happy and successful. All our dreams will come true. If we experience loss or trouble, we feel forgotten. We lose faith in God's power and promises. We doubt his love.

Believe God's Word today – he holds your life in his hands. He's proven his love by giving Jesus' life to pay for yours. He uses hard times for your good, to build your trust and prove he's faithful. He knows what you need before you ask him. He offers "treasures in heaven" surpassing anything this world might offer.

Pray for eyes to see God's goodness in your circumstances. Ask for deeper gratitude for all he's done. Believe his wisdom is higher than your own. Trust that he's with you all the time. Continue to bring him your questions and problems. He'll fill you with peace as you depend on him.

Lord, keep our faith strong no matter what happens. You're always good, always here, and always enough.

Amen.

November 12

Truth That Lasts

The grass withers and the flowers fall,
but the word of our God endures forever." (Isaiah 40:8)

Fashions change every season. Powerful leaders rise and fall. Investments build and collapse. Friends grow close then move away. Fresh, romantic bouquets wilt and die. We grow in strength and weaken with age. Nothing we see or try to keep will last forever. There's nothing in this world we can depend on with certainty.

Hope is found in the God who never changes. His Word is always true. His character is always holy. His love never fails. When he makes a promise, he keeps it. His plans will come to pass. He's your anchor and your rock.

Where is your security today? What are you holding on to, to feel happy and safe? What are you the most scared to lose? Pick up your Bible, your priceless gift from God. As you read its verses, remember, "They are not just idle words for you – they are your life" (Deut. 32:47).

It will never fail when you need wisdom. It will restore the joy of your salvation. It will keep your eyes on the future, when our Lord Jesus returns. When everything else passes away, God's Word will endure.

Lord, thank you for your enduring, eternal Word. Let it be our hope, our source of truth, and our life.

Amen.

November 13

The Anatomy of the Church

If the whole body were an eye, where would the sense of hearing be? If the whole body were an ear, where would the sense of smell be? But in fact God has placed the parts in the body, every one of them, just as he wanted them to be. (1 Corinthians 12:17-18)

Perhaps you feel like nothing special. Your spiritual gifts seem small. You're not sure if you can make a difference. The abilities of other believers seem more useful and important. Be encouraged today – God has placed you just where he wants you to be, with exactly the gifts that are needed.

You're a unique, special part of God's design for his church. He has a purpose for placing you in his family today. "For we are God's handiwork, created in Christ Jesus to do good works, which God prepared in advance for us to do" (Eph. 2:10).

Resist the temptation to compare yourselves to other people. Instead, pray for strength to serve God faithfully right where you are. Ask for wisdom to know his assignment for you both, and willing hearts to carry it out. Thank him for uniting you into one body by his Spirit.

Lord, thank you for building your church and making us one. Show us how to love and serve each other in your name.
Amen.

November 14

Joy in the Journey

Be joyful in hope, patient in affliction, faithful in prayer. (Romans 12:12)

Not every mountain is climbed in a day. Suffering wears us down with no end in sight. Tension and conflict can escalate until peace seems impossible. Our needs and longings go unfulfilled – we wonder if we should just give up.

It's useless to trust in your own ability to solve your problems. You can't dull the pain of life with money, food, or distractions. In Christ you find hope through his power to overcome. The One who conquered sin, death, and hell is fully able to overpower whatever you face today.

The Lord will soothe your spirits with his offering of joyful hope and patience. He invites you to meet him in prayer. Your grieving, frustration, and disappointment can be replaced by strength to carry on.

Find joy as you place your hope in God, who promises to work everything for your good in the end. Be patient as you walk this road of trouble, knowing God is in control and sees the future. Take every emotion, question, and problem to God in prayer. Place your heartache and burdens at his feet. Invite him to display his power in your situation.

Lord, this struggle feels too hard. It's tempting to give up. Restore our faith to believe you're with us. Renew our hope and strength as we trust in you.

Amen.

November 15

Lifted Up

"So do not fear, for I am with you; do not be dismayed,
for I am your God. I will strengthen you and help you;
I will uphold you with my righteous right hand." (Isaiah 41:10)

Just when you thought your situation couldn't get worse, it did. More bad news. The support you were counting on never came. The voices of worry and doubt are getting louder in your ears. You're so tired from trying to cope, you have little left for each other.

Fear doesn't have to take over today. It's not the time to quit. It is the moment to give your struggle to God. Pray, trusting he's with you in the middle of the mess. Tell him all about it. Ask for help – stop pretending you can handle it on your own. No matter the outcome, he'll give you strength to make it through.

God is still on his throne today. He'll keep you standing if you hold on to him. He'll give you strength to do the right thing. He'll keep you together in the fight. He'll make sure the pain isn't wasted as you grow in faith. He'll show you his love and power. Have hope and courage to move forward with him.

Lord, we're feeling beaten down by this trouble. Lift us up today as we trust in you to help. Thank you for staying with us through it all.

Amen.

November 16

Matched by Love

> The LORD God said, "It is not good for the man to be alone.
> I will make a helper suitable for him." (Genesis 2:18)

"He's my better half." "She's my one and only." "He completes me." "We're a perfect match." We all seek a partner who's a good fit for our values, personality, and dreams for the future. In God's wisdom, he joins us together and makes us more than we could be alone.

Husband, remember anew why your wife is a blessing to your life. How does she serve you each day? How has she supported your work, parenting, or ministry? What would you miss the most if you were alone? How do her strengths complement your weaknesses?

Wife, are you helping your husband today? How is God challenging you to serve and support him? Take a fresh look at the responsibilities on his shoulders. Ask the Lord how you can encourage him along the way.

It's comforting to know that marriage was God's idea from the beginning – he knows the countless benefits of sharing a life together. Praise him today for creating your relationship. Ask him to deepen your appreciation for all the ways you're blessed by each other.

Lord, when you created our relationship it was for our good. Thank you for giving me a partner to love and share my days. Make us thankful for the gift of our marriage.

Amen.

November 17

The One We Can Count On

> Do not be far from me, for trouble is near
> and there is no one to help. (Psalm 22:11)

The pain of our problems grows deeper when we feel alone. A friend can't rescue us from unemployment or bankruptcy. Our parents can't patch a friendship back together. Our church family can't reverse a hopeless medical diagnosis. A husband or wife can't undo the mistakes of the past. We find ourselves discouraged and lose hope for tomorrow.

When troubles loom too large for anyone to solve, our God is with you. Your struggles make you feel weak and isolated, yet "the LORD your God is with you, the Mighty Warrior who saves" (Zeph. 3:17). You can find contentment and peace in the middle of the storm because "God has said, 'Never will I leave you; never will I forsake you'" (Heb. 13:5). Place your lives in the hands of God – not other people – because he is your help and deliverer (Ps. 40:17).

When the Lord is your only hope, he's the only hope you need. Take every wound and worry to him in prayer. Have faith that he'll stay by your side every moment. Let his peace and comfort fill your heart today.

Lord, we're suffering through trouble with no one to help. Help us, encourage us, and give us faith to believe you're always here.

Amen.

November 18

Eat, Drink, Remember

In the same way, after supper he took the cup, saying, "This cup is the new covenant in my blood; do this, whenever you drink it, in remembrance of me." For whenever you eat this bread and drink this cup, you proclaim the Lord's death until he comes. (1 Corinthians 11:25-26)

Our hope for the future is found in the past. The Lord claimed us as his own before he created the world. Jesus came to die over 2000 years ago, to pay the penalty for our sins. The miracles of yesterday give us confidence in God's power today. For our faith to endure, we must remember all he's done.

Remember God's promise to send a Savior. Remember Jesus, the fulfillment of that covenant. "But he was pierced for our transgressions, he was crushed for our iniquities; the punishment that brought us peace was on him, and by his wounds we are healed. We all, like sheep, have gone astray, each of us has turned to our own way; and the Lord has laid on him the iniquity of us all" (Isa. 53:6). Remember his death that made you alive.

Remember who you were before knowing Jesus – the fear, guilt, and confusion that filled your life. Remember to share in communion, keeping the knowledge of Christ alive in your mind and heart.

Lord, you suffered and died so we could have life forever with you. May we never forget.

Amen.

November 19

Gaining and Losing

"Who has ever given to God, that God should repay them?"
For from him and through him and for him are all things.
To him be the glory forever! Amen. (Romans 11:35-36)

God is the source of everything we have. Our health. Our kids. Our money. Our house. Our circle of friends. Our job. We're thankful and celebrate his goodness in our lives.

But when we're forced to give up a blessing, it hurts. It's hard when our car is totaled. Or when company layoffs leave us in the cold. When a pregnancy ends too soon. When our loved ones move or pass away. When we're injured or suffer chronic pain. It feels unfair and undeserved. We secretly wonder if God knows what he's doing.

All you've received has come from him, through him, and for him. His wisdom for both giving and taking is greater than you can understand. Whatever you gain and lose is for his glory in the end. Trust that he loves you.

He has no plans to harm you. He's holding your eternal reward in his hands. Offer him your loved ones, your possessions, and yourselves today.

Lord, may this be our prayer: "Whatever were gains to me I now consider loss for the sake of Christ. What is more, I consider everything a loss because of the surpassing worth of knowing

Christ Jesus my Lord, for whose sake I have lost all things" (Phil. 3:7-8).

Amen.

November 20

Wise Words

Nor should there be obscenity, foolish talk or coarse joking, which are out of place, but rather thanksgiving. (Ephesians 5:4)

When we find salvation through Jesus, the Lord purifies our hearts and our lives. A sign of his work is in the purity of our words. Once we place our faith and trust in the God of heaven, we no longer need to swear by anything in the world.

We recognize his beautiful gift of sexual intimacy, silencing crude humor and remarks. We understand how each person is made in the image of God, so insults and slander turn to honor and respect for everyone. Foolish talking falls away as we grow in knowledge of his truth.

Let your words be a useful measurement of your faith-walk with God. If angry profanity is creeping in, let him restore your patience and peace. If complaining and worry are filling your conversation, ask him for gratitude and faith. If coarse joking and innuendo are fun or entertaining, ask God to help you cherish the purity of your marriage bed.

Listen closely to what you're saying, "for the mouth speaks what the heart is full of" (Matt. 12:34). Speak words of love and life as you walk with Jesus today.

Lord, let our words be a reflection of our lives in you. Fill our conversations with honor, thanks, wisdom, and love.
Amen.

November 21

The Foolishness of Fighting

Don't have anything to do with foolish and stupid arguments, because you know they produce quarrels. And the Lord's servant must not be quarrelsome but must be kind to everyone, able to teach, not resentful. (2 Timothy 2:23-24)

Before Jesus returned to heaven, he prayed. He asked God to make us one, just like he and his Father are one. His heart's desire as he left this earth was for his people to live in unity.

He knew we'd find plenty to argue about. Churches bicker over how to celebrate holidays. How to spend money. Who to put in charge. Which music to sing on Sunday morning. What the pastor should drive, and how his wife should dress. How to decorate the lobby. Our brothers and sisters get upset about the little things, ignoring what matters most.

Today, choose kindness. Give people room for their feelings and opinions. Refuse to be dragged into foolish debates. Have patience, forgiving people who want their own way. Know the Word so you can teach others what's true and right. Serve as peacemakers, showing God's love to everyone.

Lord, let our marriage and our church be unified in you. Keep us from foolish fights that tear us apart. Teach us your kindness and love.

Amen.

November 22

Filled by Love

> Let them give thanks to the LORD for his unfailing love and his wonderful deeds for mankind, for he satisfies the thirsty and fills the hungry with good things. (Psalm 107:8-9)

When you look at your life, does it feel like something is missing? Do you think you could be content if you had a bigger house, a better job, or a nicer mother-in-law? Do you believe a child, a degree, or a healthy retirement fund would bring satisfaction to your soul? Do you suspect God is holding out on giving you things that could make you happy?

God himself is the answer to your dissatisfaction. Name the ways he's shown his love to you. Consider how he's brought you to where you are today. Remember his forgiveness and freedom from the sin that enslaved you. He's given you his Word, his Spirit, and hope for the future. Your deepest desires can be fully satisfied in him.

Trust the Lord to continue working in your life. Believe he'll give you the desires of your heart as you delight in him (Ps. 37:4). Remember that he loves you now, is with you today, and is accomplishing his will for you in this moment. You don't have to wait for tomorrow to discover his joy and peace.

Lord, teach our hearts to be grateful for all you've done. May we find perfect satisfaction in you.

Amen.

November 23

Inner Beauty

Your beauty should not come from outward adornment, such as elaborate hairstyles and the wearing of gold jewelry or fine clothes. Rather, it should be that of your inner self, the unfading beauty of a gentle and quiet spirit, which is of great worth in God's sight. (1 Peter 3:3-4)

It's a gift from God that true beauty isn't found at the gym, the makeup counter, or the plastic surgeon's office. Age and weight, height and style have no bearing on your worth in his sight.

God's priority is the inner self – only he can look past the surface to see your faith, motives, and love. Put on kindness and generosity with your outfit. Build your knowledge and truth through the Word as much as you build strength at the gym. Weave words of peace into your conversation even as you style your hair. Adorn yourselves with gentleness along with your accessories. Your words, attitudes, and generosity will become your "look" and display Jesus to everyone.

Take time to meet with God through prayer and his Word every day. He'll renew your heart and mind, creating true beauty that lasts forever.

Lord, forgive us for putting our focus on our outer appearance instead of our inner selves. Teach us your gentleness as you continue to make us more like Jesus.

Amen.

November 24

Christ Alone

One of you says, "I follow Paul"; another, "I follow Apollos"; another, "I follow Cephas"; still another, "I follow Christ." Is Christ divided? Was Paul crucified for you? Were you baptized in the name of Paul? (1 Corinthians 1:12-13)

The Lord raises up godly pastors to lead his Church. Wise teachers instruct us in the Word. Dynamic speakers fuel our passion to serve Christ. Authors fine-tune our understanding of the heart, mind, and calling of a Christian. Yet we must not let God's servants take the place of our Savior.

Receive others' teaching but read the Scriptures for yourself. Grow in knowledge of God's character, but know him through prayer and experience too. Respect your spiritual leaders, but give God full authority over your life. Admire and support God's servants, but honor and worship the Lord above all.

Our salvation is found in Christ, not people. "His divine power has given us everything we need for a godly life through our knowledge of him who called us by his own glory and goodness" (2 Pet. 1:3).

Who are you following today? Pray and ask for undivided devotion to Jesus. Listen to his voice and go where he leads you.

Lord, you bless us through people's teaching. But we want to follow you most of all. Be our true source of wisdom and knowledge today.

Amen.

November 25

The Battle Within

What causes fights and quarrels among you? Don't they come from your desires that battle within you? You desire but do not have, so you kill. You covet but you cannot get what you want, so you quarrel and fight. You do not have because you do not ask God. (James 4:1-2)

Sometimes we want what we want! We give way to anger, manipulation, and selfishness, demanding our way no matter what. When our "wants" collide and create friction in our marriage, something has to give.

What is your desire today? How is your patience wearing thin as you wait for it? Do you feel like your spouse is standing between you and what you want? Have you become more attached to your desire than to the one you love?

The Word challenges you to take your needs and desires to God in prayer. When you depend on him as your source, you put yourselves in his hands. Trust that he knows what's best for you. Submit to his timing. Don't depend on others to make you happy. Be set free from the strain and stress of fighting for what you want. Find peace and contentment in him.

Lord, give us patience to wait for what we want. Teach us to trust you to meet our needs and satisfy our hearts.
Amen.

November 26

Your Best Gift – Yourself

Therefore, I urge you, brothers and sisters, in view of God's mercy, to offer your bodies as a living sacrifice, holy and pleasing to God – this is your true and proper worship. (Romans 12:1)

We're in awe of God's goodness and love. He created a beautiful world. He blessed us with our marriage and home. He listens to our prayers and takes care of us. He gave up his only Son so we could be saved. He's preparing a place where we can live in joy with him forever. We could never count all the ways he's shown mercy. How can we tell him how much we love him too?

Today, worship him by giving him yourselves. Offer your bodies as living sacrifices. Serve and give with willing hands. Stand firm together against temptation. Move your feet to walk where he leads. Use your mouths to tell of his great salvation. Share pure intimacy with each other. Use your strength to carry others' burdens. Kneel side by side in prayer. Give God your whole selves as you obey him in everything.

Jesus set the example of sacrifice. He "loved us and gave himself up for us as a fragrant offering and sacrifice to God" (Eph. 5:2). Love the Lord as you offer yourselves to him.

Lord, teach us to give up ourselves to you. Let us love like Jesus without holding back.

Amen.

November 27

Growing Together

> "If your brother or sister sins, go and point out their fault, just between the two of you. If they listen to you, you have won them over." (Matthew 18:15)

Your loved one isn't perfect. They let you down. They can be rude and self-centered. They lose their patience. They say things they regret. They fail to show integrity. You see the good, bad, and ugly in your spouse as you live together each day.

How do you respond to your partner's sins and mistakes? You can complain to your friends, looking for sympathy. You may share your frustration with family, hoping they'll justify your anger. You can criticize them in front of the kids, stirring up conflict at home. You can make sarcastic remarks to your neighbor, making your partner look foolish. You can grow resentful instead of showing concern for their struggle.

Today, consider how you both might be falling into sin. Take a private moment to share what you see. Speak the truth in love about how you're losing your way. Tell how their choices affect you and your home. Offer forgiveness and understanding since you both need God's grace. Pray together – confess your sin and receive a clean heart.

True love desires Christ's freedom and power for one another. Live in that love today.

Lord, show us how to encourage each other today. Let us grow in faith and obedience as we share our lives.

Amen.

November 28

Dearly Devoted

Husbands, in the same way be considerate as you live with
your wives, and treat them with respect as the weaker
partner and as heirs with you of the gracious gift of life,
so that nothing will hinder your prayers. (1 Peter 3:7)

Someday we'll be able to worship God face-to-face. Until then, our love for him is expressed in how we love others. Husbands are called to cherish their wives – their devotion is an amazing mirror-image of how Jesus loves his church.

Your love is to be considerate in the day-to-day routines of life. Notice if her gas tank or phone battery are low. Help out with errands if she's running ragged. Show common courtesy in how you pick up your laundry and dishes. Stick up for her if the kids are disrespectful. This kind of thoughtfulness is love in action.

Love is respectful. There's no place for sarcasm or criticism. It keeps her secrets and speaks highly of her in public. It treats her body as God's creation. It stands with her when she suffers abuse or insults from others. Your honoring words and actions are marks of love like Jesus'.

Love wins God's favor. Rejection, rudeness, and abuse create barriers in your relationship with God. Work out your faith by serving and loving your wife in his name.

Lord, fill our home with respect and consideration for each other. Teach me to be gentle, kind, and loving all the time.
Amen.

November 29

The Weapon of the Word

> The weapons we fight with are not the weapons of the world. On the contrary, they have divine power to demolish strongholds. We demolish arguments and every pretension that sets itself up against the knowledge of God, and we take captive every thought to make it obedient to Christ. (2 Corinthians 10:4-5)

The world and the enemy attempt to crush our faith. Political powers limit people's religious freedom. Scientists attempt to disprove the truth of the Word. Intellectuals deny the historical facts of the Bible. Advertising sells style over substance. Organizations push their own agendas to deny what's holy and right. We're told to fit in with the culture and live to please ourselves.

Set down the world's weapons today – money, influence, and human reasoning – and pick up the Word of God. Its power will crush the lies of the enemy. Its wisdom will tell you what's true. Its goodness will instruct you to know right from wrong. It will move you to mercy and love in a world full of hate.

"Unplug" today from the pride and foolishness around you. Turn off the news, the speeches, and social media's ranting and raving. Be still with the Lord. Pray together. Read God's words. Worship. Let him renew your mind so you can stand firm in Christ.

Lord, Jesus' love and truth are nonsense to the world. Renew our minds so we can obey you in every way.

Amen.

November 30

Rescue and Rest

> I sought the Lord, and he answered me;
> he delivered me from all my fears. (Psalm 34:4)

The world is a frightening place. The news is filled with threats to national security, natural disasters, epidemics, and crime. Jobs can be precarious, health can fail, and accidents harm the ones we love. Anxiety and worry can dominate our thoughts and emotions. Exhausted, we wonder if peace can be found.

Security is found in God alone. Cry out to him in prayer with every burden on your heart. Name your troubles; confess your fear. Call on him as Deliverer, Savior, Helper, and Healer. Ask for greater faith in his power and promises. Let him meet you in the darkness of fear and bring you into the light of his peace.

What are your deepest fears today? What shakes your confidence in the future? Who or what are you trusting in for security, outside of God himself? Let him be the rock you build your life upon. When the winds blow and beat against your house, it cannot fall (Matt. 7:25).

Lord, you know what's bringing fear and doubt into our lives today. Deliver us from every threat. Teach us to trust you completely as our loving Father. Give us your peace.

Amen.

December

December 1

At Jesus' Feet

> As Jesus and his disciples were on their way, he came to a village where a woman named Martha opened her home to him. She had a sister called Mary, who sat at the Lord's feet listening to what he said. But Martha was distracted by all the preparations that had to be made. (Luke 10:38-40)

We look around and there's so much to do. The hungry need food. The homeless need shelter. Children need care and teaching. Churches need serving. The lost need preaching. Our time, money, and energy are in demand as the cries for help never end.

But before you rise up to serve and give, you need to sit with your Savior. Listen to what he says. Study his Word to tell you what's true. Take time to pray – confessing your sins, asking for help, seeking his will. Worship and express how much you love him. As he heals your wounds, makes you clean, and gives you knowledge and wisdom, you're prepared to serve those who need his love.

Take time to be still with God today. Pray. Read. Listen. The busyness will wait.

Lord, teach us to be quiet and spend time with you. Prepare us in the stillness to go out and serve you well.

Amen.

December 2

Gifted to Serve

> Each of you should use whatever gift you have received to serve others, as faithful stewards of God's grace in its various forms. (1 Peter 4:10)

When we're saved through believing in Jesus, we're given the Holy Spirit. The Spirit gives each believer a unique, gifted ability to serve the family of God. As each one uses their gift, the body is blessed and made complete.

Today, you have a gift to share. God has created a way for you to help, encourage, teach, or lead your brothers and sisters in Christ. Your gift, used in love, will give them strength to obey more fully. It will give them hope in hard times. It will demonstrate God's heart of kindness. It will lift up the scriptures as God's own Word. It will relieve suffering, resist the enemy, and build up the faith of the church.

Pray together to recognize what the Spirit has given each of you. Study the Word to "unwrap" your gift and understand what it means. Commit to serve faithfully as God directs you. Encourage one another as you discover his purpose and plans.

Lord, thank you for adopting us into your family and giving us a way to serve. Open our eyes to our spiritual gifts. Make us strong and faithful to use them in love for your glory.
Amen.

December 3

Turning from Trouble

My brothers and sisters, if one of you should wander from the truth and someone should bring that person back, remember this: Whoever turns a sinner from the error of their way will save them from death and cover over a multitude of sins. (James 5:19-20)

A guard rail on a mountain road keeps drivers from plunging over a cliff. Powerful medications prevent disease from taking human life. Crossing guards protect children as they travel home from school. We depend on doctors, public servants, and common sense to keep us safe each day.

We're threatened by spiritual dangers as well. We battle temptation to sin. False teachers challenge our faith in God's truth. Relationships compete for our heart's devotion. Suffering brings doubt in God's goodness. It's impossible to keep our faith strong and sure without help.

Who has brought you back when you've wandered from God in the past? What kind of help do you need today to remember the truth and turn back from sin? Reach out for help before you lose your way.

Who in your life is struggling with temptation or doubt? Who is the prodigal needing a hand to pull them out of the pit? Ask God for courage to meet them in their confusion today.

Lord, our faith is in danger on every side. Surround us with godly believers to help us remain in you. Let us encourage those who are losing their way.

Amen.

December 4

Hope, Joy, and Peace

> May the God of hope fill you with all joy and peace as you trust in him, so that you may overflow with hope by the power of the Holy Spirit. (Romans 15:13)

We can't trust political leaders to shield our land from poverty, violence, or corruption. Our boss can't guarantee personal success or job satisfaction. Our families can't promise perfect harmony or support from day to day. Our kids can't ensure healthy childhoods full of constant fun and smiles. The only true source of hope, joy, and peace is our Father in heaven.

We serve a God of hope who offers joy and peace in the middle of our struggles. He fills us with hope that's overflowing – not mere optimism or wishful thinking. He's worthy of our faith in his promised salvation and the glorious future to come.

Are you losing hope for tomorrow? Are the news headlines and your personal issues dragging you down? Name your fears and give them to God in prayer. Cry out to him in your pain and receive his comfort. Trust in his awesome power and unfailing love that never changes. Let him fill you with true joy and peace as you believe in him.

Lord, let us trust you with today's troubles and the uncertainties of tomorrow. Fill us with joy, peace, and overflowing hope as we put our faith in you.

Amen.

December 5

Help and Healing

> A Samaritan, as he traveled, came where the man was; and when he saw him, he took pity on him. He went to him and bandaged his wounds, pouring on oil and wine. Then he put the man on his own donkey, brought him to an inn and took care of him. (Luke 10:33-34)

In the troubles of life, it can feel like you're bleeding on the side of the road. You're knocked down, helpless, with no hope in sight. People looking on might say you got what you deserved. That you should stand on your own two feet. That their own concerns are more important. You're desperate and waiting for someone to care.

If your loved one is hurting, show compassion today. Have empathy for the overwhelming stress of their job. Speak words of affirmation when they're insulted and criticized. Offer help and comfort during sickness and pain. Stand up as their defender when they're under attack. Hold them close when they're grieving or depressed. Soothe their fears through encouragement and constant prayer.

You never want the guilt of walking past your spouse as they're hurting. Stop and help, no matter the cost. Be God's hands of help and healing until all is well again.

Lord, give us compassion in our marriage. Show us how to comfort and help when it's needed. Bring your perfect healing to our pain.

Amen.

December 6

Hold on Tight

To the married I give this command (not I, but the Lord): A wife must not separate from her husband. But if she does, she must remain unmarried or else be reconciled to her husband. And a husband must not divorce his wife. (1 Corinthians 7:10-11)

You can feel like life is tearing you apart. Your dreams collide, pushing you in opposite directions. Busy schedules leave no time to connect. Kids, friends, and family compete for your attention. Conflict over money and sex builds tension between you. You've lost what you had in common. It's tempting to think you'd be better off apart than together.

Today, believe God wants you to stay. He remembers your vow to love each other for life. Do the hard, humbling work of naming your mistakes. Make peace through confession and forgiveness. Take a fresh look at your calendar and priorities – choose to put each other first. Let go of trying to have your own way. Be kind and respectful. Be willing to try.

Pray for God to bring you closer than ever before. Ask for a fresh commitment to your marriage. Search the Word and find wise counselors to help you find unity. Trust in God's love as the source of your own. In him, you can find your way back to each other.

Lord, give us courage to stay together no matter what. Teach us how to love like you.

Amen.

December 7

Light in the Darkness

Even though I walk through the darkest valley, I will fear no evil, for you are with me; your rod and your staff, they comfort me. (Psalm 23:4)

Sometimes the pain is so deep that it blinds us to everything else. Our situation is so dark we can't see the way out. We feel threatened and attacked by forces beyond our control. The enemy assaults our trust in God and hope for the future.

Hope is found in God's guiding hand. He never leaves you to walk the road alone. You don't have to know what to do – his wisdom is there for the asking. You don't have to win every battle – he fights for you with his mighty hand. You don't have to fear that you'll stumble and fall in the dark – his Word is a lamp for your feet, and a light on your path" (Ps. 119:105).

Find comfort and courage in God's presence with you today. Reach out to him in prayer. Place your hand in his as he leads the way through the valley. Trust him as your strong Deliverer. He will keep you until the very end.

Lord, in these difficult days all we can see is darkness. Our fears are overwhelming. Guide us every step of the way. Give us your peace and comfort as we put our trust in you.

Amen.

December 8

An Unbreakable Bond

I appeal to you, brothers and sisters, in the name of our Lord Jesus Christ, that all of you agree with one another in what you say and that there be no divisions among you, but that you be perfectly united in mind and thought. (1 Corinthians 1:10)

The oneness of marriage gives glory to God. Shared purpose, selfless love, and spiritual unity create a beautiful picture of the One we worship. As children of God – brothers and sisters of Jesus – you can experience agreement and peace in your relationship.

You find unity when you hold to one truth, the Bible. When you serve God together without holding back. When you choose to love each other before yourselves. When you're seeking God's perfect will instead of having your own way. When you're humble, thankful, and prayerful. When you love him with all your heart, soul, and strength.

Choose to agree today. Lay down your rights and let go of what you're fighting for. Pray and ask God to lead your life together. Repent of sin that's dividing you from each other and the Lord. Study the Word to share knowledge of the truth. Let the Holy Spirit join you together in "mind and thought" today.

Lord, make us one as you are one. Tear down any walls that divide, and unite us in every way.

Amen.

December 9

A Place to Belong

Though my father and mother forsake me,
the LORD will receive me. (Psalm 27:10)

God knows the blessing that parents should be. Yet children suffer abandonment. They know the fear and pain of abuse. They experience hunger and sickness as physical needs are ignored. They're pushed to achieve, and punished if they don't live up to expectations. They're overlooked in favor of parents' careers, relationships, and selfish priorities.

If you're struggling with your parents' rejection today, find comfort in God's love. Our heavenly Father is always near. He gave his own Son so you could be his children. He's paying attention to every part of your life. He's a faithful provider for your needs. He's always available when you want to talk to him in prayer. He tells the truth and keeps his promises. He loves you without holding back.

Run to the Father's embrace when you're pushed away by your parents. Trust in his truth when you're manipulated or lied to. Rest in his acceptance when you're criticized or shamed. Depend on him to care and provide in every situation. Allow the perfect love of God to heal the wounds of the past.

Lord, parents can break our hearts. Give us strength and grace to forgive. Let us know your perfect love that never lets us down. You're our true Father today.

Amen.

December 10

Thirsty for Life

> Jesus answered, "Everyone who drinks this water will be thirsty again, but whoever drinks the water I give them will never thirst. Indeed, the water I give them will become in them a spring of water welling up to eternal life." (John 4:13-14)

Nothing in this world can promise permanent satisfaction. The most elaborate feast can't ward off hunger forever. Our dream home eventually needs updating and repair. Our energetic health in spring is forgotten in winter's flu. The passionate romance of our honeymoon gives way to apathy and stress. The only source of lasting life and joy is Jesus Christ himself.

It's tempting to depend on your spouse for love and security that only God can give. When you're forgetful and careless, he is faithful and keeps every promise. When your moods and motivations are unpredictable, he is the same yesterday, today, and forever. While you may be forgiving and understanding of each other's weakness, only Jesus can atone for your sins and offer saving grace.

Set your marriage free from the pressure to give what is only found in Jesus. Love one another out of the love you receive from the Lord today.

Lord, thank you for providing all we need for life and salvation. Teach us to place our hope in you instead of the blessings you've given. Fill us with love for you and each other.
Amen.

December 11

Sick with Shame

Because of your wrath there is no health in my body; there is no soundness in my bones because of my sin. My guilt has overwhelmed me like a burden too heavy to bear. (Psalm 38:3-4)

We know what we did when no one was watching. We remember our ugly words behind closed doors. We regret the broken promise that let our loved one down. We're ashamed of our lies and the secrets we keep. The guilt is a crushing weight, stealing our peace and joy.

God loves you too much to let sin come between you. He gives his Spirit to convict you of wrong. He gave you Jesus to pay for your sins. He uses the consequences of your actions to teach you right from wrong. He's ready to wash you clean and set you free.

Be honest with yourself, the Lord, and each other today. Confess your sin. Be forgiven. Receive a clean conscience. Trust in God's love and mercy that never ends.

"He does not treat us as our sins deserve or repay us according to our iniquities. For as high as the heavens are above the earth, so great is his love for those who fear him; as far as the east is from the west, so far has he removed our transgressions from us" (Ps. 103:10-12).

Lord, our guilt is heavy since we sinned against you. Thank you for your love and forgiveness.

Amen.

December 12

Love and Respect

However, each one of you also must love his wife as he loves himself, and the wife must respect her husband. (Ephesians 5:33)

*I*t's hard for a wife to respect a man who's self-serving, arrogant, or unkind. It's hard for a husband to cherish a woman who puts him down or disrespects his role in the home. An honored man will love with all his strength, and a well-loved woman will value and praise her husband.

Are respect and love fading from your marriage today? Wife, ask God to open your eyes to the strengths and good character of your husband. Husband, ask God to show you ways to care and show devotion to your wife. Let the Lord fill you with a new measure of gratitude for each other.

Husbands are called to love their wives more than they deserve. Wives are called to respect their husbands more than they deserve. Offer the gifts of love and respect for Jesus' sake. Just as he gave of himself while you were still sinners, you can give to your partner as an act of obedience to God. We love because he first loved us.

Lord, without you, our love and respect for each other is incomplete. Make us like Jesus – able to honor, serve, and care for each other without holding back.

Amen.

December 13

God's Perfect Plan

> That night the word of God came to Nathan, saying: "Go and tell my servant David, 'This is what the LORD says: You are not the one to build me a house to dwell in." (1 Chronicles 17:3-4)

It's hard to hear God say "no" when we want to do great things in his name. He knows our hopes and good intentions, but he's the author of our faith. "For we are God's handiwork, created in Christ Jesus to do good works, which God prepared in advance for us to do" (Eph. 2:10). Ask him, and he'll give you the assignment that will please him the most.

Pray to know God's good and perfect will for your lives. Resist the temptation to compare your gifts and calling to that other believers. Focus on the Word and how it directs your unique situation. Find joy in glorifying God in every way, big and small.

God's plan for the world and his church includes every believer. Praise him for giving you a part to play in his kingdom. Whether you stay or go, sow or reap, lead or follow, find joy in living for your King.

Lord, make us glad to do whatever you ask. Show us your perfect plan so we can obey you in everything.

Amen.

December 14

Hearts Revealed

A good man brings good things out of the good stored up in his heart, and an evil man brings evil things out of the evil stored up in his heart. For the mouth speaks what the heart is full of. (Luke 6:45)

Our words will give our hearts away. A greedy heart will ask for more. A bitter heart will spew anger and spite. A fearful heart will worry and fret. A deceitful heart will lie and manipulate. A prideful heart will brag and put others down. A lustful heart will degrade other people. An unbelieving heart will deny the truth of Jesus.

What is coming out of your hearts today? Pray for the goodness of God to fill you by his Spirit. Speak words of joy and gratitude. Say what's true instead of lies. Make peace instead of arguing. Be gentle and quiet instead of shouting in anger. Keep gossip, slander, and boasting out of your conversations. Let your loving words reveal God's love in you.

Pray to be a "good man" and a "good woman" today. Store up goodness by reading God's Word. Meditate on wisdom and truth. Remember the love and grace you've received through Jesus. He'll fill you with himself.

Lord, fill up our hearts with your goodness and love. Let our words show that goodness to everyone.

Amen.

December 15

Let It All Out

> I cry aloud to the LORD; I lift up my voice to the LORD for mercy. I pour out before him my complaint; before him I tell my trouble. (Psalm 142:1-2)

Sometimes it's all too much to handle. Demands on our time and energy never let up. Conflict builds tension and stress. Cars break down. Bills come due. Sickness strikes. We feel out of control, with nowhere to run and no hope in sight.

The Lord invites you to bring your struggles to him in prayer. You can pour out your frustration, worry, and grief. He responds to your cries with compassion and mercy. There's no pointing finger of accusation. No rejection or "I told you so." You'll never be told to just get over it, or to pull yourselves together. He draws you close as your loving, patient Father.

What is your complaint today? Take the problem to God instead of trying to solve it by yourselves. Give him your emotions and receive his peace. Leave your troubles at his feet, knowing he cares for you.

Lord, we're at the end of our rope. Our burdens are too heavy — we need you to carry us through to the end. Thank you for your mercy and for listening to our prayers.

Amen.

December 16

Praising in Prison

> After they had been severely flogged, they were thrown into prison, and the jailer was commanded to guard them carefully. About midnight Paul and Silas were praying and singing hymns to God, and the other prisoners were listening to them. (Acts 16:23, 25)

Do you feel beat up today? Do you feel trapped in an impossible situation? No matter how much you give, you're accused of being selfish. Your hard work is criticized and disregarded. You're lonely and ignored by those who should care. Financial pressures weigh you down. The doctor has more bad news about your health. Your burdens are so heavy you're afraid you'll be crushed.

Even in this "prison" of difficulty, God is there. He's full of love and compassion. He hears your prayers for help. He'll keep his promise to use your struggle for good in the end.

Praise God's name in this troubled time. Thank him for his empathy for your weakness, since Jesus suffered too (Heb. 4:15). Tell him how grateful you are for his presence. Ask him to use your life to show others his power and love. Express your faith in his plan, knowing he's in control. Sing and worship as you put your hope in him.

Lord, we don't like the painful place we're in today. But we're grateful that your love and power are with us through it all.
Amen.

December 17

Pressure to Please

> Fear of man will prove to be a snare, but whoever trusts in the LORD is kept safe. (Proverbs 29:25)

Do you regret taking someone's advice? Have you ever been talked out of following God's direction? You're pressured by others who say, "Everyone else does it this way." "You need to take the safe, easy road." "You should trust the experts – they know better than you." "Do what feels right – God wants you to be happy." "You don't want to be some kind of religious fanatic." When you choose man's way over God's way, you become lost and trapped.

Do you feel torn, not knowing whose voice to listen to today? God's wisdom is higher than any other. He loves you the most, and sacrificed everything to purchase your life. He's worthy of your total trust and obedience. Pray for strength to submit to him in everything. Believe his Word and follow his leading. Choose godly friends and mature believers for wise counsel.

Pray and seek God before acting on others' opinions. No matter what anyone thinks about your choices, have peace knowing you're right with the Lord.

Lord, we're told it's foolish to trust you and obey your Word. Give us courage to live for you alone.

Amen.

December 18

The Money Trap

*Those who want to get rich fall into temptation
and a trap and into many foolish and harmful desires
that plunge people into ruin and destruction.* (1 Timothy 6:9)

You've seen how chasing money ruins people's lives. Sibling bonds are broken as they fight over their inheritance. Children are ignored or left to nannies while parents build a career. Cheats and thieves find themselves in jail. Gambling leaves families in poverty. The desire to get ahead is a trap in disguise.

Find freedom in Jesus today. Count his blessings in your life. Cherish the soul-satisfying love of your friends and family. Remember your treasures in heaven that can never be lost or destroyed. Pursue what really matters – a life of joy, hope, and love in Christ.

Let this be your prayer today:

Keep falsehood and lies far from me; give me neither poverty nor riches, but give me only my daily bread. Otherwise, I may have too much and disown you and say, 'Who is the Lord?' Or I may become poor and steal, and so dishonor the name of my God (Prov. 30:8-9).

Lord, guard our hearts from loving money. Let us live in freedom as we trust you to provide all we need.

Amen.

December 19

Hearts at Rest

> The LORD is my shepherd, I lack nothing. He makes me lie down in green pastures, he leads me beside quiet waters, he refreshes my soul. He guides me along the right paths for his name's sake. (Psalm 23:1-3)

Are you feeling depleted today? Your motivation is gone. You're stressed and tense. You're worried about making the right decisions. You think more time and money would solve your problems. It seems like your prayers stop at the ceiling. You forget what it feels like to truly stop and rest.

This is not the life your Shepherd has in mind. He wants to be your guide so the future doesn't rest on your shoulders. He wants to deliver you from the dangers of sin. He wants you to "lie down" instead of striving to get ahead. He wants to feed your soul with his Word. He wants to provide for your needs. He wants to show he can satisfy your deepest longings with himself.

Let the Lord take your hands and lead you together today. Find peace in his forgiveness. Let his love bring comfort. Let his strength hold you up, and his wisdom take you where you need to go. Find rest in him today.

Lord, we're wearing ourselves out trying to live without you. Teach us to trust you, follow you, and love you as our Shepherd. Amen.

December 20

A Little Goes a Long Way

"Here is a boy with five small barley loaves and two small fish, but how far will they go among so many?" (John 6:9)

It was hard for Jesus' disciples to believe a kid's lunch would feed thousands. We ask the same question today – "How far will they go?" How far will our money go when bills are piling up? How far will our time go when work is overwhelming? How far will our patience go with our stubborn child? How far will our commitment go when our spouse is hurt and angry? How far will our strength go in sickness and pain? The little we have leaves no room for hope.

Put the little you have in God's hands. Pray, giving him your troubles and needs, hurts and fears. Pray for faith to believe he can do more than you ask or imagine (Eph. 3:20). His grace is enough for what you're going through. He'll show his perfect power in your weakness.

"Trust in the Lord with all your heart and lean not on your own understanding; in all your ways submit to him, and he will make your paths straight" (Prov. 3:5-6).

Lord, all we have is a little faith. We believe in your power, we trust in your love, and we rest in your will.

Amen.

December 21

Growing Up

> Instead, speaking the truth in love, we will grow to become in every respect the mature body of him who is the head, that is, Christ. (Ephesians 4:15)

Share the truth of the Bible as a gift of love in your marriage. When your spouse is stressed and afraid, encourage them to be strong and courageous because God is with you wherever you go (Josh. 1:9). If harsh anger is taking root in your house, hold each other accountable.

Tell how human anger doesn't produce the righteousness that God desires (James 1:20). If lust is polluting your intimacy, remember God's call to honor your marriage with purity. If you're falling into debt or materialism, hold to the Word: "No one can serve two masters. Either you will hate the one and love the other, or you will be devoted to the one and despise the other. You cannot serve both God and money" (Matt. 6:24).

In your love, build up each other's faith. Depend on the Bible to guide your family. Let it protect you from sin and painful mistakes. Count on it to help you grow in obedience, trust, and knowledge of God.

Lord, teach us how to speak the truth in love. Let our family live by your Word.

Amen.

December 22

A Happy Home

Finally, brothers and sisters, rejoice! Strive for full restoration, encourage one another, be of one mind, live in peace. And the God of love and peace will be with you. (2 Corinthians 13:11)

God knows you want to love him, follow him, and honor him in your marriage. He's waiting to fill your home with his love and peace.

Today, praise God for his salvation. Thank him for the gift of your marriage. Give him glory for bringing you this far. Thank him for his strength to keep your vows and grow in love.

Be reconciled to God and each other. Confess your sin, pride, and selfishness. Name the ways you've hurt and let each other down. Choose to forgive and begin again tomorrow.

Encourage each other to follow Jesus. Give cheerfully, serve willingly, and take every opportunity to share God's love. Trust him through times of grief and trouble. Take all your worries to God together in prayer.

Find unity in the Spirit today. Work through conflict with humble hearts. Seek God's will and obey him together. Lay down your rights and put each other first. Pray to be one in body and mind.

God's love in your home will shine his light in the darkness. His peace will give you rest and comfort in every situation. He is with you always, to the very end of the age (Matt. 28:20).

Lord, let us always praise you, obey you, trust you, and live as one in your name. Be with us, filling our home with your love and peace.

Amen.

December 23

Safe and Secure

As for God, his way is perfect: The Lord's word is flawless;
   he shields all who take refuge in him. (Psalm 18:30)

Our ways are far from perfect. We get lost and confused. We hurt when we want to help. We lose our keys and our patience. Our best intentions get buried in regret. No matter how much we try to be strong and do the right thing, we don't have what it takes.

God loves you so much, he gives you what you need – the truth of his Word. Its wisdom never lets you down. It's filled with grace when you're ashamed. It shows the way to salvation and refuge in the Lord.

Are you tired from trying to make it on your own? Have you run out of energy to try? Are you hurting and far from God and each other? Pray and ask for help. Depend on the Word for wisdom. Believe God's promises to love and protect you. Put yourselves in his hands instead of handling life on your own. He is your peace, comfort, and security today.

Lord, everything falls apart when we go our own way. Teach us to live by your Word. Be our shield and refuge from trouble. Amen.

December 24

Lives Made New

> Then King David went in and sat before the Lord, and he said: "Who am I, Lord God, and what is my family, that you have brought me this far?" (1 Chronicles 17:16)

God knows the baggage you carried into your marriage. He recognizes the sins that trapped you for so long. He wept with you in your pain. He heard the hateful words and accusations you suffered. He saw the broken dreams and disappointments. He was there when you gave up hope for tomorrow.

Yet through all your trouble and heartache, God has been writing a story of victory. He set you free from the power of sin and death. He healed your wounds. He reconciled broken relationships. He proved that "in all these things we are more than conquerors through him who loved us" (Rom. 8:37).

Today, praise God for bringing you this far. Thank him for the work he's done to renew your heart and mind. Celebrate how you've stood against the enemy, resisted temptation, and overcome the past. Have joy in how he's sustained your marriage and family. Worship him for loving you, and for all that's still to come.

Lord, without you, we'd still be lost and blind. Thank you for lighting our path so we can find life in you.

Amen.

December 25

A King Is Born!

The angel said to them, "Do not be afraid. I bring you good news that will cause great joy for all the people. Today in the town of David a Savior has been born to you; he is the Messiah, the Lord. (Luke 2:10-11)

That heavenly announcement is just as glorious for us today: No fear. Good news. Great joy. A Savior born to us. The Lord is here!

Fear of punishment and death melts away in God's grace and the hope of heaven. The future holds no dread when we're promised eternal joy through Jesus. Forgiveness and mercy take guilt and shame away. Our Deliverer has come – what can Satan or this world do to us?

Just as the angel brought the greatest news the world had ever known, we're able to tell a lost and hurting world that Jesus has come. Share how you've been set free. Declare how he's rescued you from trouble. Praise his name for the joy he's brought to your life. As his people, you're a light in the darkness when you celebrate the Savior born to us all.

Praise God for sending Jesus to you today. Stand in awe of his great power and love. Take hold once more of the joy of your salvation.

Lord, we praise your name for sending Jesus, setting us free from all fear. Let us tell your good news to everyone with joy. Amen.

December 26

Truth You Can Trust

"To God belong wisdom and power;
counsel and understanding are his." (Job 12:13)

Life is full of tough decisions. Where should we live? How should we educate our children? How should we spend our money? How do we care for aging parents? How do we handle conflict in the workplace? How do we keep our priorities in order? How are we to serve the Lord? What does the Bible say about our situation?

Thankfully, you don't have to depend on your own common sense. You're not doomed to fail for lack of knowledge or experience. You serve a God who offers all the wisdom you need for whatever you face. He knows the plans he has for you. He'll guide your steps because he loves you.

Today, resist the urge to make a hasty decision. Let go of the need to take control. Receive advice from others, but allow the Lord to have the last word. Pray and ask him all your questions. Read the Word to know what's right. Trust him to navigate the road ahead. Lean on his strength to go where he leads.

Lord, we need your wisdom today. Let us understand what to do, and give us power through the Spirit to do it.
Amen.

December 27

The New You

> Listen, I tell you a mystery: We will not all sleep, but we will all be changed – in a flash, in the twinkling of an eye, at the last trumpet. For the trumpet will sound, the dead will be raised imperishable, and we will be changed. (1 Corinthians 15:51-52)

We share Paul's struggle in Romans 7: "I have the desire to do what is good, but I cannot carry it out. For I do not do the good I want to do, but the evil I do not want to do – this I keep on doing. What a wretched man I am! Who will rescue me from this body that is subject to death?" (18-19, 24). No matter how hard we try, we fail. We hurt the ones we love. We betray our conscience. We're sick and tired of our own weakness.

Find hope today – the battle is almost over. Jesus is coming to make you new. He'll set you free from sin. You'll be fully alive in God. You'll receive resurrection bodies that never die. You'll see your beautiful Savior's face.

Have patience in the waiting. Even now your life is hidden with Christ. He's transforming your mind by his Word. Your old self is being put off for the new. You have the Spirit – God's seal declaring you're his forever. Pray to keep believing. Keep watch – he's coming!

Lord, we're tired of the battle to do what's right. Restore our hope in your coming.

Amen.

December 28

The Haven of Home

> Then they can urge the younger women to love their husbands and children, to be self-controlled and pure, to be busy at home, to be kind, and to be subject to their husbands, so that no one will malign the word of God. (Titus 2:4-5)

If marriage and parenting were easy, we wouldn't need advice. We wouldn't need mature believers to teach us how to love and care for each other. We wouldn't need the Spirit to give us strength to love our family well.

Today, ask God for a teachable heart. Pray for eyes to see the unique qualities and needs of your loved ones. Speak words of encouragement. Seek counsel for how to overcome anger and grow in patience. Practice respect. Be busy building a household that's safe and inviting. Let your love create a sanctuary for your family in a hard, hostile world.

A home that's filled with Jesus' love is a light in the darkness. Your words and actions display the truth of the Word to everyone watching. When you grow in kindness, purity, and self-control, it proves the transforming power of God.

Lord, without your help, our family will miss the love and joy you have in mind. Fill our house with your goodness so we can bless each other and shine your light.

Amen.

December 29

Comfort and Care

The LORD upholds all who fall and lifts up all who are bowed down. The eyes of all look to you, and you give them their food at the proper time. You open your hand and satisfy the desires of every living thing. (Psalm 145:14-16)

When you love someone, their grief gives you pain. Their problems burden your heart. Their sins and doubts make you anxious for their future. Today, place your friends, families, and neighbors in God's hands.

Pray for your friends who feel like giving up. Ask for God to restore their hope for tomorrow. Ask him to open their eyes to see he's with them all the time. Pray for God to heal their wounds, comfort their grief, and quiet their fears.

Pray for those in need. Ask God to show himself as their provider. Let him direct you in how to give and help. Pray they would find peace by trusting God to take care of them.

Pray that your loved ones will walk in the truth. Ask for the Spirit to teach them right from wrong. Encourage them to believe God's Word – it holds power to save and wisdom to guide their way.

God knows the ones you love by name. He's faithful and strong to watch over them today. Keep praying, believing he'll open his hand and satisfy their hearts.

Lord, the people we care about are suffering. Let them know how much you love them. Lift them up today.

Amen.

December 30

Claiming Christ

By faith Moses, when he had grown up, refused to be known as the son of Pharaoh's daughter. He chose to be mistreated along with the people of God rather than to enjoy the fleeting pleasures of sin. (Hebrews 11:24-25)

We can base our identity on many things. Our family's status in the community. Our education, job, and achievements. Money, cars, and houses. Our appearance and image. Our social circle and popularity. What are you known for today?

Pray that you're named as followers of Christ today. Obey the Word without apology or compromise. Forgive those who insult your faith in Jesus. Strive to please God instead of other people. Give when others are taking. Speak the truth in love. Share the good news of salvation. Respect those in authority. Serve the church with your gifts. Live your lives to shine God's light in the darkness.

You're called to pick up your cross and follow Jesus. You'll be mocked, hated, and misunderstood. Yet it's worth it all in the end. "Set your minds on things above, not on earthly things. For you died, and your life is now hidden with Christ in God. When Christ, who is your life, appears, then you also will appear with him in glory" (Col. 3:2-4).

Lord, give us courage to call ourselves your children. Make our lives a witness of your truth and love.

Amen.

December 31

A Beautiful Blessing

"The LORD bless you and keep you; the LORD make his face shine on you and be gracious to you; the LORD turn his face toward you and give you peace." (Numbers 6:24-26)

When God adopted you as his children, he promised that his grace would overflow in your lives. Take a moment today to remember his many blessings. Pray, thanking him for how he's kept you safe and rescued you from trouble. Praise him for keeping your faith secure, even during seasons of doubt or discouragement.

Praise the Lord for how he's shown you favor. Remember how he's rewarded your work with success and the respect of others. Consider the responsibilities and relationships you're entrusted with.

Express your gratitude for grace. Remember the gift of Jesus, who paid the penalty for your sins on the cross. Thank God for his forgiveness and the promise to make you clean and new.

Praise God for answered prayers today. His face is turned toward you – you're never abandoned or forgotten. Thank him for his constant presence.

Finally, pray for God's peace that passes understanding. Ask for faith to believe he'll carry you through the storm. Find rest in God's mercy and faithful love.

Lord, your blessings are too many to count. Thank you for your love that gives us peace hope for the future.

Amen.

Rob and Joanna Teigen
have been married for over
20 years and are the parents of
two sons and three daughters.
They are the authors of
A Dad's Prayers for His Daughter
and *A Mom's Prayers for Her Son*.
Rob and Joanna enjoy homeschooling,
exploring new places, and laughing
with their kids. They make their
home in West Michigan.